Fools and Children

EDWARD T. FRYE

iUniverse, Inc.
Bloomington

Fools and Children

iUniverse books may be ordered through booksellers or by contacting:

iUniverse
1663 Liberty Drive
Bloomington, IN 47403
www.iuniverse.com
1-800-Authors (1-800-288-4677)

ISBN: 978-1-4620-2415-5 (sc)
ISBN: 978-1-4620-2612-8 (ebk)

Printed in the United States of America

iUniverse rev. date: 05/27/2011

Contents

Author's Note vii

Acknowledgments ix

Preface xi

Introduction xiii

Chapter 1 1

    Big Horse, Medium Dog, Small Town 1

Chapter 2 19

    Straight From The Pages Of Mark Twain 19

Chapter 3 37

    Of Hills and Caves 37

Chapter 4 56

    Life and Death in Black and White 56

Chapter 5 76

    God Takes Care of Fools and Children 76

Chapter 6 96

    Of Banks, Bullies, and Boxing 96

Chapter 7 114

    Bullies R Us 114

Chapter 8 133

    Down On The Farm 133

Chapter 9 154

    Millheim — Again 154

Chapter 10 176

    It's Just Sinful 176

Chapter 11 189

    Endless Days of Summer 189

Chapter 12 210

    Hormones Rage, Are You Listening? 210

Chapter 13 226

    Early Efforts At The Birds And Bees Thing 226
Chapter 14...251
    Nothing Gold Can Stay 251
About The Author..267

Author's Note

This book is a slightly fictionalized account of my early childhood. Slightly.

Few and small fictions prevent me from identifying this book as a memoir, a genre requiring highly-principled veracity. There is just enough vermouth in this vodka that I must call it a martini. Just a splash. In intent and creation, however, Fools and Children resembles a memoir much more than a work of fiction. It reads like a memoir, it relates real stories, events, and characterizations like a memoir, and it is as close to the truth as my own faded and jaded memory allows.

Yet I will call this a "constructed autobiography" – some sort of mixed genre -- to avoid controversy. As a writer, I rank truth as the Holy Grail behind credible, compelling story-telling and reader enjoyment. Still, anytime I violated veracity, I had to convince myself that it was for the best of everyone concerned – the reader, the involved people or event, and me. I was careful here. So, it is all true, except for just a little bit.

Certainly, the single largest distortion of fact involves the characters. Almost all the names have been changed for several and obvious reasons. A few names are unchanged; I did not change Herb Bierly's name, and he agrees with that.

I have melded two or more characters into one, or deleted someone on certain occasions. I did this for my own convenience. I allowed myself this prerogative to tie things together or retain a crispness or clarity to a venture.

One or two of the tales are amalgamations of several events taking place at different times. I simply finessed a few story elements into one telling. That is also true of my use of direct quotations, and/or the sequencing to the next tale. After I became more accepting of characterization changes, I allowed myself to foul about three stories to create a seamless, worthy offering. (He who will steal an egg will steal a chicken.)

There is no philosophical or artistic principle involved here. I have long believed that the division of literary "genres" – especially the somewhat arbitrary distinction between fiction and non-fiction -- is a theoretical construct. Such distinction allows for some convenient classification and critical review, but the choice it presents writers can be untenable, as several memoir writers have found, to their chagrin. The line between absolute veracity and story-telling can be a thin and gray one. For some, but not for me, verisimilitude is more critical than enjoyment.

Having made that disclaimer, I advise the reader not to ponder just how much of this book reflects reality. Virtually all of it reports people and events of my beloved Millheim in the 1950s. If perception is, in large part, reality, then this is my reality.

So, Reader, just relax and enjoy. If one shared the 1950s with me, these offerings will unleash some dusty, similar, but suddenly vivid experiences in other lives and places – perhaps yours. For those not around in the 50s, you are about to learn just how your parents and grandparents enjoyed the flowers of their youths in a simpler time.

Ed Frye

Acknowledgments

Writing a book is a lonely task, but few writers truly do it alone, I think. A writer needs the support of closest family members — in my case, my wife and two grown daughters. They patiently waited for normal life to resume following the tunnel vision I necessarily adopted to complete the book. They moved over and allowed some space for this intrusion into our family life. So, Doris, Danielle, and Brina, I thank you for your forbearance.

My mother and sister, Bari Deaven, were of extraordinary assistance. Being a partial family history of sorts, this text required all the memories I could tap and exploit. Mom was a really good sport, even though she learned some things about her little boy that she did not know back then. She did not live long enough to see this version. Being a bit older than I, Bari was able to validate some memories and events better than I could have done alone. Together, they provided innumerable remembrances, facts, and details — a patina for the tales.

Bari and I with Mom on her ninety-first birthday.

Perch Gramley, the erstwhile bartender at Penns Tavern and informal town historian, provided both facts and stories. So did Don Smith, a half generation older than mine. Both were generous in the provision of time and knowledge to this undertaking.

Two friends, Rosa Marinak and Bette Zook, read early versions of this manuscript, offering editorial review at the most needed time. Rosa represents exactly the audience for whom the book was written. She helped me determine the readability and acceptance of the effort. Bette is one of the world's great proofreaders. She, and my wife, Doris, (who knows how I think) caught numerous usage infractions that my readers will now never get to see.

Then there are all those friends who for years encouraged me to write this book. They suffered through all those storytellings and continually urged me to commit the litany to writing. They are just too numerous to mention.

I certainly thank the great folks of Millheim themselves – those persons with whom I shared a town and my boyhood years. They are really the essence of this book. Would that everyone could share this world with such wonderful and colorful folks. My intent has certainly not been to disparage or denigrate them. I trust that those who are still alive will laugh with me through these tales of the time we spent together.

Preface

"I know who you are," she said, emphasizing both the "know" and the "you." In a small town reputations and identities die hard.

In Millheim, mine wasn't so much a bad reputation, but a colorful one. So, here I stood, more than fifty years removed from those childhood days, and town residents still looked knowingly at me when I returned. While many of the names and faces in the town have changed, those of us who grew up there never really become strangers.

I was in the post office. It wasn't always the post office. It used to be one-half of the Hosterman and Stover Hardware Store. But times change. Now I was in the new post office, trying to do a good deed for my mother, eighty-eight years of age. On my way through town to visit her, I thought I would just stop by the post office and pick up her mail. One can't do that just everywhere, but this was Millheim. I thought that if I explained who I was the kindly lady would save my mother a trip of her own.

Well, I didn't have to explain who I was. Before I could even say "Ruth Frye's son," the postmistress had interrupted me. That was embarrassing; I didn't know her, even after she told me who she was. It was a family name I knew, but I just didn't remember her.

This tiny event was a galvanizing epiphany for me. It spurred me to attack an idea I had been too busy to address for years and years. "I'm going to write that book," I said to myself, pretty much right on the spot. Myriad little things jumped across my mindscape – memories, events, people, and Millheim itself, in the 1950s. "Yep," I said again, "I'm going to write the book."
Here it is.

Introduction

I don't know if I focused on Bierly or Queeny first. They were together, of course, she padding along just five or six inches behind his leg as they slogged through the slushy snow toward my house. One would think I'd consider him first, another kid who appeared to be about my age and headed for my house. But the eye of a seven-year-old who loves dogs but doesn't have one probably goes to the dog, not the boy.

I liked the look of the dog. I had concerns about the boy. I was sitting on a big mover's box gazing out the picture window of our new, rented home in a strange town. It was one of those days between Christmas and New Years Day, the waning of 1952. My parents were unpacking stuff in the kitchen, my sister was upstairs, organizing the bedroom she and I would have to share, and I was just sitting on that box, sullen and angry. I didn't want to move here, and I was showing my parents just how tough a customer I could be when I was unhappy. I had chosen not to help. I was going to sit on my cardboard perch, in this funk, and wallow in my gloom.

My dad had taken a new job. That is why we moved, so it really was his fault. I happened to know my mother wasn't happy about leaving State College. It had become her home. She had sisters and friends there. It was the only place she had ever lived since she left her ancestral farm in Huntingdon County. She was putting on a happy face, but I knew she wasn't thrilled about the situation. And Bari? Who knew? She was a ten-year-old girl; whether she cared or not didn't much matter to me.

All I knew was that they had moved me to Millheim. Twenty-one miles away from my comfort zone and power base. I had just gotten all my friends organized on West Beaver Avenue and in Corl Street Elementary

School. I was the undisputed leader of both kindergarten and first grade – I knew all my classmates, guys like Sam Greer, who followed me, played with me, and did what I wanted to do.

Now, all that was gone. I didn't know anyone. This new house was odd, the gristled old man who owned it was odd, this little town was odd. It was going to get worse. Christmas vacation was going to come to an end, and I was going to have to go to a new school. Worse, I had to ride a bus to get there. The school was in someplace called Coburn, almost two miles from Millheim. I didn't have to ride a bus in State College. Corl Street Elementary was right out my back door. I walked out the kitchen door, across the yard, over the alley, and into the school. No muss, no fuss, no stinky school bus. I was going to miss all that – my friends, my organized social order, the convenience, the comforts of the known. I was pretty miserable.

And then Bierly came shuffling through the snow, with Queeny's nose at the back of his knee.

Queeny was a mongrel, no doubt about that. She appeared to have some collie in her, but she wasn't nearly as tall as a collie. She wasn't a dainty border collie either. Queeny wasn't refined or dainty. She was thick and low to the ground with wide, working dog feet. That's why her nose came only to the knee of a seven-year-old boy. She was broad; she had the look of some herding dog. I remember her as too heavy for us to carry very far, but small enough to sit between Bierly and me in the cab of his dad's pick-up truck when we rode downtown.

She was mostly white with hair long and thick enough to get matted if we ran her all day in the woods behind Sheep Hill. She had a bit of tan over her perpetually smiling face and a little color down her throat. Brindle bits splashed down her front legs and her right thigh. But mostly, she was white.

As she followed Bierly, she seemed to rise right up out of the four or five inches of slush on the alleyway. She and the three-day-old snow were the same hue. Forget that refrigerator white of newly fallen snow. That pristine color had given way to dirty white, the result of traffic and the splashing of mud that was working itself into the old snow. That was the color of Queeny. As an act of love I will call it off-white.

So here the two of them came, up the alley toward the house. There was another thing. This strange new house of ours sat in an alley, right behind Old Man Brindle's huge, Victorian house. Old Man Brindle built our two bedroom Cape Cod, with-a-dormer and had rented it to the Fryes. It turned out that Bierly lived just three houses down the street from Brindle, so he only had to come out his back door and slog up three hundred feet of unplowed alley.

I had this all figured out. His mother had sent him up here to introduce himself. She sent Queeny along because little boys like dogs. She would have said something to her son like, "Make nice to the new kid. He's probably lonely, remember, and he is in a strange, new place. Don't forget that his dad is the new principal of the elementary schools in the area – like Coburn – so it wouldn't do to be too smarty-pants or obnoxious. Just go by and say hello."

Only known photograph of Bierly and Queeny

I could have gone outside and intercepted him if I had wanted. But, instead, I waited for him to knock. That was another thing about this strange house. It had no doorbell like our old one in State College. It didn't have one of those little mail slots in the door either where the postman could slide the mail through when he came by twice a day. It turned out that such a slot would never have any use in Millheim because they didn't deliver the mail in Millheim – townfolk had to go and get it at the post office. What a burg this was.

So I let him knock. In fact, I let him wait a few seconds and have to knock again, because I did not want to seem too eager. Then I opened the door. He had come to the nearest door, the one at the end of a narrow hallway that split the first floor in two and led either outdoors or down the steps to the basement. It was a poor choice actually, but he had never been there before, so it was hard to blame him for not knowing which door to try.

I remember all of that vividly. What I can't remember is one word of conversation in those first moments of our new friendship. I am sure I fussed over Queeny. I am sure we shared vital facts about our families. I am sure we established that we were the same age and, therefore, in the same grade. I am sure he told me how close he lived, and I am sure he described the town and promised to take me on a tour. I am sure we traded interests and favorite activities and what not. I am sure that I learned his name was pronounced "Beerlee," regardless of how they spelled it and that old phonics rule that says, "When two vowels go walking, the first one does the talking."

But I do not really recall any of that. I know we went down to the basement and shot baskets at the new hoop my dad had just put up the day before.

The hoop, complete with its string net, was a Christmas gift. We had celebrated that holiday at the State College house just before we moved. Dad put the hoop up in the basement as soon as we moved, as an act of good will. I think he wanted to show me just how much I was going to enjoy this new home in this new town. Of course, it wasn't regulation height, but neither was I. The problem was that the basement ceiling was as low as Old Man Brindle could make it, so we had to keep the arc of our shots shallow or we would hit the beams that separated us from the kitchen.

Anyway, I remember shooting baskets for awhile. I am sure we did not engage in a competitive game of basketball. We were too new of acquaintances to try anything so risky to egos and bodies.

The good news was that we hit it off pretty well. Bierly and I both sensed that we were beginning a long-term friendship. And that was really good for me because the holidays ended, and real life in Millheim began. In January, 1953 I went off on a school bus to Coburn School. I only knew one person in the whole place. He rode with me on the bus, told others who I was, and got me into Mrs. Shreckengast's classroom without incident. I was now a second-grader in a new land.

***

A family relocation makes an indelible impression on a child of seven years. It forms a line in the sand of one's childhood – in my case, pre-Millheim and Millheim. My memories are clearly separated into events that either took place in State College or in Millheim. What is lost, probably because it wasn't important at the time, is exactly how old I was when specific experiences occurred. I remember the transitional days and much of the first year or two as I became attuned to my life in Millheim. But then the timeline breaks down. When I share my childhood escapades, people invariably ask, "How old were you at the time?" I think the purpose behind this question is really, "Weren't you old enough to know better?" The answer to the second question is "Yes, I guess I should have been." But the answer to the first is just too hazy. All I know is that, if it happened in Millheim, I was seven or older and, for purposes of this book, younger than thirteen. That is the best I can do with regard to specific timing of things.

That makes storytelling a bit dicey. Austere chronology aside, something I report as the noodling of an eleven-year-old may have actually occurred in a nearby time zone – perhaps when I was a year younger or older.

Anyway, discounting the first six years of my life, I grew up in Millheim. I graduated from the consolidated high school that served all the little towns in the three or four tight valleys that formed the new school district. I am a child of the '50s. I lived a childhood that, until relatively recently, I always thought was typical of people my age. I have come to realize that such is not the case. People seem to relate to this or that from my stories, but I find that few seem to have experienced the rich, full, childhood freedoms those of us in small town America have enjoyed. This is my story of that childhood.

Chapter 1

Big Horse, Medium Dog, Small Town

"How about we just go and catch ourselves one of the FBI's Most Wanted Fugitives?" Bierly suggested. That sounded like just the plan for this sunny summer morning. I agreed, and we headed off to the post office to identify our prey of the day.

That's how lots of trouble would start for us. Bierly would get some notion, and I would buy right in. We often spent the day extricating ourselves from some fix the plan set in motion.

It had become the three of us, all the time, everywhere: Herbie Bierly, Eddie Frye, and Queeny. We wandered all over town in search of adventure and mayhem. That was the beauty of living in a small town. Two boys, aged seven, and a dog had the run of the place. Little kids could do that in the '50s.

In summertime, when school didn't use up our days, Bierly and I — and often one or two others — would hook up somewhere in the morning, usually down by the old mill. Our mothers did not expect us back before lunch, if then. We would roam about town, go home to eat something, and then head to the swimming pool. There we'd spend the afternoon, along with virtually every other kid in town until closing time at five o'clock. After a quick family dinner, we headed out again, often up to the field behind the high school where we would play baseball until dark. Then home, a snack, bed, and another day just like the one before it.

Queeny was with us, all day, every day, padding along right behind us, her nose at our heels. She never knew a leash. She always walked just one and one-half steps behind us, never straying from the sidewalk, never running after another dog, never checking out a squirrel, never stopping to sniff a piece of trash by the roadway. We never worried that Queeny would leave the sidewalk to cross the road after a cat or a bird, or a pie sitting on a window ledge. Queeny always stayed right behind us, shadowing our every move.

When we would stop into a store, we simply told Queeny to sit down and wait for us. She did. She'd plop down in the shade of some storefront overhang and wait patiently for us to return, for hours if necessary. More than once we would go in the front door and out a back or side one. We didn't mean to, but now and again we would forget Queeny. Then we would remember, and we'd go back. There she would be. Waiting.

Never a bark, never a growl, never defiance. In the afternoon, when we'd go to the pool, she would traipse along and find some shade underneath the trees that lined two sides of the pool. There she'd sleep the afternoon away until Bierly and I called for her.

Bierly and I had quickly become best friends. By the time the summer of 1953 had mercifully arrived and freed me from a dismal second grade school year, Bierly and Frye had become inseparable. We would take off on those summer mornings looking for adventure. If we couldn't find it, we invented it, and that made for trouble often enough that we became the scourge of the local merchants and many of the residents.

So off we were then, on one of those adventures. We were going to catch a fugitive from justice. Our goal was to return him for a sizable reward. We knew who these fugitives were, and we knew the bounty on each of them. All that information was available at the Millheim Post Office.

The post office was a small storefront three buildings down from the town square.

The federal government always displayed wanted posters in the nation's post offices. These posters were complete with the typical black and white photographs from three sides and a description of the felon's physical features — height, weight, color of eyes and hair, distinguishing characteristics like scars and tattoos — and, for some reason, fingerprints. If we wanted to know who were the most dangerous guys in America, we just went into the post office and walked up to the bulletin board. There they were. And the FBI wanted our help in apprehending these renegades.

That is exactly what Bierly and I decided to do. We weren't that busy. We had been casting about for adventure, but nothing seemed to capture our fancy. We also had some limited options. Of the fifteen or so stores lining the Millheim diamond – that's what we called the intersection of the two roads coming into town – Bierly and I were currently persona non grata in eight of them. So, browsing was not much of an option. The last time we "browsed," we were considering a candy purchase in the 5 and10 store. While Bierly was leaning on the glass top of the bin that held the orange slices, he shattered it, pretty much falling all the way into it, face first. This, of course, rendered all the candy underneath worthless for consumption. The proprietor, Gerald Waters, was vehement in his suggestion that we take a little sabbatical from his premises. That is not at all how he phrased it, but it is the jest of what he meant. Similar, if not as dramatic, events in stores all across the square had limited our access to daily commerce.

Anyway, catching one of those most wanted guys would be fun, and we could put the reward money to good use. Bierly had a fledgling stamp collection that needed some underwriting. I was seeking funding for a new baseball glove that I longed for since seeing it in the hardware store — a black leather, Clem Labine Signature Edition, made by the first name in baseball gloves, Spalding. I had already removed it from the very modest sports department and had hidden it in the glassware section so that no other kid could buy it before I had the necessary resources.

So, we went to the post office. We perused the posters until we found an interesting felon. I certainly do not remember his name or the dastardly deeds for which he was wanted. All I recall is that he looked very much like he could be the kind of guy who would end up in Millheim. We made sure the postmaster and Rae McNair, an old lady who hung out in the building, weren't watching. Then we ripped the poster from its counterparts, Bierly jammed it in his pocket, and we left with a spring to our step. We had no idea that we had just committed a federal crime. It was just the kind of discourteous act that had us outlawed in those other stores up and down Main Street.

We spent the next thirty minutes surveiling Millheim. We sat down on the restaurant steps and studied every man who passed us. We held the poster out in front of us to compare the side-view photograph with our latest suspect. When that didn't render any results, we stood up and faced passers-by directly, so that we could use the more trustworthy full-frontal view.

Still, no luck. We discussed this and decided that perhaps our prey was wearing a disguise. We thought we might be licked. No way could we solve that problem. To avoid having to deal with such an insurmountable issue, we simply created a more solvable problem.

We decided we were being stupid to think that one of the most wanted men in America would be walking down Main Street, Millheim, Pennsylvania in the middle of the morning. He'd know his face was hanging in the post office. Why hadn't this occurred to us before? The answer was as simple as apple pie. He would be hiding somewhere around here, fearful of being recognized.

So, all we had to do was find his hiding place. Now we had a problem we could tackle. If anyone knew anything about hiding places in Millheim, it was the team of Herbie Bierly and Eddie Frye.

And that is how we had the little misfortune with Albert Stover's famous Tennessee Walker.

Albert Stover operated the big half of The Hosterman and Stover Hardware Store. The Hosterman in the store's name had been bought out long ago. The other half, part of the same building but separated by an open doorway, belonged to Albert's father, Lucius Stover. Customers could go into one hardware and have the benefit of shopping at two.

Albert's side had all the cool stuff – housewares, sporting goods, toys, models, appliances, equipment, tools, and such as that. The other side seemed to feature lumber, stoves, pumps, pipe, and fittings.

Albert Stover was influential businessman, involved in municipal and church affairs. He was a short, little man standing no more than five feet, four inches. Most of that modest height was used up by an upper torso and a head, both of which appeared to be oversized for such a small body. He had very short legs; Bierly once joked that Albert's legs were so short that they barely touched the ground when he stood. He had thick jowls and wore large, rimless glasses. He had a Teddy Roosevelt look about him, imperial and assured, jaw jutting into the issue, and all of that. Except for the mustache of course.

Now horses were somewhat numerous in town. Benny the Barber had one, Drew Gearhart had one, as did John Rishel and Harry Ebbots. These folks had even organized a riding club – The Black Panther Riding Club, named after a local legend that alleged such a rare animal lived in the hills near town. Some residents actually claimed to have seen the elusive feline on one or more occasions. These claims were never really substantiated. In any event, there were lots of horses around town.

But only Albert Stover owned the special and unique Tennessee Walker.

Tennessee Walkers feature a gait during which, unlike other breeds, they land flat-footed with only one foot hitting the ground at a time. Meanwhile, the head nods forward with each step, seemingly smoothing out the discomforting, non-rhythmic gait of more everyday breeds. So, the rider, even when galloping or cantering, enjoys a ride judged by many to be simply superior.

Tennessee Walkers are the result of very selective breeding programs that have carefully integrated the better qualities of Standardbred, Morgan, and Thoroughbred heritage. Back in the ante-bellum south, plantation owners, spending hours in the saddle perusing their acreage, were looking for less continual trauma on their derrieres. The Tennessee Walker was a solution to that problem. As a bonus, this breed also cut a dashing, regal, almost majestic attitude as they pranced along, reflections that certainly suited the lord of the realm sitting atop.

Albert's horse was so special that it was the only horse in town referred to by its breed name. People would say, "Oh, that is John Rishel's horse," or "Isn't Carol Highman's horse pretty?" But Albert's mount was always referred to as "The Tennessee Walker." Of course the horse had a name – Tony – but his identity was "The Tennessee Walker."

I just didn't share this widespread appreciation of the artistry and majesty of that horse. When Albert would ride by in the annual Halloween or Christmas parades, he and his horse always looked strange to me. From the side it looked to me as if the horse were in a fit of palsy, slamming each foot down independently from the rest. His head was always moving out of rhythm with the rest of the animal. His elegance and grace were lost on me, a young kid who wanted a horse to look like the amazingly agile steeds my favorite cowboys rode — simple standardbreds or quarter horses. Of course I never attached any real value to either one of the two Cadillacs in town either. I wanted the old Ford Jim Wineheart had all customized.

Albert stabled his horse in a small barn at the downtown end of my alley, where it turned right and ran along Elk Creek to intersect with Main Street at the bridge. Lots of the houses along Main Street had small outbuildings bordering the alley, and this one was built as a two-horse stable.

It was a convenient place for Albert to keep his horse because he lived only one-hundred yards away, across Main Street and up a driveway to his Victorian house. The stable was also close to Albert's hardware store only twelve buildings from the Elk Creek bridge.

The House of Tony, the Tennessee Walker

Bierly and I often used this alley to go downtown. After all, it bordered my front door and his back door. At the bottom, we would stop to pet Albert's Tennessee Walker.

We'd perch on the half-door and fuss over him. We'd talk to that horse as if he were Mr. Ed from the television show: "A horse is a horse, of course, of course, and no one can talk to a horse, of course, that is, of course, unless the horse is the famous Mr. Ed." Tony never talked back, but we'd jabber on about his jet-black mane, his huge brown eyes, and his blue-blood bearing as he thrust his neck out between us.

Albert never locked up his stable. Why should he? No one stole anything in Millheim. No one in town even locked a car. Besides, if Albert had locked the door, the poor animal would be totally penned in, unable to stick his head out the top half of the doorway. There was a common understanding that one stayed out of other people's sheds and horse stalls.

Bierly and I knew this well-bred and highly-strung horse didn't like people in his stall with him, especially at his rear end. But we had already decided that the rogue we sought had probably sought sanctuary in the second floor hayloft of this shed. That section was filled with hay and straw that could be dropped right into the stable below via a trap door. What a great hiding place for one of the FBI's Most Wanted fugitives! Clearly he would choose this spot to elude capture. We knew of other, equally-qualified hiding spaces around town, but this one had convenience going for it. This would be a great place to look. We knew we had to go into that shed, Tennessee Walker or not.

When we arrived, the Tennessee Walker seemed a bit more agitated than usual. He moved about his confines restlessly, tossing his head wildly enough that we could not pet him. He was antsy. Well, that sealed it for Bierly and me. Clearly our quarry had gotten this horse excited with his comings and goings.

We began to whisper and to communicate with gestures. We had no way of reaching the second story access door on the outside of the barn. Our only way to get to the loft was to climb in with the horse and use the wooden ladder built onto the rear wall.

Bierly produced our only weapon, an official Boy Scout pocket knife that he had recently acquired. I had nothing with which to conduct this assault. But we were committed. The first step was to get into the stall and up the ladder on the rear wall.

Bierly climbed over the lower half of the door first; after all, he had the weapon. I followed. That's when things sort of broke down.

The Walker did not look favorably on Bierly's intrusion this day. He began to shuffle about, and I saw a bit of white in the corner of his eye. But I assumed that Tony knew us and would settle down.

Now the lower half of the door was fastened by a large iron hook that dropped into a hasp. This device did not tightly secure the door; it was actually intended to provide easy access. The door always could rock back and forth several inches as the bent rod lay loosely in the oblong ring. I crawled over it.

And in doing so, caught the long metal latch with my U.S. Ked, pulling it right up and out of the hasp.

The three of us shared that stall for about two seconds. Then Tony decided to leave.

We never did determine if the man on the FBI's Most Wanted List was actually in that loft. Our priorities changed. Albert Stover's Tennessee Walker was on the loose, and he was feeling pretty frisky about it.

Tony had two choices. He could turn left and go up the alley past Bierly's house and toward mine, then into the huge field behind all the homes on our end of the street. Or, he could go right and run down the short end of the alley to the bridge.

"Go left," I prayed out loud.

He went right. Bierly and I gave chase. That probably did not help.

When the steed hit Main Street, he did not look for traffic. He simply took a hard left in that distinctive cantering gait of Tennessee Walkers and headed for greater downtown Millheim, PA. There went any chance that nobody would see him, with us giving chase. Straight up the street Tony galloped, with the Saturday morning motor traffic of Millheim (probably eight or so cars) making accommodation for him. Horns started honking, and people started shouting and pointing. Pedestrian life on the street came to a halt. The Walker was headed due west on Main Street, straight toward Albert Stover's hardware store.

Where Albert was putting up an outdoor display of gardening equipment — a shovel, rake, and hoe combination worth much, much more than his advertised special price. Albert heard the commotion, looked up, and saw his Tennessee Walker about to run the only red light in town. Confused and scared, the horse never acknowledged Albert's presence; he kept on going, headed for Spring Mills. Albert shouted for someone to get a car and pick him up, and then gave chase on foot.

Bierly and I disappeared. We had followed the horse up the alley, across the bridge and half of the way up Main Street. But when we saw Albert outside, we decided discretion was the better part of valor. We turned the chase over to him and decided that he did not need to know how anxious we were to help.

So we peeled off Main Street at the little alley that separated the post office from a little house. We stopped behind the post office and caught our breath. We decided we were not noticed by anyone because all eyes were focused on Tony. Certainly Albert had not seen us; we had seen him first. So, sticking to the alleys, we worked our way back to Bierly's basement where we waited for the heat to die down.

Albert successfully captured Tony. I do not know how long it took, or how he did it. I wasn't there, and I chose not to show too much interest in the topic in the days that followed. Thankfully, the horse was none the worse for wear, but we knew the potential for real catastrophe had been averted. I felt badly about it for a while. Bierly always laughed about the incident.

I do know this. The next time we wandered down the alley to pet the Tennessee Walker, there were some technical up-grades made to the door. An entirely new and heavier metal hasp now held a forged steel latch, all of which was secured by a commercial grade Masterlock.

Later, Albert Stover asked me if I knew anything about a black left-handed baseball glove, but he never asked me if I had any part in loosing his prized Tennessee Walker.

***

So there we were, Bierly and I – sharing a small town with nine hundred other residents, their animals, their possessions, and their interdependent lives. I guess it is more accurate to call it a village. Our town was surrounded by even smaller little hamlets such as Madisonburg, Smullton, and Coburn. These were our versions of suburbs to Millheim, central to them all.

Located one mile from the geographical center of Pennsylvania, the town stretches for about a mile in the eastern end of the expansive Penns Valley. Lush farmland is cupped on two sides and at its eastern end by the long, low-slung Allegheny Mountain range. Millheim straddles Elk Creek, a fast-moving, fifty-foot wide stream that flows south from the mountains above town. It effectively bisects the town into western and eastern portions. Slicing through the very middle of town, and the valley, for that matter, is Route 45. It forms a natural separation of the town into northern and southern hemispheres, and in cooperation with Elk Creek, forms almost equal quadrants of town, each with its own personality.

Millheim during rush minute

The section of Route 45 that ran through town was referred to as Main Street. Intersecting Main Street was Pennsylvania Route 445, running more or less parallel to Elk Creek although not directly beside it. In town the road had two names. Beginning at the only red light in town, at the diamond – where it intersected Rt. 45 — it was known as Penn Street as it headed toward Coburn. As it trailed north through the mountains toward Rebersburg, it was named North Street. However, that end of town was more widely known as "up Texas."

This strange designation was the inadvertent result of a malcontent who used to live up there in the 1920s. This ill-tempered drinker would come into town and head straight for the earlier version of Penns Tavern where he would rant and rail incessantly to other patrons about how he was going to leave Millheim. He hated Millheim, and he was going to move to the state of Texas where he had real opportunities for success.

While he did this regularly, he made no real plans to move to Texas, and it soon became obvious to those who had to listen to him that he was going nowhere. So, when he'd rise to leave the bar, they began to ask him if he was going to Texas. When he came in, they asked him how things were "up Texas." North Street had a new name. To this day few residents call it North Street.

Anyway, that was pretty much it. The town was basically t-shaped, defined by the two highways that passed through it.

From its inception, Millheim was all about mills. The name is the German equivalent of "Home of the Mills." Back in the mid-1700s an early settler named Jacob Hubler built a flouring mill, better known as a grist mill, near Elk Creek. Two other grist mills were built just a bit later. Of these three only one, The Brick Mill, exists. The Brick Mill guards the lower end of town on a small alleyway, now more civilized and called Mill Street. In its early days the town also sported three mills on North Street, a planing mill, a saw mill, and a woolen mill. They were long gone by the 1950s, replaced with tidy homes.

Two remaining artifacts of those days often figured in my childhood. The first was the Brick Mill itself. The second was the man-made concourse of water to power it.

In early days, of course, most mills were water-powered. They were usually built close to streams so that water could be easily diverted into them to operate the milling machinery. An exception was the Brick Mill, built by

Philip Gunkle in 1798. For some reason Gunkle built it several hundred yards from Elk Creek, on that alleyway off Penn Street. To power his mill Mr. Gunkle had to build a small canal from Elk Creek to the enterprise. What he built was a millrace – town folk called it simply "the race." The millrace snaked right behind the tiny business district of town, diverting water from the creek at the bridge and threading it behind the gas station, the restaurant, and the bank. Then it ran right under and then alongside Penn Street down to that alleyway at the southern edge of town. The millrace was approximately eight feet wide and about three quarters of a mile long.

It entered the old mill, turned a paddlewheel that turned something else, and then found its way back to Elk Creek. Long ago abandoned, the old mill was a staging area for many of our childhood escapades, created while we met, loafed and schemed.

In the 1950s Millheim was a self-contained town, boasting all the services and products necessary for rural life. On the four corners of the diamond were the hardware store, Farmers National Bank, Nieman's clothing store, and John Cooner's grocery and sundry business. Up and down Main Street there were two barber shops, a drugstore, three grocery stores, a five and dime, a restaurant, a jewelry store, a gas station, Stanley C. Bierly Appliances, Heating and Plumbing store, Elmer Ivine's shoe repair, and two of the four bars in town, The Millheim Hotel and Penns Tavern.

The Millheim Theatre, seating up to 600 patrons, offered an early and a late movie for fifty cents on Saturday nights only. Vic Stoler and his sons sold and repaired farm implements at the eastern edge of town, directly across the road from Dot and Jake's, a tiny restaurant and teenage hangout. Doc Henninger practiced medicine in a big, white house on Penn Street, and Dr. Stein, the optometrist, opened his near-the-diamond office once a week when he came down from State College. *The Millheim Journal* was published weekly from a building down Penn Street, right behind the bank. There were three churches in town. It did not escape my notice that Millheim boasted more bars than churches.

Millheim, with this much commercial development, was the major social and shopping center in Penns Valley. People from the neighboring villages would flock to town on Wednesday and Saturday evenings, when the stores remained open until nine o'clock. These were the days before shopping malls, Wal-Marts, and Home Depots. State College, Lock Haven, and Lewistown all provided more selection and brighter lights, but the people of the lower valley met most of their needs in Millheim.

A sort of weekend shopping tradition had developed for those living on farms or in Aaronsburg, Fiddler, Woodward, Madisonburg, or Georges Valley. Entire families would come into town on Saturday evening. Dropping the kids off at the theatre for the early show, parents would shop for food, clothing, and whatever until the movie let out. That generally left time for a drink at Penns Tavern, conveniently located in the diamond right next to the bank. In addition to the hotel, other choices were the Legion or the Firemans Club, both up Texas right behind Niemans and sitting side by side. On Saturday evenings, the town bustled and brimmed with people. The sidewalks were crowded, and one could count on encountering long time acquaintances.

Or someone to whom they were related. The original German and Scotch-Irish immigrants who built the mills and cleared the farmland in Penns Valley really were few in name and number. Their progeny stayed and expanded over the years, solidifying the area's Pennsylvania Dutch roots. Whether farmers, millers, or merchants, the founding families married and intermarried so much that only a few surnames covered a disproportionate percentage of citizenry. The area teemed with Hostermans, Stovers, Bierlys, Breons, Millers, Vonadas, Mussers, and Bresslers. Certainly, however, there was more Hosterman and Stover DNA in the gene pool than anything else. It is no surprise that a business partnership such as the hardware store had to be The Hosterman and Stover Hardware.

The lineages became rather arcane, yet most valley folk could explain exactly the relationship between themselves and someone else. "Yeah, Bill Hosterman. He's my second cousin, once removed, on my mother's side."

To a newcomer, it seemed as if everyone was related to everyone else in town. This was actually close enough to be true. It was a lesson my father learned early in his career in Penns Valley. After he arrived to become the principal of all thirteen elementary schools in the area (many of which were one-room affairs), he quickly learned to keep his own counsel. He learned his lesson the hard way. He was complaining to one of his board members about a parent who was giving him grief over some educational issue. Following Dad's brief foray into character assassination, the board member said, "Yep, he can be trouble, that one. I know, because he is my brother-in-law."

With so few surnames, the given names of newborns became a study in redundancy. Each generation produced a new set of Jim Stovers, Charley Vonadas, Bill Hostermans, and so on. When all the good Christian names were worn out, several families started to use two common surnames. That is how I ended up with a friend named Stover Musser and came to know a house builder named Meyer Brungart. I am surprised there wasn't more of that.

There was much use of nicknames. Perhaps a nickname was a way to separate one generation of Stovers from another, a way of keeping a junior version of a Hosterman separate from the senior with the same Christian name. I'm not sure.

This I do know. During my years in Penns Valley I called dozens of my friends and acquaintances by nicknames that, in most cases, lasted their entire lives. Here are just a few that I remember: "Bugs" Vonada, "Hap" Stoler, "Pickle" Johnson, "Pudge" Weber, "Mouse" Ripka, "Tic" a.k.a. "Spider" Revis, "Elmer" Worth, "Moon" Dinges, "Spit" Ungar, "Pappy" Ungar, "Chappy" Walker, "Sparky" Walker, "Spaget" Auman, "Hat" Knight, "Chickie" Lamey, "Chippy" Homan, "Snip" Strouse, "Pony" Stover, "Chile" Peebles, "Dump" Hosterman, "Fritz" Hosterman, "Perk" Stover, "Fat" Meyers, "Whitey" Horn, "Dinger" Foust, "Tubby" Trucot, "Skyxx" Keen, "Rock" Ungar, "Perch" Gramley, "Goose" Adams, "Maynard" Stover.

Life was simple and good in Millheim. The town perfectly reflected the general good will and heady, expanding affluence that America was enjoying in the '50s. The citizens of Penns Valley enjoyed a robust commerce within their own community. All in all, valley folk featured fierce independence and obstinacy, mollified by good-heartedness and generosity. They were a hardy and hard working breed. They enjoyed a rousing church service and a good beer.

Which is not to say they were perfect. The town had its share of scandals and social misfits. It was a bucolic setting, not an idyllic one.

Soon after we arrived in Millheim, several influential townsfolk led a mean-spirited and surreptitious campaign to run Doc Lenker out of town. Doc Lenker was longest serving of three doctors serving the area, and he enjoyed early popularity. However, someone got the notion or talked to someone else who had the notion that Doc was treating clients while under the influence.

To me, this seemed a bit of a stretch. I remember Doc Lenker only vaguely. I recall him looking like the undertaker in one of those early westerns we saw at the theatre: a tall, thin man, always dressed in black. I recall him as a serious, brooding type, stern of visage and way. That is probably what did him in.

Adults all over town reacted to this allegation of Doc's drinking by either denying its possibility — after all, they knew the man well enough to know if that was occurring – or denouncing him as a charlatan whose medical license ought to be lifted.

We kids heard rumors, but we were not exactly in the information loop of either camp. Doc Lenker had a daughter, Georgie, who was my sister's age. They were friends — she played in our house. I remember feeling badly for her during this period, especially after the Halloween parade. In it someone with a black mask and other disguise stood and staggered on the back of a flatbed truck holding a doctor's bag labeled "Dr. Lenker" in one hand and a bottle of booze in the other. As he rode down Main Street, the clownish figure, with an obvious slur in his speech, asked spectators along the parade route if they needed any medical treatment.

Dr. Lenker left town.

Millheim also had its own prostitute – at least that was always the story. A gal nicknamed "Noodles" lived at the western edge of town. Reportedly, she serviced the constant parade of truckers who passed through town on their way to somewhere else. She also was said to ply her trade down in Lewisburg where a more, well-traveled trucking route headed north to New York. We kids heard stories of "Noodles" even though I must say I never even knew her to see her, which I probably did. We'd hear the constant jokes among the adults about her and fantasized about what it might be like to be with such a woman. We heard rumors of some of the town's leading citizenry's consorting with her.

Occasionally, a scandal involving infidelity or business chicanery would surface. A bank employee was once accused of embezzling funds, and more than one citizen stole another's wife. Such local news seemed much more important than national issues.

Most of the nation's battles and history were being conducted in places far away from Millheim. Townsfolk read about and discussed these things and formed their own opinions. The exception to that was Korean War, of course, which was beginning to wind down. Several local boys, known to everyone, were part of that "military action," so that topic certainly involved Millheimers.

But most of America's issues just weren't part of the warp and woof of the town. Even we children were aware that some bigshot named Joe McCarthy was hunting communists and that was all related to something they called "The Cold War." We knew that Edward R. Morrow, someone we did know from his "See It Now" television program, helped McCarthy make a disgrace of himself in his irrational and dogged pursuits of "Commies." We knew that our country was at odds with Russia, and that is where the commies were. We were told that the commies may bomb us. We heard how hard our government was working to prevent this. Our leaders had just executed a couple named the Rosenbergs because they were working for the "Godless Commies." Then, in an even more public and daring move, our government delivered a big blow to communism everywhere. They added the words "under God" to The Pledge of Allegiance, something we said in unison at the start of every school day. While we kids suffered the inconvenience of having to insert the words into our already-memorized version, we knew we were striking a blow for freedom and the American Way.

We never really found out how the commies survived this onslaught. The government did not send us a memo on any result. And, we couldn't exactly ask a commie, because we did not know a single one in the town. We didn't even know what they looked like.

We read that a black woman named Rosa Parks had challenged the segregation policies of the South. That is the first we even knew about racial tensions and inequalities. Heck, most of us didn't even know what "inequalities" meant until then. But in 1954 we learned about segregation from the U.S. Supreme Court ruling that "separate but equal" schools were just plain unconstitutional. The Brown vs The Board Of Education of Topeka, Kansas decision was informational, but not very applicable in Millheim where not one single black person resided. But this racial tension business just kept itself before us. Jackie Robinson, Althea Gibson, George Wallace, water fountains and toilets, and voting rights were stories that just magnified this notion that it was different in other parts of the country. This was a much more complicated picture of black and white people than the one we were studying in school – like Jesse Owens and the black guy who could do four thousand things with a peanut. Of course we rural, somewhat isolated, kids were naïve in such matters, having no personal experience. But what struck us most was not the issue itself but the fact that it was a issue – thankfully, one in places far, far away, and not much connected to daily life in Millheim. Where the hell was Topeka, Kansas anyway?

Chapter 2

Straight From The Pages Of Mark Twain

"I'd like R49 please." I was calling Bierly on Millheim's version of the Bell Telephone System. It was not exactly state of the art – even a kid like me knew that.

Through the early '50s (and I don't know for how long before that) the telephone system in Millheim was operator-driven. Homes with telephones had large wooden boxes, enclosing all the marvels of modern communication, attached to the wall. On the front was a microphone into which the caller spoke. A metal crank protruded from the right side of the box; near it hung an earpiece.

A call was made by removing the earpiece, cranking the handle, and waiting for a woman (it was always a woman in those days) to say, "Operator." Then one leaned toward the microphone and made a "request," comprised of a letter and at least two digits. The operator would make the connection, if she were so inclined.

This antiquated phone system was another one of my annoyances with Millheim. State College had already abandoned that dated technology. There, we had already moved to black desk phones with the straight, cloth-wrapped cord that connected both the speaker and earpiece in one convenient, hand-held unit. We could contact my Aunt Edna directly, with no operator, just by dialing Adams 709. Now we had moved to

Millheim, and I had to talk to some lady sitting on the second floor of the hardware store before I could contact Bierly.

And I knew those ladies listened in. It just made sense. These operators knew everyone's business in Millheim. They were local residents, and there just weren't that many homes with phones. They recognized voices, and of course, they remembered many of the most-called numbers. Actually, I seldom used Bierly's number. I would crank the crank and wait. When the operator came on, I would say, "I want to speak to Bierly." She'd say, "Okay, Eddie, hold on," and she would make the connection. Or, she might say, "Oh, Eddie, Herbie isn't home now; they went down to see his Aunt Orie and Uncle Lester." She knew who I was, she knew "Herbie" wasn't home, and she knew where he was – at the Rote's mill and home west of Coburn.

I really didn't know to whom I was speaking. And one never asked. Operators were very busy people; no small talk with them. So, they either connected the call or told why they weren't going to bother.

Customers were supposed to respect that. In those days, there were consequences if one fooled with Ma Bell. One of my dad's favorite stories involved an old timer down in Coburn who forgot that fact.

Apparently, these old style phones, simple by today's standards, still were beyond the ability of some to handle. Now residents of Coburn, the little village south of Millheim, were served by our local exchange. An old codger, whose name I never learned, just could not deal with this new-fangled system without getting unnerved and angry. One day, for some reason, he became infuriated with the operator who was attempting to assist, or not assist, him with his call. Whether he was angry because he could not complete a call, or was being charged for a long distance call, or could not locate the correct number he needed is not important to the story. He was upset.

So upset and frustrated that in a rage he told the operator that she should just, "Stick this phone up your ass!"

Well, anyone who remembers Lillie Tomlin's parodies of tho: and the phone company on those 1970s *Laugh In* shows reali... ... old fool was not going to get away with that. The telephone company was going to respond.

They did. Representatives went directly to his house and confronted him about the incident. He readily admitted that he had said just those words to "that woman." The telephone company employees told him that he would have to apologize to the operator. Failure to do so immediately would force them to remove his phone. They could do so then because the phone company owned all the equipment and simply charged a rental rate for that service – due at sign-up of course. Surely planned, the phone guys told the old man that the operator was working at that very moment and could take his call.

The old geezer thought about it long and hard for several seconds. Then he picked up the receiver and cranked up the operator. She answered. "Is this the operator who I told to stick this phone up her ass?" he asked.

"It is," she replied.

"Well, Honey, get ready, because they are coming with it."

I assume that is how he left it.

Anyway, I called Bierly because I was ready to play. We were probably about eight or nine years old at the time. We met in the alley behind his house and, with Queeny, of course, headed downtown. It was a spring day, a Saturday or a Sunday. It had to be spring because Elk Creek was running riotous. The creek is typically a fast-moving stream, but in the summer it is quieter and, in the early fall, almost serene. In the winter it freezes over, not fully, but very close to it. But that is another story. This one involves the spring water level, a torrent of deep, swift current. (In hindsight, I realize that the creek in springtime was a dangerous place for kids our size – actually, anyone. Were one to fall in, that current was going to hurry one downstream in rude fashion, providing opportunities to meet rocks and old tree stumps along the way. One could drown there.)

Still, Bierly and I spent hours along the creek, skipping stones, building mini-dams, wading and searching for crayfish and salamanders under the rocks. While neither of us enjoying fishing, we loved playing in and near the creek, no matter the season.

Elk Creek and the millrace gate

The stretch of millrace that caused some problems

We were particularly fascinated with the mouth of the millrace. Just out from under the erector set steel bridge that carried Route 45 across the creek, the mouth of the race veered off to the right. It began at the top of the five-foot dam that cascaded the water on through the lower side of town. The mouth of the race was about six feet wide, contained by concrete walls on both sides. I suppose this wall and a tiny patch of grass yard kept Derwood Climb's home from eroding into the race and the creek. That concrete wall continued down one side of the race for most of its trip along the alleyway behind all the downtown businesses. From there it turned and headed due south to the old Brick Mill.

On the creek side the concrete wall encased the race for only several yards, gradually becoming a ground embankment. Now this embankment was discernibly lower in height than the other side – perhaps a foot or more lower. That seemed strange, but it was not supposed to matter. The level of the water in the race was never to exceed a certain level. That level was well below that dirt bank on the south side of the race.

The water level was determined at the mouth of the race, back at that six foot opening. There, straddling the entire raceway was a large, solid wooden gate, hinged on one side so that it could be opened or closed to varying degrees – blocking or unblocking the water entering the race. Someone in town – we never really knew who exactly – was responsible for monitoring the gate.

This was not a daily job. It was really more of a seasonal one. In the spring the gate needed to be virtually closed because of the high water and rapid speed of the creek. Plenty of water found its way into the race to keep it running at a soft, even two-foot flow. In the summer and fall the gate needed to be pushed open – almost fully open — so that more water could enter the race.

Bierly and I changed all that on this bright spring day. We got to fooling around with that gate. I guess we decided to let a bit more water head down the race. Maybe we didn't even think about more or less water; we just wanted to change the current setting to see what would happen.

Nothing happened. We changed the gate setting – we opened it wider than its normal spring setting. But that made no immediate difference. So, we played around the gate for awhile, splashed each other with the frigid seasonal run-off, and got bored with the race and its gate.

We left, and did not think another thing about it for four days. That is when we heard that many residents of Penn Street were experiencing ground water flooding in their yards and basements. All those beautiful old Victorian residences down the left side of Penn Street began collecting water that was seeping in from all around their properties. This was a shock because the spring did not seem abnormally wet. Nor was the previous winter particularly snow-filled – certainly not enough to cause a melt that could flood Millheim. And why did it seem to be restricted to just one part of town – to one side of the street?

Eventually, someone noticed the race. It was swollen with water. So swollen that it was overflowing the lowest sections of its south side ground embankment. Once over the bank the water sluiced its way across Lucius Stover's yard and on across his neighbors' yards further down the street. For three days it sluiced, apparently without notice. On the fourth day, it began to flood yards and basements. The town fathers corrected the problem: They simply closed the race gate back at the bridge.

On the fifth day, Millheim's version of a lynch mob began an attempt to identify the infidels who changed the gate setting. Fingers were pointed everywhere. Someone had to pay. Penn Street residents were in an uproar.

Bierly and I lay low. The obvious worry for us was that Derwood Climb might have seen us. He would have fingered us if he could, no doubt. But apparently he saw nothing. All he could contribute to the situation was that he had seen us there before, and, in fact, had shooed us away on at least one other occasion.

But that was only circumstantial evidence, and everyone knew it – the town fathers knew it, Derwood knew it, and Bierly and I knew it.

We decided a good defense was a good offense, so we joined in the discussions about how such a thing could happen and who was to blame. Benny Benfer, the barber, lived about five houses down from the race, on the left side. His was one of the homes affected. I happened to need a haircut around this time, and when I went in, he grilled me pretty hard for information. He obviously had heard from Derwood Climb. Well, I launched into animated, hands-punching-the-air attack on whoever would be so stupid and thoughtless as to do such a thing. I sympathized with Benny all over the place, and told him I thought he had every right to whip hell out of the cad who flooded his basement.

This sympathy seemed to mollify him a bit. Bierly told me later that he had a similar discussion with Doyle Summers, a mechanic down Penn Street who wanted to know if Bierly knew anything about the debacle. Bierly told Doyle that from now on he and I were going to keep an eye on that race so this sort of thing didn't happen again. He said Doyle seemed good with that.

***

With Bierly a little knowledge was a dangerous thing. When he got a fact or two, he leaped to some activity, quickly and with all absence of due consideration.

One summer morning (it had to be morning because we went to the pool in the afternoons – always) Bierly and I were down at the old mill hanging out with several other kids.

"Hey, you know where oil comes from?"

"Yes, I do. It comes from the ground," I answered.

"Yeah, yeah," he says, "but do you know what it is?"

"No."

"Well, it is decayed vegetables and leaves, and other dead stuff. What happens is all these weeds and plants and trees got stuck under the ground a long time ago and rotted. When they got all rotten, they turned to oil."

"Cool."

"Yeah, cool. But think about it. We could make some oil if we wanted to."

Now we already knew that people who worked in the oil business were rich. There was money in oil. (Incidentally, this knowledge preceded the old television show "The Beverly Hillbillies" in which other small town folks stumbled onto that fact.) So we quickly decided that we ought to get into the oil business. After all, if all that oil just happened to be some old, rotten, squashed vegetable gunk, we could manage that.

With dollar signs in our heads we implemented our get-rich-quick plan. We trekked up to Bierly's house and requisitioned about six potatoes from the pantry. We cut each into eight or ten little chunks and put them in a paper sack. We grabbed his dad's garden shovel and off again we went, across Sheep Hill to the Brick Mill.

We went around to the back of the deserted building. The ground there was stony and high with weeds. Being obscured from the street and homes by the mill itself on three sides, the area was the site of many nefarious, youthful deeds. Many of us tried our first cigarettes there, perhaps a beer, and often a first kiss. The area was strewn with broken glass. It was sunny and hot on that side, but it was just the place we needed.

The old mill looks better today than when we were in charge of it

Bierly had read that the vegetable matter needed to be under pressure to turn into oil. We figured the stones there, plus some short lengths of boards and a few broken cinderblocks would weigh down the oil-conception pit just about right.

Taking turns with the shovel, we dug. We dug as deeply as we thought necessary. It was tough digging so it was not difficult to convince ourselves that eight or ten inches would be plenty.

We threw the hunks of potato into our trench-like hole. We covered them with dirt and placed some old pieces of wood on the site and jumped up and down on them – just to increase the pressure. Then we tossed on some big pieces of stone and cinderblock and sat down on them – more pressure.

We planned how to spend our money. We agreed that all the profits would be split fifty-fifty. We shook hands and decided that we would wait a few weeks and then inspect the area to determine if our oil was ready. Bierly had read that it took someone else's oil thousands of years to form, so we knew there was no big rush. On the other hand, we did not want to wait too long either. All the town kids came to that area, and we didn't want any of them to find our oil.

They didn't. When we finally remembered to get back down there to check the fruits of our labor, we did not get fruit. We got vegetables. There behind the Brick Mill were about five of the nicest potato plants in the world. Well, that is not quite fair. There were about five all right, but they were scrawny and only slightly green, twisted into grotesque shapes from working their way up through all the offal we had placed on top of them. But they were there – instead of any sign of oil, whatever that might be. One look at those plants and we knew that any plans we had of becoming oil barons were pretty much dashed.

***

Bierly and his schemes. He once read how important it was for folks to be prepared for mishaps and accidents. Apparently the article extolled the virtues of having a quality first aid kit at one's disposable. That's all it took for Bierly. He decided that he was going to carry a first aid kit with him, all the time, just so he would be ready for any calamity.

He began small enough. He found himself a small cloth bag with a drawstring around the top. This was just perfect for carrying several band aides, a few cotton balls, a tiny bottle of tincture of iodine, and a small roll of adhesive tape. He figured he was all set; after all, he already carried a pocketknife, as we all did then, so he had a sharp blade to dig foreign matter out of wounds and to cut his adhesive tape.

The first time I saw him with his new addition, it was swinging from his hip with the drawstring looped over his belt. It seemed a pretty good arrangement, but somewhat incomplete to me.

"But, Bierly, do you think you have everything? Think about it. Splinters are better pulled with tweezers rather than dug out with a pocketknife. Punctures should be cleansed with peroxide, and you need Ace bandages for twisted ankles. What about broken bones? Splints, right? How about aspirin for headaches?"

Bierly allowed that all these were important considerations.

The next time I saw Bierly the little, dangle-at-the-belt kit was gone. Bierly had expanded his first aid capabilities, having acquired all sorts of new stuff from Doc Forsythe's Drug Store. He had obtained the tweezers, Ace bandage, and the aspirin that I had mentioned. But he also had sprung for a small bottle of Witch Hazel, a folding cup, and a length of hermetically-sealed cloth strips/bandaging. There were a few other items also, some of which could serve the double function of both first aid and general assistance in the situations in which a young boy periodically finds himself. There was now cord string (tourniquet), a pair of small scissors, and a magnifying glass.

For this Bierly needed a bigger container. He solved that problem by appropriating, from his dad's store, a gray metal box that had previously held those old, long red electrical fuses that filled fuse boxes everywhere. The box was about ten inches square and had a sturdy metal fastener to keep it closed. It also sported a convenient metal handle for easy transportation.

By the time I saw it, Bierly had already painted the box white and was planning on adding a big red cross on the hinged cover. Now, he decided, he was set for life's travails. Whatever might befall us, he was ready with medical help.

So wherever we went for the next week, that medical kit went along. He had outlined the red cross on the top of the box, all ready for painting, but that never happened. Inconvenience happened first. Bierly had trouble carrying it and doing anything else. He couldn't skip stones across the creek and hold that thing. He couldn't eat an ice cream cone or drink a bottle of pop and reach into his pocket at the same time. He had to set the box down often. Sometimes he'd forget to pick it up. We'd be halfway up the hill toward home, and he would remember that he had left the first aid kit sitting in the five and ten cent store. Back we'd go for it. I will admit now that I was not sorry when his gusto for that box began to wane. After all, we never once needed it. We only seemed to hurt ourselves when we were the most ill-prepared to do so.

We talked about and actually tried different ways to fasten the kit to Queeny's back. We thought she could carry it for us like a Saint Barnard carried rum in those pictures we had seen. Just as an experiment, we tried tying it on her with one of Bierly's belts and a length of rope, but it kept slipping. Besides, Queeny didn't like it.

One day we headed out over Sheep Hill without the first aid kit. I never saw nor heard of it again.

***

In retrospect, Herb Bierly was Tom Sawyer to whom I played Huck Finn. This is more than a convenient comparison; it also is one I never made during our youth. It did not occur to me until I was in college and read both those classic Twain tales in American Literature, 101.

Bierly was a unique romantic. He was, like Tom, a bit impractical, headstrong, and impulsive. Add a dash of petulance. He was bright, and he knew it. He was quick-witted and admired by both kids and adults for that. He was creative. He was "a man with a plan," always with a new scheme. Most featured that unmistakable Tom Sawyer aspect of connivance. He was adaptable. He feared nothing and would have been equally reliant in any urban, suburban, small town, or forest setting. His ability to forge his immediate environment to his own tastes and conveniences made him the lightening rod of all events about him. He was in charge of any grouping even if he didn't know what he was doing. He was to become the quarterback on the high school football team – what else?

His interests were wide, but seldom deep. He stayed with new things for only short periods of time. When we were done with something, we were done with it – the FBI fugitive, the millrace, the oil scheme, the first aid kit.

Bierly was thin and wiry. He was in constant motion and engaged in several activities at once. He could not simply walk anywhere. "Walk" is just not sufficient to describe his loose-jointed, helter-skelter, limbs akimbo style of ambulation. He cut a wide swath, needing lots of space because he found it impossible to navigate in a straight line. He simply

30

required space to negotiate anything. Walking down the sidewalk with him was a study in bumps and nudges. His arms would swing away from his body, his legs would stretch far in front of him in an exaggerated stride, and his head would bob and weave like a boxer's. His eyes were always darting from side to side, surveying the entire landscape in front of him. When he ambled down a long hall – say the type found in a high school or a hospital – he was likely to brush up against both walls if he was going any distance at all.

Not that he was spastic. Far from that. Bierly was a wonderful athlete. As we grew older, he led the football team and became a star wrestler, competing at 127 lbs. In all athletic endeavors he was experimental and daring. We used to joke that he had some form of brain disorder that was causing both his originality and his lack of fine motor control. We may have been correct. We just didn't know as much about such things in those days. I now believe he was a perfect specimen of hyperactivity.

His hair was a tight knot of interlocking wires, curly, springy, and tight against his head. He could make it stay in place for about the length of a church service, if the preacher kept the sermon within reasonable limits.

He needed glasses by age nine. He selected big, round caramel-colored plastic frames with red, green, and yellow filaments lacing crazily through them. On his small face they made him look like a cartoon earthworm with huge glasses.

His mother was very concerned when Bierly went public with his glasses. For some reason she feared that we would make fun of him and call him "four-eyes," or tease him such that his fragile little ego would be damaged. Only his mother could worry about abuse to Bierly's self-confidence. When I showed up for the premiere of his new look, his mom quickly took me aside. She gently, but with an edge to it, told me not to offend him during this difficult time of transition. I remember laughing in her face. Bierly upset? Give me a break! Nevertheless, I pledged my allegiance to her sensitivity edict and waited for Bierly to show in his new eyewear. When he did, I dutifully said something like, "Hey, you look good, Man." He looked at me and then at his mother who was, naturally, in the vicinity. Then he emitted an off-hand snort, and we headed over Sheep Hill. That's the last we ever talked about his caramel-colored glasses.

Bierly's individuality was reflected even in his name. He was the only person in town, kid or adult, who could get by on just one name. From the day I met him, he was always known as just "Bierly."

There were Bierlys spread all over Penns Valley, Brush Valley, and the mountainside. There were young Bierlys and old Bierlys; there were Bierlys marrying Bierlys, and Bierlys producing new Bierlys. Millheim sported at least five Bierly families alone. Herb's dad owned Stanley C. Bierly's Heating and Plumbing store just four doors up from the red light on the diamond. He was known by everyone. Bierly had an older brother, Curt, who was equally well known.

But all these Bierlys were known by their first names. Herb Bierly was known by "Bierly." Even as far away as Rebersburg, where there were lots of Bierlys, all of them went by first names – Kip, Roger, Keith, Sam. The only Bierly in the valley, young or old, who went by surname only – enough to identify him to anyone – was Herb Bierly. His mother and, occasionally, an operator, a teacher, or a saleswoman may call him "Herbie," but even that was rare.

Bierly had what my mother termed a "strong personality." He could change the focus of his attention quicker than Elizabeth Taylor was changing husbands in those days. However, he had real difficulty changing his mind about anything that he "knew for real." What he "knew," he held as gospel. He did not want to be confused with additional facts. After all, he already had acquired some information to form his opinions, and that was good enough for him.

He had many closely held inaccuracies. For a while, he was fascinated by foot and mouth disease. He was convinced that it was "foot in the mouth" disease. I think that is why he found it so interesting. I tried, to no avail, to correct this notion, but he would have none of it.

He made me hunt with him all over Millheim for the elusive but deadly Black Widow Spider. It didn't seem to matter to Bierly that the Black Widow Spider was not indigenous to our part of the country. He wanted to capture one because he figured we could scare all the girls in town with it and then sell it for a small fortune to some museum, circus, or zoo. We climbed around barns and sheds, looked under old boards and around rock outcroppings. We dug holes in the ground near the crumbling remains of several old building foundations down on Penn Street. A wasted effort, of course, although we did unearth two garter snakes, myriad spiders, earthworms and millipedes by the hundreds.

Once we argued for days about which was the largest snake in the world.

"The boa constrictor is the largest snake in the world," Bierly pronounced.

"Well, Bierly, I just read in a *National Geographic* at Doc Reber's office that an anaconda is the largest thing on its belly."

"No, no, no. The boa constrictor is the biggest. I read it in *Boy's Life*."

"Bierly, one of these magazines is wrong, and I think it is yours."

Didn't matter what I said. Bierly could never let that go. The boa constrictor is bigger. Whatever. I let it go at that.

The same thing happened regarding his conception. We were considering that one day, so he marched me up to his parents' bedroom to show me how he was conceived. He probed about his mother's side nightstand and pulled out this tube of lubricating jelly (what did we know about "lubricating?").

"See, my mother puts this inside her, and then she gets pregnant, and out comes a baby. That is how I was made."

"Seems pretty easy, Bierly. And what does your dad do, watch? I think you are wrong here. There is something else going on." I was gently trying to move him to the concept of sexual intercourse.

"Oh, no," Bierly answers. "My mom just uses this ointment."

To be sure of myself, I checked this out. I went to see Paul Lingle. He was two years older than I, and he knew stuff. Paul Lingle had two sisters, both older than mine, and he often filled me in on how things were accomplished. As a matter of fact, some of that previous knowledge was probably why I balked at Bierly's explanation.

Anyway, I went to Paul and asked him where babies came from. He gave me an amazingly accurate story. I found out later that he was pretty much right on the money. So, I went back to Bierly to tell him the truth about his conception.

He freaked. Jumping on me, throwing both fists and profanity, he says, "My dad loves my mother. He'd never do something like that to her." I tried to tell him that he was missing the point here, but he just kept flailing away, and I was too busy defending myself to keep arguing. Let him think what he wanted.

I have no idea how long Bierly was able to cling to the notion that he came from a tube of K-Y Jelly.

The Bierly's lived well. They always had a new car – two actually, in a time when that was not exactly common. His home always showcased the newest things – automatic dishwasher, a new and improved television set, and all those household gadgets. Some of this was the natural result of his dad's appliance store, but such accumulation carried over to clothing, toys, and cash as well. Bierly always seemed to have money. His spending habits were definitely more flamboyant than mine. Bierly had stuff. If he didn't have a suitable product for his newest need, he would craft one. He was creative and driven to experimentation in his childhood, mixed up world of fantasy and fact.

In contrast to all of that, I was Huckleberry Finn. Compared to Bierly's impetuous nature, mine was much more practically oriented. I tended to ponder things a bit more. I usually viewed Bierly's little brainstorms with a wide-angle lens. I attempted to discern both the impacts and consequences of our plans. For example, could we possibly die doing this? Is this trouble? Who else gets involved here, and can we withstand that? I was more meticulous.

I was simply slower to make up my mind. Actually, I was slower, period. He could run faster, swim faster, understand faster, and decide faster than

I could in all arenas. He was always at least two steps ahead of me. Bierly galloped; I loped.

Wasn't he a beautiful child? Probably better looking than Huck

I was thicker in stature than Bierly. While we were about the same height, I was always heavier, by five, then ten, then fifteen pounds. By the time we got to high school and joined the wrestling team, I competed in weight classes at least two or more divisions above Bierly's. In football he was the quarterback. I was the center. My job was to give him the ball so he could do his magic. If we had been horses, Bierly would have been the Tennessee Walker and I the lowly workhorse.

My role in our relationship tended to be one of modification and mollification. Bierly would initiate a wild activity or create an outlandish plan. I often needed to suggest changes that would make it more survivable. I was the ways and means guy. I had to be careful not to insult him by demeaning his "off the wall" vision. That would be an affront to Bierly. One could never tell him that his latest idea was just plain stupid. I needed to frame my contributions so as not to tame the original concept to a point that it no longer interested him. Keeping Bierly's schemes viable was no mean feat.

In contrast to the lifestyle of the Bierlys, my family lived a sparse and frugal life, fashioned by my mother. We lived such that we could endure the next depression. My dad was a school administrator in the days when school administrators were not well compensated. My mother did not work outside our home. Discretionary funds were not vast.

If Bierly's lifestyle featured largesse, mine reflected parsimony. The differences in the homes, I think, promoted the different outlooks we brought to our lives. Bierly had more means at his disposal; he was not shackled by necessity. I, on the other hand, had been taught to be cautious in all things.

So it was for Tom Sawyer and Huck Finn. The first was always more flamboyant, the second more restrained. Tom always had answers, Huck always had questions. Tom was rather self-absorbed; Huck had self-doubts. Tom looked out for Number 1, Huck worried about others. Tom was an idea guy; Huck was a problem-solver. Tom was impulsive while Huck was methodical.

Bierly and Frye.

Chapter 3

Of Hills and Caves

Sheep Hill was an important piece of real estate in our world. This sloping piece of farm field stretched from the edge of our house right down the alley, past Bierly's, all the way to the creek. There Sheep Hill was so steep that it forced Elk Creek to make a hard right turn to run down behind Penn Street. At our end the rise was very shallow, but by the time it got to Bierly's, it had developed a large, steep hump. Mid-way into that hump was an outcropping of rocks and undergrowth – weeds, sumac trees, and briars. This wicked terrain ran like a spine right from the middle of the hill to the creek. In front of that thicket was open field; behind it was a fenced-in pasture used by a local farmer.

Sheep Hill: Sledding in front, bull pasture on top, widow maker on right.

When Bierly and I wanted to go to Penn Street, especially to the old Brick Mill, Sheep Hill was the preferred route. Instead of going down the alley, across the creek, down to the diamond, and then left down Penn Street, we could just cut directly up and then down Sheep Hill. It was the hypotenuse on a right triangle. We could cut up that way, pass Roger Hosterman's house overlooking the creek, and cross the footbridge that he had built to access Penn Street. We could be at the mill in about ten minutes.

Unless the bull was in that pasture up behind the sumac trees.

That upper quadrant of Sheep Hill was cordoned off with rusted barbed wire fence. Whoever owned or rented that piece of the hill pastured a fast and mean bull in the small hilltop clearing. Because of the contour of the sloping land and the three sides of sumac and weeds that surrounded it, the bull was not always in sight. Bierly and I had to crawl through the wire fencing and begin to cross the small pasture before we could determine the bull's whereabouts. All we wanted to do was cut from the near corner of the pasture right straight through the middle to the far corner. We meant that bull no harm.

He did not share our ecumenical nature. If that bull was in the field, he chased us. Always.

I was scared of that bull. Of course Bierly was a faster runner than I. That meant that if the bull were successful in catching one of us, it would probably be me. We both knew that, and Bierly used to make great sport of it. We'd arrive at the fence and he would say, "Are you feeling fast today, Fritz? You better be able to reach that far corner in fourteen seconds, because the bull can do it in fifteen."

On all but one occasion I successfully outperformed the bull. Usually, I was victorious because the bull would be in one of the further corners of the field and simply had to cover too much ground to make it a real contest.

However, one day this was not true. Bierly and I had climbed through the fence, meaning to cross the field as usual, right through the middle.

Queeny squeezed in under the lower strand and followed at our heels. We progressed up the rise carefully, attempting to locate the bull before he located us. As luck would have it, he was standing almost in the middle of the field, looking directly at us. That was a singularly bad placement.

Now the correct course of action was to turn around and exit the field from the same corner we entered. It was close, right behind us, only about twenty yards back. But, of course, that was the opposite direction from our destination – the old mill – and that would have been an inconvenience.

"Come on, we'll make the corner easy," Bierly said, almost nonchalantly.

"I think we better go around," I offered.

"Pansy. Come on, let's just go." End of discussion. I knew that because he just began to move forward.

Gingerly, I followed Bierly about ten more yards into the pasture, with the bull standing dead still watching us with that black-eyed, impassive stare. I was hoping that he was not even the slightest bit interested in us, that he was just casually observing our passing. For a moment I thought we were just going to pass directly off to his right and take a gentle curving route to the far corner of the pasture.

Not so. With no warning whatsoever, he charged. No pawing the turf, no snorting, no shaking his huge dusky head. He just charged.

At Bierly.

I was walking on Bierly's left, about six feet from him. The bull charged from a distance of about fifty feet. He had taken a bead on Bierly, veering toward him immediately. Perhaps he had been mulling this victim selection while he just stood there glaring so intently at us.

"Ah, shit!" Bierly yelled. "Look out! That prick's got me!"

Bierly peeled off to his right in a dead run for the near side of the pasture, the sloping downside of Sheep Hill. Queeny followed him; I do not think she yet sensed any danger. Bierly's goal was to clamor through the three-strand barbed wire fence and reach the sumac outcropping on the other side. He didn't seem to care much which way I went.

I broke off in the opposite direction, up the slope and toward the top of the pasture. Once I was assured that the bull wanted Bierly instead of me, I straightened out my route and cut right through the middle of the pasture, near where the bull had originally stood. I stopped in the middle of the field to see how Bierly was making out.

Not so good. He had beaten the bull to the barbed wire fence. I don't know if he had tried to jump the fence, crawl under it, or climb through the strands of wire. Whatever he had selected, he was about ninety per cent successful. He had gotten most of his body on the safe side of the fencing. However, his left leg was hung up in the barbed wire. Somewhere between his knee and ankle his dungaree had caught in the fence wire. His leg was captured there like a fallen branch. Luckily, however, he was lying perpendicular to the fence with just half of one leg hanging over it where the bull could attack. Queeny had taken the role of guard dog, but it was not a station to which she was born. She moved about frantically, barking herself off her front feet, but staying a respectful distance from the combat zone. She was like a mother robin flitting about when someone goes near her little babies in the nest. But she really had nothing but noise to offer.

Bierly was kicking and hollering to both the bull and me.

"Get me out of this wire! Get this prick off me! Get the hell away from me, you prick! Don't do that, you stinking cow! I'll kick your teeth out! Stop that! Where the hell are you, Fritz?" A mixture of fear, annoyance, and bravado.

I wasn't sure that the drooping barbed wire or Bierly's shouting and kicking about would deter that bull for very long. But animals do not like barbed wire. That is why Joseph Farwell Glidden invented it back in 1874. And Bierly was making a hell of a racket. For the moment, he and the wire seemed to be holding off the bull.

I could see the bottom of his PF Flyer sneaker pushing and pulling forward and back as he tried to free his leg. Bierly always wore PF Flyers. I always wore U.S. Keds. Bierly swore by his PF Flyers, claiming, of course, that they provided more speed than my Keds. "You'd run faster if you just wore the right sneaker." Since he was already faster afoot than I, we had no way of determining this.

Anyway, the bull halted his charge at the fence and butted Bierly's sneaker with his head. He pawed at it with one then the other front leg, but he couldn't get quite close enough to Bierly's leg without getting into the barbs himself. That he was unwilling to do. He shuffled a bit to the side and tried a different angle, but the same barbed wire that was holding Bierly prisoner was also protecting him from the head thrusts and the leg stampings. Bulls seldom bite, so Bierly was safe on that account.

I watched this horrifying scene from a safe distance. I had moved to the fence row below the conflagration and had begun working back toward them. At the first sign of trouble, I figured I could safely bail overboard. I looked at Bierly. His face reflected as much surprise as fear as he considered his predicament. He was flailing his arms to cause a distraction; he was trying to kick the bull in the snout with his semi-trapped leg. And he was looking for me to help. Amid all that other stuff, I heard him appeal several times, "Fritz . . . . ?"

So I helped. Best as I could. I picked up a fallen sumac branch, a partially rotten length of limb about five feet long. Immediately the thin end fell off, but I still had most of the length. There were a few fronds hanging off to both sides, but they were dried out, and of no additional weight.

I moved into the field a bit, further away from the fence than I had hoped would be necessary. My initial idea was to get close to the bull and spear at him the way a bullfighter does. After all, seeing such a thing on television was my only experience in making a bull do what he doesn't want to do.

But the closer I got to him, the more I realized that was not a good idea. First of all, I was leaving my safety net, the fence, at a distance that was just plain unwise. If the bull turned on me, I would never reach the other side of the barbed wire in time. Second, I knew the old limb was not sturdy enough to penetrate the bull. It would snap again somewhere out near its dull, broken end. No, the matador-in-the-blazing-sun routine was not going to save the day.

Better it was, I decided, to attempt to irritate him into surrender. This plan provided me with the comfort of being on Bierly's side of the fence. I liked that part. Close as we were, better Bierly than I. An awful thought, but there it was.

So, I ran back to the fence and climbed through the bottom two wires. For a second, Bierly thought I was going to exit the area completely and let him to his fate. Again I heard an imploring, "Fritz . . . ?"

But then he saw me drag the old branch through after me, and he started to realize the plan.

I ran up to him and straddled his body. In his thrashing about with his raised, trapped leg, his knee hit me several times in the groin. While that hurt, I could not exactly ask him to lie still and provide the bull a sitting target.

I lifted the stick and started jabbing the bull in the face with it. When he turned away, I jabbed his shoulder, then swung clumsily at his legs and hit him with a glancing blow. He looked back at me, either angered or bewildered. I repeated the sequence again.

And that did it. Irritated, frustrated, and beaten, the bull simply backed straight away from us and the fence. He snorted one time and walked up along the fence row.

I unhooked Bierly from the wire. Queeny came near to sit beside Bierly. She had a look of satisfaction that would have led a newcomer to surmise that she was the heroine in this gig. Bierly pulled up his pant leg to check for bodily damage. Just some long scratches and a little blood. "My frigging leg burns."

We knew that under normal circumstances he should receive a tetanus shot – that old barbed wire was rusty and filthy. But each of us already had current tetanus shots. Kids like us always had that protection. Knowing that "kids will be kids," our parents periodically had Doc Henninger shoot us up. So that was of no concern.

One would think that little drama would have cured us from crossing that pasture ever again. It did not. As a matter of fact, we sat there and relived the event with great satisfaction. Then we noted the location of the bull in the far front corner of the pasture. We walked on up Sheep Hill and crossed the pasture at the high end; letting the bull in contemplation of how he missed the best chance he was ever going to get at Tom and Huck.

We continued to use that short cut to the old mill for years.

$$***$$

But all of that happened in the far reaches of Sheep Hill. Only that postage-stamp corner of the hill bore us malice. The rest of Sheep Hill was for sledding. Many of the kids in town, certainly all who lived up East Main Street, did our sledding on Sheep Hill. It was the best hill in Millheim for that, especially if Warren Fox, who rotated crops in this rented field, had not planted corn the previous summer. If he had, we simply needed more snow to cover the old shocks that were left from corn-picking. If we got enough snow, even that didn't matter. Sheep Hill was a sledder's paradise.

The hump in the hill, just out Bierly's back door and beside the edge of the sumac and stone outcropping, was perfect for us. We would take our sleds down that hump for hours – until our gloves got wet, our feet numbing cold, or until our moms called us home for dinner.

We all had our own sleds. My sled was a short, stubby Lightning Guider, unique on Sheep Hill. I believed then and still do today that it was the fastest sled on the hill. When I lay down on it, half of my legs would hang out in space off the rear – that's how short it was. But it was fast. It was like the sports car of the sledding world – much smaller, much more maneuverable, and much more fun to drive than those behemoths of my chums.

Many of the other kids also had Lightning Guiders. From nearly the turn of the century forward The Standard Novelty Works in Duncannon PA produced Lightning Guiders. That information was stenciled right on the underside of the sled. Most of them, like Bari's, were longer than mine. Common to most sleds of our era was the red thunderbolt painted across the wooden slats. That distinguished a Lightning Guider from all other sleds on the hill. Some kids had Flexible Flyers, another popular sled. I much preferred the Lightning Guider, mostly, I suppose, because I owned one.

We had faithfully waxed the runners of our winter chariots. We used either the expensive sled wax available at the hardware or good, old-fashioned soap straight from the bathtub. I think Bierly used Crisco just to be different. It didn't matter much, even if he thought so. His sled, like my sister's, was the longer, conventional model of the Lightning Guider, and he could never really compete with me in the pure speed department.

The bigger kids knew how to "groove" a hill, packing the snow just so. The establishment of a base coat of snow turned to packed ice made for better sledding. Preparing that snow was the responsibility of the older, more experienced kids. We younger kids were told to wait at the top of the hill until Curt and Lee and Leonard and Barry worked in several trails down Sheep Hill.

"Go!" Curt's final clearance for takeoff would rumble across the hill, and everyone – there were often thirty or more kids — would leap onto our sleds. The games had begun. Queeny, bless her huge canine heart, would stand with us until the sledding started in earnest. Then she was all over the hill, chasing one and then another sled down the slopes, but never getting too far from either Bierly or me.

Then we would get inventive. Early in the season and early in the day, riding down the hill in our Lightning Guiders was just the ticket. But after about an hour we were ready for some variation. We would turn to three such alternatives.

The first involved finding unconventional ways of going down the hill, beginning with how many people we could get on one sled. The second involved experimentation with various non-traditional forms of transportation upon which we could traverse that hill. The third involved adding to a deadly level of difficulty and danger in the route itself.

When the day started, we usually went one on one down the hill. One man, one sled – just as the specifications from The Standard Novelty Works dictated. We would make our first few trips down the hill by lying down in the conventional form of sledding.

Soon, however, we would try sitting up, using our feet to steer our missiles down the hill. That increased the difficulty and, therefore, the risk. It was high drama to see someone lose his balance and tumble off into the snow from this up-right position. So interesting was this that we would soon try standing on the sled and steering it with the towrope. Soon, someone would try going down backwards, first lying, then sitting, and finally standing. All this resulted in what seemed like spectacular crashes.

Then we started adding people to the mix. The more, the better. First, we would stack two, then three riders on one sled like lengths of wood. The bottom guy would always complain of being "squished." That was usually a foreshadowing of the loss of control that was sure to occur somewhere down the slope. We would take the bigger sleds and put several riders on, all in various positions, one standing, one lying, and one sitting. The results were predictable.

We also formed "trains." We would line up our sleds at the top of the hill. The first person would lie down on his sled and hook his feet into the front of the sled behind him. We would link up several sleds this way and then have someone start the entourage down the hill. We could make a big sweeping turn that would challenge the riders in the rear sleds to stay aboard. Often they did; sometimes we had what could be called a multiple crash.

When we tired of these innovations, we moved to the second variation. We experimented with equipment not designed for sledding in the first place. If it looked as if it could slide down the hill, we tried it. For example, someone would bring a big cardboard box. First, we would place it on a sled and put someone, or several someones, in it. That way, any rider would be going down the hill blind. Later, we'd forego the sled and just push the box down the hill. We'd do this until the box shredded or someone was injured.

Then we would go over to Bud Rigger's garage that sat at the edge of his property on the alley at the bottom of Sheep Hill. Bud repaired cars in that garage, mostly bodywork. Outside his garage was a pile of discarded fenders, doors, or hoods from cars of all makes and models. We would select from the pile any odd thing that might make a decent conveyance.

Once we dragged the slightly crinkled hood of a '54 Plymouth up the hill. We had to smash off the hood ornament so it would not dig too deeply into the snow when we turned the thing upside down. The greasy underside of that hood was not comfortable, what with its several rough metal protrusions sticking up at us. These small metal knives would cut us even before the ride became bumpy or, worse, interrupted violently by a sudden stop, a roll over, or change in the distribution of the payload. I do not think our intended usage was what Chrysler Motors had in mind when they designed this several-tiered engine cover.

All that made it the perfect device for sledding. We rode that lime green and chrome hood down Sheep Hill in all configurations. That old hood would spin around in wild circles like those new aluminum dishes, only the ride was much more unpredictable. I once watched Bierly and a few others ride that hood down the hill, completely over the bank of snow plowed off the alley, and right into the pile of discarded auto body parts from which it had earlier been taken. Home again, but with blood.

Still, this experimentation with non-conventional vehicles got old. So we moved to the next level of adventure. This one was stupid.

Right beside our regular trails was the beginning of the sumac and rock outcropping that ran down the second half of the hill. It was rough terrain. There were small gullies and deep ruts in the steep hillside. Big rocks protruded from the ground. There were sumac trees of all sizes and various nondescript weeds and bushes. Worse, there were strands of old barbed wire running through the sparse tree line. Apparently, in years gone by that section was part of the upper pasture that lay behind it and up the hill. Some of the barbed wire was still attached to the trees in the copse; some of it had sagged to the ground and lay under the snow. This, along with the rugged terrain, created dangerous landmines for anyone trying to negotiate the area on a sled. Anyone passing through there had to watch for trees, rocks, and barbed wire, some of which hung at eye level to the prone sledder.

It was a perfect venue for the reckless, impervious-to-injury sledder.

That would be the Bierlys, the Bonners, Mike Toomis, and I.

Every winter Curt Bierly and Barry Bonner created the "suicide run" over in that copse of trees. Starting at the top of the hill, the sledder would turn hard left and cut into the trees. As one entered the mini-woods, the trail dropped off quickly and the speed of the sled increased. We now had to steer around sumac trees and rocks, both seen and unseen. There were old unconnected strands of wire, a few cans, bottles, and lengths of rotten fence posts strewn about the woods. All of these could stop a moving sled dead in its tracks; the rider usually kept going.

The trick was to stay on the trail that had been created. One foot to either side was no man's land. We had no idea what dangers lurked beneath the snow.

Curt and Barry Bonner were devious engineers. They would cut the trail into short straight stretches followed by sharply veering turns, some of which started or ended with a sumac tree positioned right along the course. After a few runs these sumac trees would be barked up from repeated brushes with our metal runners. It was difficult to avoid these trees because we also were passing over, down into, and out of those gullies and ruts in the steep downward slope of the hill. All of this was just prologue to "the widow maker."

"The widow maker" was more dangerous than it sounds. It was, in my mind, the fulfillment of Barry Bonner's death wish.

In the last row of trees going down the hill there were still those three strands of barbed wire attached to the sumacs just below where Bierly had

47

his run-in with the bull. For about thirty yards the rusted fencing draped loosely from tree to tree. In the steepest part of the terrain there was a small dip or gully that passed under the fence. In this tiny section, the dip made the clearance about twenty five inches or so. "The widow maker" involved passing under the barbed wire at this highest of low points. The height of the sled and the thickness of a young boy heavily encased in snow clothes made the clearance a matter of inches. The sledder had to keep his head down for those last moments before going underneath the fence or he risked some degree of decapitation.

But that was difficult to do. The dip under the fence was guarded on the up-hill side of the run by four small sumac trees. There were two on either side of the trail, framing it like a cattle shoot. After all the maneuvering, twisting, and turning required above the hole in the fence, the rider had to ensure that his sled entered the shoot absolutely straight. If he hit the trees, his sled would stop or veer off to the side. He, however, would be launched right into the three strands of barbed wire in front of him. So, to see well enough to steer correctly into the shoot one needed to keep his head up until he was assured of his accuracy. Only at the last possible moment, a nanosecond before dipping under the wire, could the sledder lower his head.

We normally performed this maneuver with closed eyes. There are some things one just doesn't want to see. One soon found out how successfully the trick had been performed. If there were no sickening thud – if one didn't become airborne or enmeshed in barbed wire – he would open his eyes two seconds later to see nothing but the open field of Sheep Hill sloping down to Bud Rigger's garage.

We all had our wrecks at the widow maker. Some were worse than others. I once saw Mike Toomis hit one of the guardian trees. He was launched into the upper two strands of barbed wire. He actually flipped in mid-air and hit the wire with the broad of his back. We had to free him and his torn red and black plaid Woolrich coat from the barbed wire. Bierly hit one of the sumacs so hard that he broke three of the four bolts that held the front of his sled together. He had to borrow a sled to finish the day on the hill. He had to promise the lender that he wouldn't go through the widow maker.

There wasn't a mother in Millheim who would have allowed anyone she knew, let alone her own child, to use that trail. That part of Sheep Hill we just never mentioned to our folks when they asked how sledding was that day.

***

Bierly and I were "thick as thieves" as Mom used to say. But I knew most every kid in town. Of course we all congregated at the pool, on Sheep Hill, and down at the old brick mill. I was capable of getting into a fix with any of them — Davey White, for instance.

He was one of the kids who lived up Texas. Older by a year than I, Davey was a good looking kid with a dimpled smile, a quick sense of humor, and a curious streak that almost got us killed.

Davey had constructed a primitive camp up in the hills south of town, down and behind Penn Street. By primitive I mean that he had dragged some old tin sheeting and boards up into the hills and nailed them together. The result was a room about eight feet square, furnished with a wooden trunk that served as a table, complete with a oil-burning lantern, and a few boards nailed together, creating both a seat and a bed.

Every now and again Davey and I would go up there to camp for the night. My parents had no objection to this. They had never seen the place, but we told them we would be covered from the elements and that it was better than a tent.

Davey and I would pack a sandwich, grab our sleeping bags, and head for Johnny DeSoto's gas station. We would buy several bags of potato chips, about six bottles of soda, and a pack of cigarettes for each of us. We would take our treasures and head up to the camp where we would eat junk and puff our weeds into the late evening. We'd review the news.

"How do you like Elvis' new one, Heartbreak Hotel"

"Guess what I read. Willie Mosconi sunk one hundred fifty consecutive balls in a pool tournament."

"Did you see that broad on The Bob Hope Show last week? She was stacked."

Soon we'd tell each other our secrets and make up wild adventures, usually involving some of the local girls. Pretty harmless and pretty safe. The only real danger was that we would burn the place to the ground what with all those butts and the rickety, old lantern. Mercifully, that never happened.

But Davey had another idea that was not so harmless. One day he showed me some old carbide lanterns. Carbide lights were in wide use much earlier in the century, by miners, railroaders, and early automakers. Most were made of brass or nickel and came in various models that allowed them to be carried or mounted onto such things as miners' helmets.

Carbide lights worked through the marvel of chemistry. The bottom of the lantern was a reservoir holding chalky lumps of carbide, a combination of carbon and calcium formed into thick white wafers so that the caked powdery substance could be broken up and placed into the lantern well. Once we filled the reservoir with shards of carbide, we just poured in some water. That caused a chemical disturbance that produced a flammable, if somewhat smelly, gas. Now all the operator had to do was turn open a valve on the nozzle head of the light and strike a match. Presto! Light! Not very good light, but light. What was produced was a bluish-white flame that sort of sparkled and sputtered. It reflected off a circular disk behind the flame in an effort to throw the illumination forward.

Well, Davey had two of these old-fangled contraptions — small ones — but working models. He also had the calcium carbide needed to fuel them.

These old lights fascinated Davey. He wanted to find a way to use them. He knew we needed a dark place. Then he remembered the cave down near old brick mill.

Everyone was aware of the cave. It was in the hillside that ran behind the mill and nearly out to the alley that ran down that side of Penn Street. We knew little about the cave. Of course we were instructed to stay out of it. That was not a difficult order to follow. It was not a particularly attractive nuisance. Given the limestone rock that underlay the soil throughout the valley, there were lots of little caves throughout the area. We were not that interested in them. Kids seldom talked seriously about entering this particular hole. Besides, if we wanted to see caves, we only had to beg our parents to take us down to the commercial cave in Woodward. Or, we could ride a boat through nearby Penns Cave, America's Only All Water Cavern.

This cave was no match for those. It was simply not worth the effort. It did not have an easy, accessible, and convenient opening. Huge slabs of limestone had slipped down the forty foot hillside from under the upper levels of dirt and vegetation. To enter the cave one had to lie prone and slide between two huge rocks into a sliver of an opening. Then the explorer had to squeeze along rocks covered by moist, green, and black mossy goo. The trip was impossible without becoming slimed from head to toe. All of this was just prologue to the cave itself. Finally, this tight entry channel intersected with the real cave itself.

Of course we didn't know that before we attacked the hillside. We had no idea where we were headed or what we were doing once there.

No matter. We were going in. We had Davey's carbide lights, and we wanted to test them under real game conditions. Besides, we had developed this notion that no one had ever been in there before. No kid in town bragged about ever being in the cave. This was going to make us famous.

Perhaps we should have told someone of our plans. Perhaps we should have timed the lights to determine how long they burned between fillings. Perhaps we should have carried some reserve carbide with us. Perhaps we should have carried back-up flashlights. Perhaps we should have listened to our mothers.

We didn't. We assailed the cave.

Everything went well for about fifteen minutes. We slid through the gooey crevice. When we crawled to the edge of the sunlight's ability to reach back the channel, we lighted the lanterns. Then we forged ahead to the opening that joined the main channel of the cave.

The main channel ran at about a thirty degree angle to the entrance path. What was really happening was that we were crawling through a big crack in the wall of the main channel, finally merging with the channel about twenty feet from the cave entrance. Where the two paths intersected, the opening was no more than a slice in the wall through which a kid might just barely fit.

We were little, so we popped right through onto the big hallway of the cave. The very first thing I noticed was an exhausted, blue flash bulb lying on the path. There went any notion that Davey and I were the first to tread this ground.

The hallway ran to our left and right. We turned right, but there wasn't very far to go in that direction. We could walk standing up in here; in fact, the ceiling over our head was at least ten feet high. After only fifteen feet or so the hallway widened to a small room – solid rock in all directions. This was clearly the northernmost end of the cave.

We held our lights up and away from us. The room was about ten feet in diameter with a ceiling at least that high. There were rock formations – stalactites and stalagmites. Water dripped off the ceiling onto the caked clay floor. There were expended flashbulbs all over the place. We spent a few minutes there and then headed down the other direction, past the opening that brought us into the hallway.

This end was much more significant. About thirty feet down the hallway, the cave opened up in all directions. The ceiling had to be twenty feet high, about the same size as the room diameter.

This chamber was majestic. It looked like those caves we had read about in those Ali Baba stories and had seen in movies. Yellow stone walls with rivulets of running water. Several levels of stones, decks almost, on which we could perch. Great echoes and the smell of slightly stale and acrid air.

We were pointing things out to each other, from formations to flashbulbs, when Davey's light sputtered and went out, all in the space of about three seconds.

"Let's get the hell out of here."

"Right behind you," Davey's voice was one of impending doom.

We turned to retrace our steps back the channel. Almost immediately, my light sputtered and extinguished itself.

It is really dark in a cave when the lights go out. Pitch black doesn't describe it. Abject black gets closer but is still just a bit weak. I know this: A ten year old in such a situation gains a new respect for black. For about a half of a minute I thought I was going to die there. I'd like to say that my whole life flashed before my eyes, but, actually, it was too dark for that.

Now we were standing in a big, dark space. I'm not sure about Davey, but I nearly freaked. I could feel the panic rising in my throat, and I was tempted for a second to start off to my right as fast as I could, with or without Davey, with or without telling him that I was leaving. If we both were thinking the same thing, he didn't mention it.

Instead, we stood dead still and began to reason this thing out. We knew the opening we needed was to our right. But we also knew it was just a crack, not a convenient doorway with a red exit sign over it. We also knew it was not the only crack in the rock wall that formed the front side of the cave. There were fissures all along that wall, some of them big enough to crawl into even if they didn't lead very far.

The biggest fear of all, however, was that we both knew that we had not really taken very good stock of the cave. We had really just started in this endeavor. There may have been other paths that our dim lights had not yet revealed. There may be cuts in the wall that led to other rooms, or to pools of water, or deeper into the hillside away from the mouth of the cave. We only knew of two paths, the entrance slice and the main hallway. What if there were more?

We spent a moment or two considering our fate, were we unable to find our way out. First, we would get cold. Then we would get thirsty, then hungry, then weak. Days later, after extended and agonizing suffering and self-recrimination, we would die. Actually, one of us would die first, and the remaining one would have to decide where he stood on the subject of cannibalism.

Sadly, nobody would find our skeletons for fifty years, and that would be by sheer accident, because no one would ever think to look in the cave for us.

No use contemplating such scenarios for too long. We needed to try to find our way out. So, with each of us advising the other and working very close to the other in that pitch black, we backed up to the wall behind us, turned and put both hands on it, and began feeling our way toward the room at the other end of the hallway.

The trick would be to find the right slice in the wall. The challenge was that we had not made any real mental note or calculation of how far down the wall it was when we first entered. It seemed to me that it was closer the other end of the corridor than to this one, but that was really just a guess. What if we went by it? Could we find it again on the way back? What if we somehow got going off on another hallway that we had not noticed when we entered? After all, those stupid lights weren't too bright. My mind was dancing with terrible possibilities.

We moved slowly, feeling our way along the wall with Davey in the lead. Abruptly, he stopped. "I found it. This is it!" he declared.

I stepped around him and felt what he was feeling. Geez, it only felt like a small slice in the wall. This couldn't be it. It didn't seem nearly big enough for us to climb up into. Surely we didn't come through here. It just didn't feel right.

"This is it. This is it." Davey was adamant.

"It better be, or we are really going to be lost,"

We climbed up into the narrow passage that started about a foot off the cave floor. I didn't remember that either, but on through we climbed. It was a tight squeeze; we were crawling across solid rock coated with that muddy slime. It was a scary minute or two when we left the only thing in the cave that we knew, the main corridor. I kept telling Davey that he had better be right about this.

Davey was right. We clamored along the angled rock formation, forward and slightly upward, waiting to see some shaft of light ahead. Mercifully, it finally appeared, and we emerged into the full sunlight. We sat there awhile to gain our composure. We discussed a few errors we had made in the conduct of this venture. I handed Davey the defunct light I was carrying.

"You know what you can do with this frigging light . . . ?"

Then I offered a suggestion.

We went our respective ways, told nobody about our adventure, cleaned up, and waited for dark. Then I crawled between the sheets in my moonlit bedroom, listened to the crickets outside my open window, and cried.

Chapter 4

Life and Death in Black and White

"Contrary to what any of you may think, this man is dead. I can assure you all of that."

With those words, George Reiff certified my first personal experience with death. That little step toward adulthood transpired on a Saturday night in front of Stanley C. Bierly's store. For some reason my memories of that event, and all the deaths and danger I was personally near, are in black and white.

Bierly and I had been to the first showing of the movie at the Millheim Theatre. Most kids near our age always went to the Millheim Theatre on Saturday nights. The first screening always started at seven o'clock with the second showing coming sometime after nine o'clock. While westerns and World War II movies dominated the slate of offerings, *The War of the Worlds*, *Ben Hur*, *The Blackboard Jungle*, *On The Waterfront*, and other great offerings visited Millheim, even if they were screened well after appearing in more populated areas first. Young couples — some teen-agers — but mostly those serious couples in their early twenties went to the second show. We little kids sat in the lower section; the smoochers sat in the balcony, no matter which show they attended.

On the way into the theatre we often checked out the balcony just to see if any of those older women I adored were there with the losers who were trying to bed them. I was perpetually on the lookout for Betty Carlston,

Dottie Cabel, Jane Bitner, and Roxanna Revis. If they were, I'd engage them in small talk.

"Did you see my sister up here? I need to give her lunch money for next week."

Or "Is Bierly up here crawling around the floor looking for Dots?" I think they knew what I was up to. I'm sure the losers did. They always seemed really annoyed to see me.

After the movie, we walked up Penn Street to the diamond. We headed straight for Carl Blazer's restaurant for a 12 oz. Pepsi. We could add a small bag of Middlesworth Potato Chips and still have spent only twenty cents. That was our custom and our limit.

As we reached the corner and looked across the street, we saw a small commotion in front of Bierly's store, which was open for business, of course, being it was Saturday night. We hurried over, anxious to get involved in whatever was happening. There lay this guy – this big, burly, middle-aged bruiser – sprawled diagonally across the sidewalk right in front of Bierly's entrance. He wasn't moving, and none of the eight or ten people standing around him was helping him. This is bad, I thought.

It was. The guy was dead. During the next half-hour, Bierly and I were able to piece together this much of the story. The man, one Bruce Homark, had come to town to attend the viewing of a fellow World War II veteran. He had first gone into Penns Tavern where Perch Gramley served him just one beer. Then he proceeded up the street to George Reiff's funeral parlor, about four doors up from Bierly's store, where he paid his last respects to his fallen comrade. He left with a friend, presumably headed back to the tavern. He had to pass another bar, The Millheim Hotel, to do that. But he apparently had made his choice, and he was headed back to the green door. He only made it to Bierly's when he turned to his friend, looked strangely at him, grabbed his chest, and fell lengthways across the sidewalk.

I do not know what the friend did first. I do know that these were the days before mouth-to-mouth resuscitation would have been popular in a man's town like Millheim. I know that the friend did not call Doc Henninger, because everyone knew that Doc was never in town on a Saturday night. He needed his rest; for that he had to leave town on his days off.

I think the guy went into Bierly's and told Chewy Woller, who ran the store on Wednesday and Saturday evenings. I know it was Chewy who called George Reiff to come down and pronounce the man dead.

And I know that took a while. After all, George was already attending to a viewing up there. So, we all just sort of stood around there and waited. At first, the crowd grew as pedestrians came by and noticed a man on the sidewalk with his beer-belly pointed skyward. But soon, those who wanted to had seen the body and went about their business. One guy came out of the hotel and stumbled down the street toward the body. He obviously had been in the hotel for quite a while. He walked a wide circle completely around the body, contemplating Mr. Homark from every angle. Then he declared the man alive. He said he saw an eye move. "This man isn't dead," he roared, "He's had a stroke or something." Others in the crowd scoffed at him, but he kept that up until George arrived.

George Reiff leaned over the body, placed his hand along the neck, then held the man's limp wrist out, palm up, seeking a pulse. While he was doing all this, the drunk kept stumbling around the circle of on-lookers, saying things like, "See, George, what I've been telling everyone, that man isn't dead. Is he, George, is he?"

That's when George made his pronouncement. No one questioned it further. After all, George Reiff knew something about death. Mike Behr was dispatched to call the ambulance crew who would ferry the body a few yards up the street to Reiff's Funeral Home.

While all this was transpiring, the regular hubbub of Saturday night in Millheim pretty much continued. Because the movie had just left out, parents were collecting their kids at the chosen rendezvous spots and were headed for their cars. Wobbly denizens of the public watering holes were navigating among the four choices. Saturday night shoppers carried their purchases up and down the street, and in doing so, confronted Mr. Homark, lying dead there. The reactions of these passers-by created a stark little tableau. Many, mostly the men, stopped, looked at the corpse intently, asked a question or two of the thinning gathering, and then moved on. Some, certainly all the women, did not really stop. They glanced at the body, stepped off the sidewalk, and made a wide circle in the street to get on up or down the sidewalk. Some, and this included those in the process of choosing the next bar, did not let a dead body deter them from their appointed task. They came down the sidewalk, noticed a dead body in front of them, and just simply stepped over it, muttering something like, "What the hell . . . ."

All this time Bierly and I hung back, standing in the doorway to the store, just sort of watching the goings on. We traded bravado comments about the dead guy, the drunk who thought he wasn't dead, and passers-by. We particularly liked those "What the hell . . ." guys. There they were, lurching along, unfazed by something as foreign to the scene as a corpse lying about, and unimpressed by it. They got so close as to step right over it. It was a scene out of *Wyatt Earp*. Just like the Old West.

For our part, we were not feeling quite that manly. This was our first dead body – actually our first real brush with death – and, for all our bravado, it was making an impression on us. We laughed and talked big, editorializing on the behavior of the passers-by, chiding those fainted-hearted who took the wide path around the body. Still, we hung back in the doorway of the store. We were fascinated but unnerved by the whole thing, sort of like seeing that first rattlesnake in the woods. This was new ground for two nine-year-olds.

Even then, I was struck with how black and white this death scene was. Mr. Homack lay there in an absolutely white pallor. His round face, his chubby hands and stubby fingers were white, not pink, not sunburned, not freckled with age spots – white, refrigerator white. His eyes were black as they blankly stared up to space at an angle leading directly over our heads. They weren't blue, green, gray, or brown – they were black, coal black. The death scene was illuminated from the lights of Bierly's store. It wasn't bright or brilliant, but it was white, florescent light falling out the two big bay windows of the storefront. The tight circle of observers seemed to hold it in from spilling onto the street, so it shone right down and almost through the cadaver. It was white. Behind the circle of people, out into the street and across to the other side and stores there, the ambient light seemed gone. There was the body and the people bathed in white; the background was pitch black. It was weird and pretty stark for a young boy.

I finally ambled home and told my parents of this occurrence. I remember that they had some company that evening, but I cannot remember who. I do recall that I had a great little audience for my tale, and I told it well. I hammed it up when I played the drunk and showed how the tough guys stepped right over the body. They laughed and agreed with how our Dodge City-like Millheim treated death. I was a big hit. Then I went upstairs to bed. I didn't sleep well at all that night.

***

This black and white presentation of death recurred in a few other brushes with the Grim Reaper. I almost froze/drown one winter day in the raging Elk Creek. The scene, my thoughts at the time, and my lasting memories of the event, are in black and white.

Of course Bierly was involved. In fact, it was entirely his fault that I found myself in this predicament. I might still be angry about that if it weren't that he saved my life at the end of the tale.

It was a very cold winter day – it had to be February because it was that fierce cold — the numbing, deep-frozen cold that comes in the very middle of the season, not along its edges. Everything was frozen to something else. The packed, hardened snow crunched under our boots. We had to walk around our own exhaled, white breath to keep it from hitting us in the face. The air was crystal clear, with just a few huge white puffy clouds dotting a thoroughly azure sky.

Everything else was in winter black and white. The wind had stripped all but the most tenacious leaves from trees, leaving just naked black trunks rising out of months of old snow. Everyone on the streets seemed dressed with the same dark mittens, dark hats or caps, and black boots. A weather forecaster would have said, "Very clear, very cold, with no wind at all." It was a deep-freeze February day.

And Bierly and I just had to be downtown. Queeny was with us, but she wasn't thrilled about it. She was cold from her toe pads up. She'd sit on the hard snow and tuck her head down into her neck as deeply as she could. We used the alley to Albert Stover's horse barn and turned right toward the bridge. We stopped beside the dam that jutted out from under the bridge.

The water tumbled over about half of it in a rush, white and frothy, cascading down the four feet or so into the creek below. The power and speed of the dropping water kept a ten-foot-wide well of water below the falls swirling about from the constant barrage. The rest of the stream, from about half-way across both the dam and the creek to the gate of the race, was frozen solid.

The water below the falls was about as deep as a nine-year-old was high. We knew this from summertime when we could wade in the stream further back from that area. In the summer the water would come just about up to our chins. Then, on downstream it became continuously shallower until the creek was no more than a foot deep at the bend that herded it around Sheep Hill.

That looked like fun. Elk Creek usually froze over in the winter, but seldom as fully as this. We could just tell that the ice, away from that pool under the dam, was really thick and hard. It was no longer semi-translucent or even that pinkish opaque that ice gets. It was white on white on white. Just right for skating.

And here we were without our skates. Well, no matter. Bierly decided we ought to just climb down the retaining wall and slide across the ice in our engineer boots. I was reluctant. That thin ice near the unfrozen hole had me a bit concerned. But Bierly convinced me that we would just stay away from the dam. So, down we clamored and started to slide around. Queeny, wisely, waited above.

The Elk Creek falls, the Climb property nearby

We stayed clear of the falls. The thick ice downstream was smooth, excellent for sliding around. I was sufficiently distant from the falls when Bierly called from my right, the direction of the dam. He wanted me to do something, hear something, or come nearer, I don't recall. I did one of my little running slides to get over to him.

And slid right toward the dam, the watery hole, and the thin ice that surrounded it. I went much further than I had anticipated; that darn ice was really smooth. The thin ice nearest the falls gave way. Into the frigid water I plunged, straight down as if I had been dumped off my perch in one of those carnival dunk tank games.

I fell to my shoulders. My arms were outstretched on the thin ice, though pieces of it nearest my body began to break and fall away. My feet were not touching the bottom of the creek as I dangled by my armpits. My engineer boots filled with water, my jeans soaked up water, along with the pockets and liner of my brown, faux leather, Sears Roebuck jacket. I was getting heavier and colder by the millisecond.

I was facing the dam. I could see that white water tumbling down to the small strip of ice that separated me from the watery pond in front of me. Its current was sweeping my dangling legs downstream, almost up to the ice layer above them. I could feel and sense the thinnest ice – that closest to me — giving way and breaking off in all sizes of geometric wedges. Naturally, I was thrashing about, trying to hoist myself up out of the hole that I was making larger and larger by my movements. The more I splashed the frigid water, the more I accelerated the cracking ice. I tried groping more horizontally for a purchase on more ice rather than attempting to pull myself vertically up and out of the hole. Neither strategy seemed to be working.

At some moment along this several second panic and thrashing, I began to get really cold. At first, my adrenaline rush and the speed of the accident made the cold unnoticeable – sort of like when someone cuts himself accidentally and the pain doesn't arrive until after the blood commences. But now I was getting cold – and weaker. The damn ice kept receding on me, and I was clamoring after it, in the direction of the deepest water of the creek.

I knew something for sure. I knew that if I slipped away from that ice, if I lost my grip on the surface, I was going downstream under ice that was undoubtedly too thick for me to punch through. I knew the current would carry me to shallow water, but I also knew that the ice there was the very thickest. I could not count on any air pockets down there (unbelievably, I was really thinking these things because I had seen on television where someone like Houdini or whoever had been trapped under ice but found an air pocket.) That small hope was unrealistic anyhow, and I knew it. The water was too damn cold to survive even if I could get a breath of air. I had this vision of myself swept down the stream, under thick ice, and then wedged there for the ten minutes it would take someone to cut out my lifeless body.

So, there I was, clawing and scratching at a receding surface, trying to climb out and inadvertently breaking away my own path to life. The whiteness of the situation engulfed me. Anything with any color came to my numbing senses as white only. The water cascading down the falls, the ice around me, the ice forming on my jacket sleeves – white everywhere. I needed Bierly, and I needed him fast.

And, suddenly, there he was. I think he was laughing when he first saw me fall through the ice. In a few moments, however, he realized the seriousness of the situation and sprung into action.

He shuffled across the ice to me and instantly sized up the entire situation. He saw the ice breaking away in front of me, he saw my cold, he saw my fear, and he saw my danger. And then he did just what they do in the training movies.

He knew better than to rush to me. He would have simply broken through the ice himself, and we would both be goners. Instead, he lay down on his back and distributed his weight across as much ice as possible, even spreading his arms flat on the surface. Then he sort of scrabbled over to me, offering me his right foot. I grabbed his engineering boot and tugged. He slid backwards, now on his rear end and two arms outstretched on the ice. Given something of substance to hold onto, I was able to make some progress. Meanwhile, Bierly pulled. At first a large piece of ice broke off right under me, and a white jagged crack spread out to my left across the thicker ice. I thought that would be it; the entire edge upon which my torso was perched was going to go. But it didn't, and Bierly just kept pulling and yelling for me to hold on. Finally, I was hoisted out of the freezing hole.

I rolled over on my back for a few seconds to catch my breath. Then I felt the cold again. I stood up and began running, slogging really, up the hill from the bridge to home. Bierly pushed me along, now laughing at my appearance and the sounds I was making. My clothes were freezing in that frigid February air. I was developing the look of a moving, frosted, chocolate donut. The water on my brown leather jacket and jeans quickly froze to a glaze. My movements cracked this thin surface, and little shards of ice fell from me as I ran. I was panting and moaning and chattering all the time. This all was great sport to Bierly.

It was a close call, and I knew it at the time. Unfortunately, it was not to be my last.

***

So I had seen death up close. And I had a serious personal brush with a dangerous situation. That should be enough for a young boy, but, as with anyplace else, death was part of life in Millheim.

And much of it came by way of suicide. For as bland and carefree as we hear the '50s were, there sure seemed to be a lot of suicide around Millheim. Some people, apparently, were not enjoying the times as much as others. Life had closed in on them.

When I was nine years old, Jacob Myers committed suicide. I didn't know Jacob Myers. I didn't even know who he was. But when the word got about town of his demise and its nature, it stunned Bierly and me. The whole idea of suicide was unfathomable. We had seen it on television shows where a hero ends his life in the name of a war, a noble cause, or a woman. We knew it to be the ultimate act for an ultimate purpose. But it was only for heroes in desperate times. Life in Millheim in the 1950s did not seem to us to constitute desperate times.

So, what was so desperate about Jacob Myers' life? We'd never know.

Mr. Myers was the owner and day bartender of Penns Tavern. He worked behind the big green door that separated the tavern from us kids on the street, it being, of course, off limits to us. We wondered what really happened in those bars around town. They were mysterious what with all these people coming and going, drinking alcohol, and stumbling down the street to their cars or houses. The tavern was a forbidden place to us, and we often tried to glimpse inside when someone opened the door entering or leaving. But it was dark inside and the bar was in the rear, and we just could not get a handle on what actually happened in this place. And now, the owner commits suicide.

Not just commits suicide but does it in a totally unconventional fashion. Jacob Myers shot himself with a .22 rifle — about six times. Adults were abuzz with the story. It wasn't long until we kids got bits and pieces of a wild and messy ending.

Anyone who knows anything about guns knows that a .22 rifle is not the best weapon of choice for bringing down an adult. It is not a large caliber gun. To do deadly damage the bullet must be well-placed. It seems this was Mr. Myers' problem.

When those who found him found him, he was in his second-floor room above and behind the main barroom. He was sprawled across his bed with the single-shot rifle and five empty shell casings at his feet. He had apparently wedged the barrel of the rifle beneath his chin, positioning it such that it was pointed toward his brain, and then reached down toward his ankles to pull the trigger.

The first several times he hit his chin all right, but he missed his brain. Later analysis revealed that at least three bullets exited his mouth and nose. They were found in the walls behind the body. Mr. Myers obviously had difficulty holding the gun straight up from between his legs and reaching down to the trigger. So, he angled the first shots such that none was fatal.

But each was messy and probably painful. And that is what we kids could not get by. Bierly and I tried to imagine the scenario. What was the man thinking through all those botched attempts? He had to stop and reload his single shot rifle after each effort. Even in his pain he apparently did not lose his zeal for the mission. We were amazed by the trauma and the gore of it. We were drawn to the drama. We knew there was a lot of blood from all those wounds; we had heard the grown-ups talk about that. They mentioned the blood and how white the body was when they found him. There was some question as to whether he ever hit his brain or if he just bled to death. Bierly and I knew that color of white on dead people. The whole affair bothered us, and the only way we knew how to deal with it was to joke about the circumstances.

We couldn't do that a few years later with Frosty Connors. We knew him too well.

Harold Connors was one of Millheim's most prominent businessmen and citizens. Known by everyone, even the kids, as "Frosty," he owned and operated the town's ultra-slim, weekly newspaper. He also was an insurance agent, providing home, auto, and life coverage to many valley families. He was a notary public, a deacon in his church, and a member of a country club over near Bellefonte. Bierly's dad also belonged to that country club and most Thursday afternoons, when all the stores in Millheim closed, Stan and Frosty would ride to the links together. Several times Bierly and I rode along, spending the afternoon at the club swimming pool while the men played eighteen holes.

More than that, we were friends with Frosty's son, Earl, about our age. The Connors lived on Penn Street, not far from the theatre. Earl, like his dad, was blonde-haired and was already becoming known as Frosty, Jr. He was bright, athletic, and friendly.

His dad started to have business problems and, apparently, knew the whole matter was soon to be made public. Before that public humiliation could occur, Frosty Connors drove out to the beagle training grounds east of town and asphyxiated himself inside his pink and white sedan.

His transgressions were just too complicated for kids our age to understand. They somehow involved fraudulent loans or insurance on phantom automobiles. When a bank employee and a local car dealer unwittingly unearthed the ruse, Frosty Connors' life unraveled.

When he "turned up missing," it did not take his good friend, Bill McCleary, long to figure out what Frosty had done and where he had done it. The only question in Bill's mind was Frosty's chosen method. Bill went out the beagle training grounds, one of Frosty's favorite spots, and found him.

Frosty's demise affected many of us kids. We knew him, and we played with his son. He was a father – like our own fathers. Cripes, it could have been any of our fathers. That was a horrifying notion to a youngster.

I remembered the whiteness of Bruce Homark's death mask face. I kept recalling this picture of a really pale Frosty Connors with a face as white as his close-cropped hair, sitting up-right behind the wheel of his DeSoto. I always associated Frosty in a car because of those trips over to the country club; he and Stan Bierly in the front and Bierly and I in the back making snide comments to the backs of those two silvery white heads of hair.

This death was different. It was someone we knew. It was someone's dad. Poor Earl. It was so stark and sad. The whole idea of losing a father this way paralyzed us. It rendered us incapable of offering any consolation to Earl when he probably most needed it. We just were not able to get over it enough ourselves to help him. I do not remember ever saying anything in the way of empathy or kindness to Earl when I saw him after his dad's passing. Like others in town, I simply avoided the issue. I pretended that I hadn't noticed his dad was gone.

I also pretended that it could never happen in my family. Many of the kids in town adopted this elaborate self-denial. Earl, thankfully, in his decency, let it stand at that. He was always quiet, but in those months following his father's death, he became even more so, and almost incapable of carrying on a prolonged dialog or participating for any length of time in our childhood activities about town. For the longest time we didn't see him at the old brick mill, the pool, the street – nowhere. Earl just got quiet and scarce.

These suicides gave us kids a glimpse of adulthood that scared us. As kids, we thought that adults ruled their domains. Adults had money to spend, folding money, not just pocket change. They had access to bars. They drove cars, going anywhere they wanted to go. They decided how to spend their time. They made decisions for everyone in the family. Kids couldn't do these things. There seemed to be so many really neat things about being an adult. But now, we sensed a downside to all this freedom and self-direction. Adulthood must be harder than we thought. Apparently all families were at risk from some unseen set of pressures. It could happen to anyone's dad. That was scary.

Sometime after Frosty's demise, Ben Sebane, who with his wife ran the hosiery mill down on Water Street, took his own life. That one, I realized later in my school studies, had a sort of Richard Cory aspect to it, reminiscent of the Edwin Arlington Robinson poem. Ben Sebane was another man of strong reputation and public favor who was unable to cope with the pressures of leadership and responsibility. His wife, actually the real force of the factory, knew Ben was becoming increasingly despondent and had a powerless feeling he was going to do it. The day it happened, she had a sixth sense premonition, so, without going to check their house when she left the factory, she went uptown and asked John Conner to go to their house down Penn Street and look in on Ben. The news wasn't good.

To top it off, the father of one of our acquaintances, Roger Wagner, also committed suicide. That simply added more credence to our fears. Here was another father cashing out before his time.

Bierly and I tried to treat the deaths of our friends' fathers as no big deal. Certainly they did not have the drama of Jacob Myers' demise, so there was no titillating speculation on the gore and the ghastliness of the scenes. But, for all our boyhood bravado about death, these deaths subdued us. They were simply too close to home, and we could not shake them easily.

***

Until we all became teen-agers and started driving cars, these were my personal experiences with death, discounting the near-death experience of Barbie Knight.

Bobby Winchel and I saved her life one fine autumn day. It was a moment of high drama.

A kid doesn't get many chances to be a hero, certainly not in a situation that actually saves a life. Bierly and I had had an experience with a groundhog once that made us feel pretty good.

One summer day as we headed up the back path to the swimming pool we came across a groundhog in a real fix. The poor critter had apparently been trying to root out remnant food particles from an old 3 lbs. can of tomato or spaghetti sauce that he had happened upon. Somehow, the animal had managed to get his head stuck inside the can. Here he was with that can stuck on him back to his withers, flailing about as he tried to get some leverage against that can with his paws and blindly bumping into everything around him on the rocky hillside. He was experiencing no success, and he was growing more agitated while we watched this sad little comedy. He looked as if he had been about it for some time.

Well, Bierly and I could see that, unless we intervened, the groundhog's future was going to be bleak – death with prolonged misery. So we dare-to-be-brave lads sprung into action.

Wild animals stay wild even if someone is trying to help them. As soon as the groundhog sensed our presence, he became more excited and aggressive, stumbling about a ten-foot circle, rolling over, and emitting a strange little hiss. Neither of us thought it a good idea to approach his front end directly and simply pull off the can. That would put us just too close to the business end of an animal with awfully sharp teeth and a spoiled disposition. I had this mental picture of pulling the can off and being punished for my effort if the little devil decided that I was more of an enemy than the can. He might lunge for my ankle, or worse, leap up my leg to some really sensitive area. Maybe he was rabid. No, that wasn't a smart plan.

Ruling out the direct approach, we devised a simple plan. Bierly would take the back end and grab the little guy by his torso. I would then leap to the front end and tug the can off his head.

That didn't work. Knowing Bierly would be holding the animal back for a second or so, or at least twist him sideways when he released him, I felt that I could have done my part. That became an academic issue. Bierly could not do his duty. Every time he laid a hand on that blinded little ball, the groundhog would twist, squirm, and dig at Bierly with his paws. Bierly reported that the animal's rear toenails were really sharp.

We needed a new approach. We searched the immediate area for makeshift equipment. Unbelievably, Bierly found a knotted length of baler twine that was nailed to a length of old board. We ripped that from the board and fashioned a loop on one end, using a slipknot which Bierly knew how to create.

For the next ten minutes we tried to loop that around the hind quarters of the groundhog. All his thrashing about made that no small feat. Finally, however, Bierly got the twine over the animal's hindquarters, and he pulled the knot tight.

Now we could finally help the miserable creature. Bierly stood back about two feet and pulled the rope hard enough to lift the groundhog's rear legs off the ground. Of course the groundhog fought that move. As his body weight shifted forward, he began to pirouette, face down, on the bottom of the can that trapped his nose.

Now I could do my part. I advanced into his little circle of despair and seized the can in both hands. I held it firmly; the groundhog did the rest. Once I had the can, Bierly lowered the hindquarters. The groundhog dug in with all four feet and pulled back. Out popped his head and neck. Mission accomplished. Almost.

Bierly and I had not planned on what we would do after we freed the groundhog. That slipknot was still encircling him, along with about three feet of trailing baler twine. Now his head was free, and he could see us. In the instant following the extraction, Bierly was holding the end of a cord that connected him to an animal with the immediate intention of exiting the environs. The groundhog started thrashing about again, pulling first away from Bierly, and then stopping momentarily to size up his options, one of which was, apparently, to head toward Bierly. The situation brought reality to the old phrase about having a tiger by the tail.

We both knew that the animal would never allow us to hold him long enough to undo the loop over his torso. We quickly decided that the only recourse was to cut off the length of twine and let the creature leave, wearing a rope belt around his midriff.

So, that is what we did. Bierly had the only knife – in his pocket of his jeans. He couldn't fish it out because he needed both hands to maintain his sometimes offensive and then defensive manipulations of the twine. So I had to slip behind him and reach into his left pocket for the blade. This was difficult because he was dancing with that groundhog; each had an end of that twine, and neither was quite sure what to do with it. Pawing about Bierly's moving pocket created a slightly uncomfortable moment for both of us, although Bierly just had to giggle while I was fishing about

71

to secure that knife. Finally, I obtained a purchase on it and extracted it. I guardedly crept as close to the animal as I dared and cut the twine. Without thanks of any kind, the groundhog took one last look at us and scurried off into the thicket. Bierly and I decided that he was still better off than when we found him. Let him worry about how to shed his baler twine belt.

Anyway, that event provided me with my single opportunity to be a hero – excepting, of course, our encounter with the bull on Sheep Hill. But then the Barbie Knight incident occurred. Unfortunately, this tale did not receive enough public notice or attention to reward Bobby and me to the degree to which I felt we were entitled. I will say, however, that Mrs. Knight seemed genuinely grateful and pleased with our work.

Bobby Winchel, just about our age, lived with his mother and grandparents next door to Bierly, only two doors down the alley from my house. Bobby's parents were divorced – somewhat of a rarity in town at that time. His father lived on a farm below Aaronsburg. When we were in about fifth grade, Bobby was at his father's farm, helping with some farm machinery. There was some sort of accident and one of his knees was extensively damaged. Most of us never knew the whole story of the incident, but we knew that Bobby "lost the fluid" on his knee. That rendered the joint incapable of flexing, and Bobby was on crutches for several years thereafter.

But the Barbie Knight incident happened before all that. It occurred on a day that Bobby and I, for some reason, were wrestling in Bierly's yard. It was a cool day for autumn, and we were wearing winter jackets. We were in the far corner of Bierly's yard, as far from the house as the property extended. We were rolling around on the ground as boys will do, engaged in a mock epic battle for backyard supremacy. We were just fooling around, but with real gusto.

I never saw Barbie come from her house over to Bierly's. The Knights lived on the other side of Bierly toward town. Barbie was a small young thing, perhaps half our age. Her mother had her all bundled up in a white silky coat with an attached hood, all of which was lined with black mock fur that stuck out of the arm sleeves and edge of the hood. Barbie was wearing black pants and little white Keds on her feet. She paid no attention to Bobby and me; she headed straight for Bierly's fish pond.

Only a few steps from the rear door of Bierly's house was an eight-foot long, in-ground fish pond. It was shaped exactly like a footprint – perhaps of Paul Bunyan's big boot. It was about two feet wide at the heel section of the shape and about four feet wide up toward what would be the front of the boot. Constructed of concrete, it was about two and one-half feet deep. Originally built as a fish and lily pond, it never sported any fish as far back as I can remember. It was either empty or filled for us kids to enjoy. For some reason, it still had water in it, even at this point of the season.

We sometimes played in the pond, usually donning some ancient kapok life preservers from Bierly's garage, jostling each about the big shoe or floating on our backs. When we splashed out too much water, we threw the garden hose in and turned on the faucet. (That garden hose was always attached to an outdoor faucet and usually stretched halfway to the pool. We often drank from it as it was more convenient than going inside for tap water. Thirty years later I read that this was not a good idea. Who knew?)

The pond was a great place to cool off. But it also was an "attractive nuisance" as legal authorities would now say. There was no fence, no apron around it, nothing to protect a young child from wandering right in.

And that is just what Barbie did. She walked out her back door, across the driveway separating her house from Bierly's, and started to play by the side of the pond. That apparently lasted about one minute. While Bobby and I were wrestling, in she went – face down.

Barbie just did not have the strength or water experience to get her head up out of the water or her body vertical. That heavy white fur-lined coat did not help. It soaked up water and weighed her down like a coal barge. Now she was floating horizontally, face down, unable to get her feet underneath her. She was drowning.

From the corner of the property, Bobby saw this. I did not. As we were wrestling, he somehow turned to face the rear of the house. I know that he was on the bottom, and I was working him over pretty good. Bobby said later that he tried to tell me to stop, but he just couldn't get the words to come out. He tried to crawl from underneath me. That was to be expected, so I just tightened my grasp on him and continued to try to turn him over to his back just like those guys did on those professional wrestling shows on television. Bobby squirmed and crawled; he made guttural sounds which I took to be the results of the excruciating agony I was inflicting on him. He tried to point. I took his hands and pinned them behind his back. I was tough; I was Bruno San Martino.

Finally, Bobby was able to say something like, "Pond!" or "Barbie," or "Look up there!" Whatever, my attention was finally directed to the pond and there was Barbie floating face down, her arms spread out on the water. She was kicking and flailing in the water. Suddenly, she went motionless. She simply floated quietly about the narrow end of the pond.

Now we scrambled to her. Bobby got there first and lay down flat beside the pond. He reached in and grabbed the collar of Barbie's jacket. He dragged her over to the side of the pond, and the two of us pulled her out.

She was stark still. Her blue eyes stared at the sky, focused it seemed, but unmoving. Her face was white, white, white. I had seen this white before, and it did not bode well. Mr. Homark was white like this. Her jacket was sopping water; the fir of the collar and hood were matted to her neck and forehead. I thought that she was dead.

Neither Bobby nor I knew anything about CPR, artificial respiration, mouth-to-mouth resuscitation, or any other life-saving technique. Bobby moved Barbie to a sitting position and started to shake her. That did not seem quite right to me. I thought that was only going to help the water settle in her, making it more difficult to dislodge. I had this mental picture of shaking a sack while filling it so it can hold more. I knew she was full of water, but I decided to treat her as if she had an obstruction in her airway. I took her from Bobby, laid her on her stomach, and hit her on the back with my fist – several times.

I doubt that hitting her helped poor Barbie very much. However, lying on her stomach must have. Within a few seconds she started to cough up water and move her eyes.

Barbie lived. She cried like a baby, but she lived. Five minutes later we walked her home, knocked on Mrs. Knight's back door, and told her Barbie almost drowned. She freaked. She saw all that water, she saw the look on Bobby's face, and heard me tell her how lucky it was that he had seen Barbie in the first place. Mrs. Knight snatched up Barbie, thanked us profusely, and promised us that we were both going to heaven. After all the "Go to Hell" epithets hurled at me, even by this young age, that sounded pretty good.

I was able to help Mrs. Knight that day. A few years later I could not. Her husband, "Red" Knight, one of the most-liked guys in Millheim, suddenly dropped dead of a massive coronary. I remember Bierly and I walking through his house while his mother tried to console Helen Knight at the dining room table. Poor Mrs. Knight sat in a black housedress and pawed at Phyl Bierly's white table cloth, wailing and lamenting Red's passing. I remember her crying out, "What will I do? How can I get along without him? What is to become of us?" That was a sad time. There was nothing Bobby Winchel and I could do for her then.

Chapter 5

God Takes Care of Fools and Children

"T.K. Arbor called." She sounded angry. Well, a little beyond that. More like a hornet that Bierly and I had disturbed recently in his mother's snap dragon bush.

My mother was waiting for me, standing there by the kitchen window, with her hands on her hips. That was always the sign of trouble in River City.

Bierly and I survived most of our exploits without parental detection. If no one saw us or reported us, we stood a reasonable chance of dodging the proverbial bullet at home. Our personal consciences were not so keenly developed that we readily confessed to transgressions that had escaped any direct link to us. The incident with Albert Stover's Tennessee Walker, the Penn Street flooding, and the cave scare with Davey White were all good examples.

But the T.K. Arbor affair was different. T.K., himself, had called, apparently during the assault and reported us. Mom was mad. She was embarrassed. This was willful vandalism. Why would we cover T.K.'s porch with pinto beans? And what made us think we were going to get away with such a wanton act?

Well, we had no answer to the second question. The first was easier. Kids in our end of town didn't like T.K. Arbor. He had an FM radio, which he often used in the early evening. And that, we were told, caused periodic interference with the television signal we were supposed to receive from our house-mounted antennas.

Long retired from the general store business, T.K. was a semi-recluse, living just two doors down from Bierly. He was seldom seen outside, almost never downtown. He was distant and unfriendly, at least to kids.

And, besides playing that FM radio and being abrupt to us, he did not want Bierly and me crossing his lawn. Well, we had to do this often. I have forgotten why.

"Get off my grass, you punk kids! I know who you are, and I will call your parents. Have a little respect!"

Old and gray or not, T.K. Arbor was an imposing figure. He scared us. All of that put him on our short list. But, his fate was sealed with that damn FM radio.

In those days there were no television cable companies or direct TV "dishes." Television signals were airborne when they left a studio – in Altoona, Johnstown, and Lancaster – and were received by an antenna on the top of every home that had a television set. The state of the art in these early days of television still had much to solve with regard to "interference."

Enter T.K. Arbor's FM radio.

We were told, or at least formed the impression, that television signals were so similar to FM radio signals that our television sets had difficulty distinguishing between the two. So, when our sets were receiving both, or better said, when T.K. Arbor's set was trying to receive an FM signal at the same time we were trying to pull in a television signal, our TVs became confused. The picture disappeared, replaced by random lines and static, both of which obliterated any program we were watching.

I am not sure this description of the situation is accurate. Worse, I am not sure the condition actually existed. In other words, I am not sure that T.K. was to blame when we encountered interference on our sets.

But that's what people said. We'd be watching a television program and suddenly the picture would turn to snow and the sound to static. Invariably, someone in the room would say, "T.K. has his FM on again." To have our supremely entertaining shows interrupted by less than an act of God was infuriating. Little wonder then that Bierly and I cut T.K. no slack in the good neighbor or "he's aged, so let him be" departments.

Like Slinkys, hoola hoops, and Silly Putty, pea shooters became a short-lived rage in Millheim. Of course Bierly acquired deluxe models for both of us – not that there was much one could do to improve on its basic design. It was a nine-inch plastic straw. Pretty simple instructions for use, too: fill mouth with peas; hold the pea shooter to lips; blow. Ours were deluxe in that the edge of one end had been slightly rounded so that prolonged use did not allow the sharp edges of the plastic device to irritate our lips.

Prolonged use was just what Bierly and I intended. He handed me the red one, kept the blue one, and filled both our pockets with pinto beans he had purchased in Bricker's that morning. Actually, he didn't purchase them. He just had Pete Rodefer add the cost to the monthly family grocery bill. Families could do that in Bricker's – pay as they go, or run a tab.

Anyway, after about two minutes of practice, mostly on each other, we headed straight for T.K. Arbor's house. This had to be Bierly's idea.

In the last light of a chilled autumn day we unceremoniously pelted his house. D-Day for T.K. Beans everywhere. The little pellets pinged off his front windows, ricocheted off the clapboards under his porch, and bounced around his walkway and doormat. We must have reloaded ten times each. The barrage lasted at least ten minutes.

T.K. never came out. We decided he must not be home. That took some of the fun out of the attack. So we quit and wandered up to our respective homes. To our mothers with their hands on their hips.

Bierly and I were to lose several privileges for this little endeavor. First, however, we were dispatched to T.K. Arbor's house to clean up the beans. We did so, without ever seeing T.K. at all. For that we were grateful.

***

"Where were your parents during all of these shenanigans? Weren't they watching you? How could you get away with all of that? How could you run so freely and be so unsupervised? Didn't your parents worry about you – your safety and what you were doing?"

These are fair questions, asked by friends over the years, but they rise from a skewed point of reference. Such questions obviously reflect the real and extraordinary pressures on today's parents to be constantly vigilant about the whereabouts, activities, and safety of their progeny. Assuming that the same conditions prevailed in the 1950s, the questioner is actually insinuating that somehow our parents were less responsible than mothers and fathers today — that our parents simply failed to keep us on "the straight and narrow."

The real answers to these questions involve differences in time, place, and culture. By today's standards, I suppose our parents were less wary and more permissive. No doubt we were loosely tethered by very long apron strings. Maybe all our parents had read Benjamin Spock's book, *The Common Sense Book of Baby and Child Care*, but I doubt it. Published in 1946, this best-seller challenged traditional beliefs about child rearing. Spock advocated more affection, more flexibility, and less discipline on the part of parents who should realize that they were raising individuals, not automatons. The book, selling in the millions, perfectly reflected post-war America and its feel good, let everyone be free, almost cavalier attitude to any political, social, cultural, or parental undertaking. But I doubt that the book, as important a commentary on parenting though it may have been, was the major influence on the Millheim parents. They were just living out their roles in simpler times from those in which my younger friends interrogated me.

In retrospect, I point to several societal or cultural conditions that defined those years.

First of all, childhood was viewed as a self-contained time period in which kids should simply enjoy being young and carefree. Our jobs were to play, to learn how to make friends and our own decisions, and to acquire some personal responsibility and a few moral principles. The future was no more important than the present. There was no inordinate pressure on ten year olds to select a career, or identify our university of first choice.

"Give me a healthy and happy child," was the national anthem for parents. Surely, they worried about getting kids to successful futures; surely they worried about good schools. The 1950s featured the last national movement of consolidation of tiny, isolated districts into larger, more robust, learning centers. In the main, parents supported such efforts, knowing that their children would have more and varied educational experiences.

But, getting into and actually going to college was a goal of only a very few Millheimers. And doing so did not require a dedication to fleshing out a child's resume with robust personal experiences. They could not have achieved that anyway. Kids could not have participated in adult-organized experiences in soccer, music, swimming, computers, math and other specialty summer camps. Such opportunities didn't even exist near us. Our parents could not have driven us from one activity to another even if they had the requisite mini-van, which, of course, they didn't. Where would they take us? There was little league baseball; there were on-again off-again efforts at keeping Boy Scout and Girl Scout troops going. Kids could take piano lessons from the preacher's wife or trumpet lessons from the moonlighting high school music teacher. That was it, and we could walk to these paltry offerings. While this was certainly true in rural areas such as ours, it was mainly true throughout the country. "Developmental" opportunities just weren't yet the fashion.

Actually, just finishing high school was a worthy endeavor. In the mid-'50s only about one-half of the nation's youth were graduating from high school. The graduation rate for the five tiny high schools in all of Penns Valley was only somewhat higher than this national average. For example, the Class of 1956 offered ninety-five graduates. These were the remaining seniors from a class of one hundred thirty six freshmen who entered the secondary grades, a graduation rate of 70%.

Only a small fraction of those graduates ever planned on or actually went to college. This didn't matter anyway. There were lots of jobs in American mines, farms, fields, and factories. Parents of the era knew the value of education, and they knew the value of personal experiences in the formation of their children's futures. Their approach, however, was to allow these to happen, not to cause them.

Certainly, child-rearing and parental responsibility attached thereto was important. Parents weren't nonchalant about their roles. Most just thought that hovering over their children was going to be unnecessary for the extraordinary opportunities the post-war boom was offering. Whether they realized it or not, parents were following the Spock formula: teach the young the condition of the world, let them experience success and failure, further the notion that they can be anything they want to be in this era of self fulfillment, and, at least equal to all of that, develop in each child the self-reliance necessary to be fully engaged in present and future possibilities. This formula did not include unnecessary hour-by-hour monitoring of a child's movements or activities. Just let them play.

Parents everywhere wanted the best for us. They worked hard to provide it. In fact, that was the role they established for themselves. They were to work hard, to make money so the family could live well, to provide warm and nurturing environments, and to tend to their children's basic needs. They were not to organize all the events in their children's lives.

Our parents instructed us to be diligent in all endeavors, so we could be anything we wanted to be. They just weren't compulsive about rushing us to the future. "Helicopter parents" were simply a rarity.

Still we had a few.

"Sonny" Price's mother was a bit compulsive about the welfare of her only child. She required more reports home from her little boy than the rest of us had to endure. She had a "no fly" list of kids she ordered him to avoid. Of course, Bierly and I were on that list. Sonny tried to honor that mandate, but it was a small town and the pickings were what they were.

Sonny was the last kid our age to get a bicycle – just too dangerous. A BB gun? Forget it. Stay overnight at a friend's house? Maybe next year.

Mrs. Price would often follow Sonny down the street to assure that he hadn't fallen in with the wrong crowd or crossed the road without looking. One day she walked her little prize down to the diamond, up to the corner. Sonny needed a haircut and had to cross the street to get to Benny's Barber Shop. That was a worry for Mrs. Price. She was very safety conscious, and, more than that, she just didn't trust traffic lights. There were only two of them in the entire valley: one up at Centre Hall and this one on the diamond. Her fear was that these high tech traffic flow devices would malfunction or, worse, that some careless driver just wouldn't be paying attention. She probably had some concern also for Sonny's decision-making ability. So, she instructed him, for the sixtieth time, how the maneuver was accomplished.

Sonny made it, so she headed off home, fussing to herself about whether he could make it back across that light. Maybe she should have just gone into the barber shop with him. No, that would have embarrassed Sonny. Ladies seldom entered the shop. Mothers did not take their school-aged children in at all.

Her fear was misplaced. Sonny, left to his own devices, told Benny that he wanted a "flat top," like the teenagers were sporting. Sort of minimal hair styling. Benny remembered asking if he was sure and did his mother approve this. "Sure, sure," says Sonny. Benny gave him the shorn look and, somehow, Sonny negotiated the demon traffic light and made it home.

Which sent his mother right back down to the barber shop. She was in a real snit. Her little man's longish, blond hair was gone. What was Benny thinking?

Benny tried to explain, but that was difficult because Mrs. Price was chasing him around the barber chair attempting to strike him with her purse. Several other customers, waiting their turn in Benny's chair, had front row seats for this loud and animated scene. They agreed that it was one of the great moments in hair-cutting history.

Benny finally mollified the fiery, red-headed dervish chasing after him by taking the long-term view. "It'll grow out; it'll grow out," he kept offering, until Mrs. Price finally ended her enraged pursuit.

"Well, it better," Mrs. Price snorted and stomped out the door.

Now the upshot of the story is this: "It'll grow out," became Benny's disclaimer in the barber shop. Benny hung a hand-lettered sign bearing this obvious future and referred to it anytime a customer had a concern about what Benny was going to do to his hair.

This pithy, little, wide-angled view quickly made its way from the shop to the street. For many of my years in Millheim, both kids and adults quoted it to sum up the worst long-term effects of some planned action.

How bad can it be if, "It'll grow out?"

Perhaps the 1950s were more about adults than their baby boomer children who didn't yet have that name or their later huge impact on how "things got done." The 1950s concerns of adults included job stability, new products — developing exponentially after World War II — the new media of television, and an unbridled optimism about the future, despite the "Cold War." Most adults were enjoying a lifestyle that was a clear improvement from their own childhoods. These continuing improvements, of course, built upon those of the last several generations, and folks expected that the human condition in America was going to simply get better and better. Hope was a movable feast. Parents had few fears that their children would not be just fine, now and in the future.

This less-frenzied approach to parenting also recognized that kids were going to learn to deal with life's unpleasantries. No parent could help a kid avoid that. Children needed to learn that into every life a little pain must fall.

Like going to the dentist.

My dentist was old Doc Reber. His office was on the second floor of the building used by Boob's IGA market, right beside the drugstore. My dad and mom did not receive their dental care from Doc Reber. They used an old acquaintance up in State College. Bierly did not visit Doc Reber because his mother could drive him to Bellefonte for all his dental needs.

But my mother didn't drive a car. Therefore, Bari and I were condemned to Doc Reber, a terror who ruined at least two dozen days of my life.

Even before the "old days" of the 1950s, dentistry was a relatively primitive form of medical attention. Doc Reber was more primitive than his peers. With his "very old school" machinery and approaches, he lowered the bar in treatment to the human mouth.

Doc was a huge, pot-bellied, tobacco-chewing old guy who simply infused – okay, drilled — unmitigated fear into his young patients. When I had to climb the dark, wooden steps to his lair, I was the shaking, physically-sick embodiment of a knave who was about to encounter the sword-wielding king. A pain-inflicting king who had absolutely no regard for a knave's physical comfort, no compassion for his very low threshold of pain, and no interest in the knave in general.

Doc Reber was there to fix my cavities, and I always seemed to have one. God, where was fluoridation when one needed it?

These were the days of slow-moving, belt-driven drills. For Doc Reber to prepare a tooth for a filling, he found it necessary, or personally rewarding, to use about four different bits in that vibrating arm of torture. He did so without compunction or apology. He simply started drilling away without the use of Novocain. While such a local anesthetic was available (Bierly always received Novocain in Bellefonte), Doc Reber didn't believe in it. Said it was for sissies. He didn't believe in cleaning teeth either. Patients should take care of their own mouths. So, he'd just drill away. I was supposed to be a man and handle the pain, the terrible vibration in my mouth, and the sound of his big belly churning up digestive noises right beside my ear. During the procedure, Doc was likely to stop long enough to go spit in the sink across the small room. I actually looked forward to this hiatus of pain. But, he'd return and, changing from one bit to next in succession, drill me out. It was unsettling. I resented my parents at the time for subjecting me to this.

Doc Reber also pulled teeth. In my case, four at a time. I had to pry out the fifth one myself while sitting in his chair.

During this particularly memorable visit, Doc said I had several "baby teeth" that needed to come out. I knew about two of them. They were already loose. I had planned on working on them later.

But Doc Reber said we would do them now. They and three others that just had to go. So, he grabbed one of his larger picks and, without ceremony, pried out these two loose teeth. He fished about with his big fat fingers and extracted them from my mouth. Uncomfortable, but not too unmanageable.

Now we were ready to tackle the three monsters. He reached for a bigger pick and started digging under my gum line. That hurt. In due course the first two teeth gave up after relatively brief struggles. Wounded and bleeding, I thought the worst was over.

Doc had pulled both of them without removing the first one first. Now I had two teeth floating about my mouth. He inserted those fat fingers (no latex gloves in those days) into my mouth and tried to capture them. He couldn't.

"The hell with this. Let's just get the last one."

Turns out he couldn't.

From where I lay in his reclining chair and from where he leaned in over me, Doc's assault on this tooth was hampered by leverage. Doc Reber just couldn't manipulate the pick – the third and biggest used so far – into a position from which he could force the tooth up and out. He tried long enough that my mouth was sore, bleeding, and sensitive. He finally gave up.

"You do it."

I already had two freed teeth bumping about my mouth and he said to add a third. I am to do this without looking. He just handed me the enormous pick and instructed me to use my left hand to insert the monster under the stubborn subject and pry it out.

Amazingly, and under extraordinary personal stress, that is exactly what I did. I knew it was going be painful, and I saw the irony of my own self-infliction of pain. Greater good, I was thinking. Besides, that's what the old coot instructed.

Mission accomplished, I now had three little pearls banging around my oral cavity. Doc Reber didn't even try to go after them. He told me to capture them myself or spit them out in his porcelain dish. Using a combined approach, that is what I did.

Since that time I have visited three dentists. Each has in my patient file this note: "Extreme trauma with dentist of youth. Approach with extreme caution. Use anesthetic for ALL procedures, including regular maintenance."

So, learning to live with pain and disappointment was just part of growing up. It was a negative side to the all-sided fact that the freedom to learn how to make one's own way in the world included both good and bad. While parents were concerned about the physical, intellectual, emotional, and spiritual development of their children, the working thesis was that kids needed to develop most of these qualities by themselves, not by parental hovering. That is why we were sent outdoors for the day. Few parents worried about the emotional development of their children. "Work it out" was the operative term. If there was a problem, solve it. If a child "felt bad," that child should do something about it. Parents knew they couldn't fix such problems anyway. Whatever demons a child faced, they were to be faced by the child.

Certainly, our parents took us to church, however erratically. Of the three choices in town, both the Fryes and Bierlys had selected the Lutheran church. Bari and I were trucked off to St. Johns, down on Penn Street, for Sunday School, catechistic classes, and the fiery sermons of Pastor Teddy Ambrose, our young, short, towheaded preacher. With his coke bottle glasses reflecting the sunlight streaming in the windows, Teddy could throw wonderful, vitriolic, and engaging talks. His oratory demanded attention, and Bierly and I were capable of listening to most of that. We, during the appropriate ages, served as acolytes and sang in the junior choir. Even the white and black gowns that we had to wear for these duties, however, just couldn't quite tame the rambunctiousness of two boys who squirmed in our hard wooden pews, pulling at the tight, stiff collars, and trading snide comments during the solemn proceedings. We often left the services under fire from our parents about our somewhat disrespectful behavior.

Another reason parenting was different in those days was related to basic safety. Quite simply, the size and number of threats to kids were not large in the '50s. Life, truly, was less threatening.

If we separate safety concerns from behavioral concerns, we can get a better feel for why our parents let us run freely. Our parents knew that accident and calamity were larger safety issues than foul play. There were no street people, muggers, or perverts to prey on us. Our parents knew we played in numbers. That provided some security. Mothers told us not to talk to or to accept rides from strangers, but no one in town was a stranger. Parents didn't have to restrict our freedoms at nighttime because dark was no more dangerous than daytime.

Perhaps without recognizing it, most Millheim parents trusted in my mother's old saw: "God takes care of fools and children." Childhood is a risky undertaking. Young people, those lacking in both experience and good old common sense, survived their early years for several reasons. Parents believed in them, and kids knew it. The entire citizenry was engaged in raising its young, and kids knew it. And, when we got into the predicaments we did, divine intervention saved us. Certainly, there was a little community help involved, a little luck, and a bit of blessed mercy involved as kids such as Bierly and I worked our way to adulthood.

Our parents certainly did not condone mischief, social, or moral infractions. We had no free pass, and we knew that. Kids were taught to behave in public. If we violated the rules of the adult world, we expected retribution to be quick and dear. This was especially true with regard to those incidents that crossed the line between accident and malice – like the T.K. Arbor affair. Surviving an incident was one thing; causing it was another. We expected to pay the piper if we were apprehended for ill behavior. Sometimes that knowledge kept us from engaging in questionable quests. Sometimes it did not.

In disciplinary matters, mothers and fathers played distinct roles. Family policy, including behavioral limits, was set by the father – the autocrat at the breakfast table. The daily, procedural application of those policies fell, except in more critical instances, to the mother. In the nuclear families of the '50s the father captained the ship, and the mother was the chief petty officer. She ran the house, and that meant everything in it, including the children. Daily control was her domain; crisis was his.

My own parents were good examples of how this worked.

Dad was a tall, rangy figure who wore mostly dark suits. He had blue eyes, which Bari inherited, and black hair so luxuriously thick and wavy that it required copious amounts of Trol — a milky, thick, lime green hair tonic — to capture. He combed these folded ribbons straight back over his head, where they were trapped in a sleek, tightly-coiled nest of intertwined snakes.

While quiet, kind, and gentle most of the time, Dad had the thinly-veiled temper befitting an Irishman with a mother named Nellie McCracken. He used two forms of punishment when Bari or I committed an infraction serious enough to call out the big dogs. The first was one of the world's great tongue-lashings. No one has been properly "bawled out" unless Jim Frye delivered the harangue. Faced with an infraction that was less than capital but more than simple "boys will be boys," Dad would lay me low.

If I fell below par on academic performance, destroyed property, or upset one of the town citizenry, I could expect the riot act. Dad would stomp around Mom's kitchen pouring out a seemingly endless analysis of my shortcomings.

"What were you thinking? How could you ever imagine this was not going to come home to roost? (Dad liked the expression "home to roost.") Is this how you were raised?"

The emphasis of these tirades usually focused on the lack of intelligence I had brought to bear on the situation. He seemed to be more bothered by my lack of reasoning or common sense skills than by the act itself. In fact, he often said in such tongue-lashings that I didn't have one "iota of common sense" (I came to believe that common sense is measured in "iotas.") Dad's usual message to me was that he expected better of me.

His second and more serious form of punishment was apt retribution. Dad was a big believer in "an eye for an eye." He seldom grounded Bari or me or took away privileges or our allowances. That was stuff from Mom's war chest. Instead, he reacted in kind to the offense. If I damaged something, I had to repair it — broken windows, damaged bikes, and someone else's lawn furniture. If it were totaled, I had to replace it, at my own expense. If I hit someone – usually Bari – he hit me in the same spot to show how it felt. If I insulted or injured someone, I had to apologize, personally. Generic punishment was out with him. The punishment was directly related to the crime.

On a daily basis, nurturing fell to the stay-at-home moms. Mothers governed the length of the apron strings. In the main, they were the ones who turned us loose on Millheim. They were busy, too. Running a household in those days was much more labor intensive. Certainly most households had electric washing machines, primarily the ones with wringers on the top. Many had clothes dryers. Automatic dishwashers were still a bit new on the scene, and it was only families rather well-heeled, as the Bierlys, who had them. Most mothers were cooking three meals a day, hanging laundry on the outdoor clothesline, cleaning the house, and so on. In the absence of so many modern day products and tools, these tasks were simply more time consuming. Mothers saw nothing to be gained by having kids under their feet all day. Either we had to help or get out. Easy choice. All we had to promise our mothers was that we would wear clean underwear, wouldn't smoke, and would be home in time for dinner, and then later, for bed. Mothers gave us big breakfasts, hugged us, told us to be careful, and then went about their own days. Affection, not control.

There is yet another reason why our parents could be more at ease – permissive, even — when we kids set out across town. Our parents had help from lots of people around town.

A family portrait after Mom finally admitted I was her child.

The adults in town, other parents for sure, but merchants and neighbors also, kept an eye on us. Part of that was for the safety of their own property, but much of it lay in the understanding and acceptance of the old adage, "It takes a whole village to raise a child." We kids knew that we were responsible to all the adults in town. We answered to all grown-ups. No kid I knew looked at an adult and said, "You're not my dad. I don't have to listen to you." If we acted like "little heathens," as my father used to call us, my mother knew that the shop owners and residents would brace us. We were the same kids who ran with their kids or attended the same church as they. For the most part, this expanded safety net worked.

It worked when Billy Sandorf stuck his foot in the spokes of the front tire of my bike going down the Millheim hill. We took a classic tumble. My dad had told me repeatedly never to ride double on my bike. Now and then, however, I would put someone on the crossbar of my purple Schwinn. Well, Billy committed the only real sin of riding double – he dropped his foot into the spokes of a spinning front tire.

That launched us both over the front of the bike and onto the highway. Billy was okay; his flight was partially curbed by mine because I went right over top of him and held him closer to the bike. He had a few brushburns. I was not in as good a shape. I hit my forehead on the pavement. I chipped a couple of teeth and was bleeding profusely from a head wound that would take Doc Henninger two clamps to close.

So, there I sat, dazed and bleeding down into my eyes. Over the hill came John Rakin in his open air Jeep. He stopped, scooped me up, and drove me down Penn Street to Doc's. John waited with me until Doc finished, then drove me home. My mom was waiting expectantly, so I assume John also called her while I was being clamped. That's how it worked in Millheim.

If we strayed from socially acceptable behavior, our parents often heard about it from the town citizenry. More than once that meant Derwood Climb. Derwood, of course, lived beside the race in that big yellow Victorian home. He worked in the bank. He was a stern little man who always reminded me of Harry S Truman. Short, bespeckled, wispy hair, chest thrust out like a banty rooster. He only smiled at adults and then only with half of his mouth getting involved. He seemed to watch us kids as if he were guarding the town's possessions, monuments, and womenfolk from hooligans.

Derwood always scared me. I knew he would tell not only my parents but everyone else if he ever saw me violate one of Millheim's common decency regulations. I was timid about going to his window in the bank with my weekly Christmas Club deposit, fearing he would tell me I had done something wrong either with regard to my account or in some little venture that week.

Mrs. Toomis, Mike's mother, once called my mother to complain about my language on the street. She told Mom that Bierly and I swore like sailors. When my mother confronted me with that complaint and asked if it were true, I told her I did not know. I never heard a sailor swear. Kenny Climb and his older brother Donny, Derwood's grown sons, were the only two sailors I ever knew. I never heard either of them swear. Of course, they were at sea most of the time.

The lady who lived behind left field down at the ball field called my mom to report that she had seen Bierly and me publicly urinating in the snow in the outfield. This was right across from her front window, so she watched the entire episode. One of us, probably Bierly, had had the bright idea of writing our names in the snow with yellow ink – what boy has not tried that? I got to "Ed Fr" before I ran out of product. Bierly was unfairly disadvantaged with a first and middle name of considerable length. Of "Herbert Eugene Bierly" he got out "Herbert Eu. He just had to be Bierly and try to do the whole thing.

Anyway, there was no way out of that one. The lady had us cold — literally. Not only did she recognize us, even bundled up as we were, she recognized Queeny. I tried the "Boys will be boys," routine, but Mom was chagrined just the same.

The point is that our parents took solace in the existence of this large network of sentries spread across town who squealed if some youngster went afoul of normative behavior.

We youngsters exploited that sense of security a bit. We knew that Derwood Climb missed things. Take the race thing for instance; that occurred right beside his house. We knew Irv Benfer, the barber, could see the whole diamond from the bay window on his shop. But Irv was a grand guy. He really liked the town kids. In fact, he was a bit of a madcap himself, always armed with a story, joke, or tale about someone. He enjoyed a good adventure too much to ruin it by snitching on us. We knew he wasn't going to call our folks. Besides, his youngest son, Tim, was just a year or two older than Bierly and I. We played with him often. We were in deep with Irv Benfer.

***

My mother's approach to parenting was mostly typical of the era. She was undoubtedly more industrious than most moms, but her view of her job as a mother was pretty much the norm of the town.

Mom was a brown-haired, brown-eyed woman of squat proportions. She often complained that she had no hips, that she was configured like a mayonnaise jar. Mom was always happy and smiling, with a cheery word and a good thought for everyone. She loved books and often read great literature. We would see her sitting with Melville in one hand and a dictionary in the other.

Ruth and Jim Frye – they deserved better<<<

Mom was born into a farming family of nine children, almost all girls. When she compared the good years and the bad years of the early twentieth century, she believed that there wasn't really that much of a difference. Dirt farmers were always poor. When the depression hit, her family had no money, no security, and no creature comforts, just like everyone else. But, they never went hungry.

My mom had learned how to do without. By necessity she learned to cook, sew, make soap, use hand tools, and can fruits and vegetables. Throughout my childhood, she made me shirts, darned socks, and patched our pants. She was a saver and a pragmatist. She allowed no false illusions in our house. Just because my father had a college education and a professional job didn't mean that we were going to be buying lots of toys, store-bought shirts, and more than one sport coat for church. She saw to it that we lived beneath our means.

Mom had learned from her farmer/carpenter father some handy construction tricks, and, in fact, had inherited many of his hand tools. She was more mechanically inclined than my father who didn't know an eight-penny nail from a carpet tack. She spent hours in our basement, sewing, sawing, nailing, and creating.

What might have separated Mom from other parents in Millheim was her method of teaching us life's important lessons. I did not know this at the time, but over the years I came to realize that not all adults talked to their children in the strange and figurative ways that Mom spoke to us.

I think that came from her own upbringing in the hills of Central Pennsylvania. What passed for wisdom and knowledge in rural America was carried in old sayings, proverbs, and ancient saws that generalized the human condition. The people who were judged to be wise in Mom's time were those who could apply these well-known proverbs and sayings to everyday life.

Of course many of these are part of our culture. "A bird in the hand is worth two in the bush." "Every dog has its day." "Neither a borrower nor lender be." "It takes two to tango." "Every cloud has a silver lining." "Let sleeping dogs lie."

Mom's youth was grounded in these aphorisms, and that was going to be her legacy to Bari and me. She raised us on these old sayings. Now that is fine, except she started with us awfully early. Little kids have difficulty with figurative language. While they can certainly understand the words and the direct application to the situation included in the saying, kids have difficulty transferring the essence of the concept to other arenas. Some of Mom's most profound teachings were undecipherable to me until I was about thirteen years old. I just didn't know what she was talking about.

I came home one day to report, sheepishly, that I had broken one of Mrs. Knight's basement windows. (I broke a lot of windows as a kid. I shattered the kitchen window of a house up Texas with a stone from my slingshot while I was aiming at a huge planter in front of it. Then there was the window of the enclosed porch window at Dean Benner's house on Penn Street and the garage window over at Gaylord Bean's house.) Mrs. Knight's window fell victim to an errant throw during a game of catch Bierly and I were having in his back yard. While Mrs. Knight was pretty decent about it (after all I had saved her daughter's life, didn't I?), it was clear that I would have to pay for it.

So, I slipped in the door, head down, looking as contrite as possible. I sat Mom down at the kitchen table. I told her I broke the window and hastened to add that it was an accident, not intentional vandalism. I was about nine at the time. Mom looked at me and said, "You make a bed, you have to lie in it."

I was lost. Here I was talking about a broken window, and Mom was talking about a bed. I repeated myself. She repeated herself. I stared. She waited. I offered that I supposed I would have to pay to replace the window. She nodded. Later on I figured it out.

She had a million of them. Without the accompanying situations to which she applied these, here are some of her oft-repeated favorites:

A fool and his money are easy parted.
If wishes were horses, beggars would ride.
The best laid plans of mice and men sometimes go awry.
It's a poor dog that won't wag its own tail.
A faint heart never won the fair maiden.
Discretion is the better part of valor.
All that glitters can't be gold.
A good horse is never a bad color.
He who laughs last laughs best.
It's an ill wind that blows no good.
Don't stretch yourself until you're longer than your blanket.
Pride goeth before the fall.
It's a difference of opinion that makes horse races.
Don't throw good money after bad.
Some days you get the bear, some days the bear gets you.

The whole idea was that a full, meaningful, and prosperous life visited a person focused on these pithy insights.

Chapter 6

Of Banks, Bullies, and Boxing

We had been planning the bank robbery for weeks.

The concept was elegant in its simplicity. The Farmers National Bank, right there on the diamond in the middle of town, was, as the bad guys on television said, "there for the taking." Bierly and I had all the big stuff worked out. We were having problems with just three little things.

We needed a wheelman, a gun, and, of course, a stick-up guy. We had the rest covered.

We had been casing the joint for weeks. That wasn't difficult. No one was surprised to see two ten-year-olds in the bank. After all, we were regular bank customers. Both of us had Christmas Club Savings Plans. We made our deposits every Saturday morning. If one of us had to be out of town on any particular Saturday – on a business trip, for example — the other one just handled his friend's finances on his behalf. That kept us in line with the bank's interest-paying policies.

The Christmas Club was a public relations ploy perpetrated by the bank on the town youth. The advertised objective was to assure kids that they would have some money at Christmas time to buy their parents decent gifts. A second intent was to teach young people to save their shekels — the inculcation of sound fiscal management. Not so obvious was the underlying reason the Christmas Club existed: To get the next generation of Millheimers to think of Farmers National Bank when banking came to mind. The bank knew better than to eat its seed corn.

So, for several years, for about forty-eight Saturday mornings, Bierly and I toted our little green bank statement books into the bank along with our respective fifty cents. A teller, usually Mr. Bressler, but sometimes Mrs. Barnard, would take our money and make a handwritten entry into the pink and blue ledger boxes on the inside pages. Then, about the middle of December, we would go in to collect our savings. The bank provided some form of interest to us for the year. It matched one payment, paid 3%, or did something to show us how our money could grow if we were just smart enough to begin saving early. We usually ended up with something like $28. We'd buy each of our parents and our sibling a gift and still have enough left over to buy some contraband that would last well into February.

Anyway, these weekly financial visits provided an opportunity to reconnoiter the site of the heist. If we stood on our tiptoes, we could look past the tellers behind those iron bars secured to the inordinately high marble countertops that ran across the four service windows. We could see back into the vault area, through the gleaming gold and silver rods that formed a metal door to the safe deposit boxes and the interior vault that held the important papers and the big loot of the bank. Hanging open on its huge hinges was the solid metal vault door, a heavy, round, shiny, steel barrier with a large combination lock on the front with its gigantic four-handled wheel.

All that metal was there to convey the invulnerability of the bank. Bierly and I were not impressed. We had no plans to break in at night and try to pick, drill, or dynamite the lock. We weren't going to take a torch to the huge hinges on those two doors, and we weren't going to have to disarm any secret alarm system.

The Farmers National Bank, on the diamond

Nope, our idea was to rob the bank in broad daylight so everyone who was there could watch. We were going to let Derwood Climb solve all those niggling problems about the vault and its doors and alarms when he opened the bank, long before our guy arrived. That would eliminate all questions about combinations, the doors, and where the big money was. That was one of the major simplicities of the plan. So, the "how" of our plan was easily established.

We were sure our plan would work. We figured Derwood Climb wasn't going to put up any resistance. He'd scare easily enough because he knew guns could hurt people. He would probably just stand there in righteous indignation. Mrs. Barnard was a really kind lady who would probably be very helpful. It was just her nature. Russell Bressler, the other teller, would pose no threat either. He was one of our town's World War II heroes. Mr. Bressler was terribly wounded during the D-Day invasion. His legs were crippled from the ordeal, and he used aluminum crutches to stand and move. He, like Keith Hartel, our other wounded war hero also confined to crutches, was a fine gentleman who would simply be unable to move swiftly enough to cause us any real problem. Old Samuel Frabell, the Bank Manager, would probably be there. But he was far beyond spry; he couldn't chase any bank robber. He was also wise. We didn't figure that he was going to risk his life for other people's money.

We had learned all this stuff, of course, from television. Bierly and I had seen untold numbers of banks robbed on TV. Every western show on the tube presented several bank robberies a year. Several of the police dramas and private eye shows featured bank robberies on a regular basis. Bank robberies were a plot staple. We knew a lot about robbing banks just from watching those guys do it.

Most of them failed. We knew why. They had not planned very well, their guns didn't work, or they messed up by calling each other by their real names. Sometimes their girlfriends torched them, sometimes they robbed the bank successfully but later fought over the money and killed each other. Sometimes, the hero of the show just happened to be in the neighborhood, and that was just bad luck for the villains.

We didn't figure to have any of those problems. So we felt really good about our chances. However, we did have problems of our own, and thus far, these had kept us from completing what had become an obsession with us.

All of our problems stemmed from just one issue: Everyone in town knew us. It was impossible to walk into Farmers National Bank and disguise our real identities. The local telephone operators already knew us just by our voices – surely Derwood Climb would know who we were. He was already watching us carefully, ever since that little incident with the millrace. The only way we could do the job ourselves was to keep on running after we had the loot. And neither Bierly nor I was ready to leave our family and friends in Millheim.

Even if we could disguise ourselves, our size and apparent age might cause some problems. We had seen enough television to know that often some Joe Blow-Average-Citizen in the crowd all of a sudden chose to be a hero and attempted to foil the hold-up. We decided that if two little kids tried this, some hayseed would attempt an intervention that could get someone hurt. After all, there were going to be guns involved.

The guns were my idea. Bierly wanted to use knives, mostly because we both had knives. Most all the boys in Millheim carried a knife. They weren't weapons so much as tools. We needed them in daily pursuit of our youth. We had strings and ropes to cut, boxes to open, loose screws to tighten, or tacks to pry out. We had splinters to extricate, twigs to whittle, and apples to pare. There was always a knife or two in any group of three or more kids. We had already agreed Bierly's new, single-shot pellet gun was not enough firepower. There, again, we were fearful that it might only help to identify us.

Bierly's official Boy Scout knife had given way to a newly-improved Swiss Army knife. I think he got it from a promotion on one of those Saturday morning television shows. Maybe he bought it in State College, I don't remember. I know he didn't get it in Hosterman and Stover Hardware because it was just too fancy for a general store. I had a simple two-bladed knife with green fake pearl sides. My Uncle Carl gave it to me over the objections of my mother. She didn't like many of the gifts my aunts and uncles gave me. When Aunt Edna gave me a BB gun for my birthday, my mother just about wigged.

Anyway, my knife only had a two-inch blade, but I kept that thing as sharp as a razor. It was the same knife Bierly and I had used to make us blood brothers in that first summer when I got to town. We did that by slicing shallow cuts on the inside of our right wrists and then squeezing enough blood out of each wound that we could rub our wrists together and mix the blood from the two families into one unified strain of lawbreakers.

I had to convince Bierly that knives don't scare people behind marble countertops and iron bars. I asked him to name one TV show he had seen where a hold-up was staged with a knife. I reminded him that most of the kids in town could identify our knives. What if one of our knives was used in the robbery and one of the kids was in there making a Christmas Club deposit? That would be it. No, just having a knife didn't make it the appropriate weapon of choice.

Finally, he agreed to guns, but that was a problem too. Except for his pellet rifle we didn't have any guns. Neither his dad nor mine hunted. Everyone else's dad in town seemed to hunt though, so getting a gun wouldn't really be too difficult. We could just borrow one from the gun cabinet in the home of Jake Howard, Davey White, Donnie Walker, or several others. But that created a messy detail, the kind of thing that often came back to haunt those idiots on television. Some kid might tell later that we had the gun or worse, the kid's father might just be in the bank that morning, and in the middle of the hold-up, say, "Hey, that's my twelve gauge Winchester! Is that you, Eddie Frye? What are you doing with my shotgun?"

I also envisioned this Elmer Fudd image of two little guys in the bank waving rifles as long as they were. Someone could get hurt. Nah, the two of us using guns and doing the hold-up ourselves was no good. We needed an adult to do the hold-up, and he needed a gun. These were two large problems.

The third stumbling block was also related to our age. Of course we were not old enough to drive. The secret to the success of our plan was in the getaway. Millheim was rather isolated, positioned in the heart of the long Penns Valley. At the time, we had no town cop. State police cruisers seldom roamed this far from the barracks in Bellefonte — unless summoned, a more frequent occurrence as we got older. We figured that we had at least a twenty-minute head start on any uniformed patrol car. That was more than enough time.

A car leaving the diamond could be up Texas and into Brush Mountain in five minutes or down toward Coburn and into the Poe Valley mountain range in about the same amount of time. All that was needed was a good car and a "wheelman." That is what the television shows called the driver of the getaway vehicle. We needed a "wheelman."

Now the wheelman didn't have to know the area. Bierly and I could show him where to go. In fact, we didn't want the wheelman to be from the valley at all, because we didn't want anyone to recognize him or his car. That was good and clear thinking, we knew. However, it created another problem. We didn't know any strangers whom we could ask to do the job. We couldn't very well just walk up to somebody on the street in State College and say, "Hey, how would you like to come down to Millheim and help us rob a bank?" We lacked connections to the underworld, and it was giving us fits.

We knew that our man could be in and out of the bank in three or four minutes. We knew he and the wheelman could meet up with us in the mountains in fifteen minutes from start to finish. This would be a cinch.

But who to get to rob the damn place? That was even more difficult than finding a wheelman. In those days crooks were hard to come by. Yep, we needed a stranger to the town.

We considered going back over to the post office and scanning those most wanted posters for a bank robber who had somehow gotten loose. But those guys don't list their phone numbers or addresses, so it would be difficult to get in touch with any of them. Besides, our last escapade involving fugitives didn't work out so well.

Neither of us could think of anyone who would be willing to help us. Actually, I did ask my Uncle Carl from Chicago if he was interested. He was back in the State College area visiting his family, like my dad, and I thought he was just the sort who might see opportunity in a plan like ours.

Uncle Carl was the youngest brother in my father's family. There was considerable difference in age between him and my father who was at the older end of the five-sibling order of birth. Carl always seemed to me to be so much younger and carefree than my dad or any of my other uncles. Every time he was around, people told stories of his youthful exploits. Many of these involved outrunning the cops in his hot rods, upsetting outhouses, and visiting gambling halls. He now lived in the big city, and I thought perhaps he still led that slightly nefarious lifestyle. When he came to visit, he always had intriguing stories of bribing cops in Chicago, running a local trucking firm out there, and all the crime around him – all that big city stuff. So, I asked him.

He laughed. He said that if he ever robbed a bank, it would be a big one like the kind they have out in Chicago. I tried to tell him how much money I knew was in Farmers National Bank, all those Christmas Club accounts, the cash in the open drawers and all, but he was unimpressed. I'm not even sure he really took me seriously. I couldn't just keep pressing the issue because I feared he would tell my folks.

We were in a tough and irritating situation. Here we had this little country bank, just sitting there with most of its doors wide open. We knew there was a lot of money in there. Yet we could not get at it.

And so our dream died. Actually, it didn't really die so much as it just quit growing. What happened was that Bierly and I started to consider too many changes to the basic mission, and it started to get too complicated. For example, Bierly didn't want to take all the money in the bank. He wanted to let the Christmas Club accounts remain. I guess he figured our weekly investments were kept separate from all the other accounts in the bank, probably in some drawer in the big vault labeled "Christmas Club Accounts For All The Children In Millheim." I assumed he didn't want to take money from his friends. I told him to get over it. He said that wasn't the problem. He knew he was getting one payment free, or three per cent interest, or something from the bank, and he didn't want to lose that. Now how was I to tell him what was wrong with that kind of thinking?

So, we were stuck. There sat that bank, just ripe for the picking, and we couldn't do anything about it. We always wondered why some better-equipped bad guys didn't take down Farmers National Bank.

Finally, the plan began to recede in importance as new ventures unfolded.

***

We turned our attention to how to rid ourselves of the three bullies who were harassing us.

For at least two years after I moved to town, Bierly and I had been terrorized by Bobby Rishel, Billy Solt, and Leonard Moyer. All three were two years older than we were, and represented the Millheim version of gangs.

Bobby was the alpha bully. He lived across the street from Bierly in one of the big brick two-story homes that lined that side of Main Street. The other two lived up Texas. This gang of three ruled the northern alley system of town. That is, they hung out downtown, but on the opposite side of the street from the bank, the tavern, the race, and the alley up to my house.

The left side of town was open to anyone while the right side was used by kids only with the courtesy extended by the Rishel Gang.

Bierly and I did not use that side of the street much. First of all, there was little over there we wanted. Second, that is where those guys were. But now and then we needed to use that side of town to get to the downtown ball field, the upper part of the creek near the park, or from some friend's house up Texas. Anywhere from the back of the firehouse near the diamond across the creek and up that alley system, we could expect to encounter these tormentors.

Just the fear of that expectation was unsettling enough. But that fear was based on real previous confrontations. Often, they were actually waiting for us. We might be passing the West Penn Power Station and from behind the corner would slide The Big Three. Their specialization was intimidation, scaring us with implied and direct physical threats, taunts, and snide cracks about our appearance, our lack of physical toughness, our parents, or our siblings. As I reflect on it now, I realize that they seldom touched us. They certainly never simply beat us to quivering little blobs on the ground. Maybe they pushed us a little with a finger or shoved us against a wall or something. They certainly got in our faces; I can remember looking directly into those braces that Bobby was sporting. But they never beat us up, threw stuff at us (well, maybe some snowballs), or ripped our clothing. Most everything was about psychological dominance and domain.

Sometimes they pulled the same crap at the old school house on North Street where we all waited for the school bus to take us down to Coburn. I hated that bus stop.

We knew why they did it. They were big kids, and we were small kids. Besides, my dad was the principal of all the elementary grade schools in the valley. That made him, and me by association, an enemy even though none of these kids had a particular ax to grind with either one of us. None of them, to my knowledge, had come into direct contact with Dad for disciplinary reasons. It was, no pun intended, just the principle of the thing with them. Additionally, here was big-mouthed, confident, in-a-world-of-his-own Herb Bierly, with his big brother Curt who was even bigger than these guys, and their successful businessman of a father. Surely there was some jealousy and misplaced aggression behind this continuing harassment.

But they scared us, and they knew it. They made us run for our lives; they made us answer their silly questions about who reigned in this quadrant of town. We had to ask permission to leave safely from each encounter. They shouted threats and epithets at us. We recoiled in childish terror.

For months this worked. We lived in dread of these kids. We tried to avoid them.

We could have reported all this to our parents. But that would have been against the code of manhood in Millheim. Every man had to solve his own problems. Our parents probably already knew that some of this was occurring. Our little encounters were often close to home or near some neighbor's house. But parents seldom intervened in the trials of their children unless their help was specifically requested. Parents did not fight their boy's battles. And such intervention never really occurred to Bierly and me. We were raised to solve our own problems. Going to our dads would have been a sign of weakness.

We did discuss bringing Curt into the situation. He could beat them all up, especially if he recruited some of his big and tough friends. But Curt was not exactly the pugilistic type. He probably would have wanted us all to sit down in a circle and share our feelings, smoke a peace pipe, and declare ourselves above these petty turf and dominance wars. Curt was big in the Boy Scouts at the time.

No, Bierly and I were going to have to solve this one by ourselves. It was going to be the two of us against the three of them. Not good odds, but one cold winter day we made our stand. We decided, without ever really discussing it, to fight back. Our respective dignities had taken all we were capable of enduring without retaliation. The bullies should have seen this day coming.

They didn't.

Naturally, it was Bierly who waded from submission into the unknown and uncharted territory of defiance. It turned out to be just a question of looking the tiger in the eye.

On this frozen day we found ourselves behind the power station, returning from somewhere downtown. It was cold, and there was snow on the ground. We were passing the power station when out slithered our three jackals. Before a word was said, Bierly and I looked at each other and wordlessly acknowledged that today was the day. Today, we would end this bullying. I could see that Bierly was ready to fight. That meant that I had to be.

Bobby, as always, did the talking. He started in as usual: What were we two wusses up to today? What were we doing on his side of the road? Did we think we were tough or what? Billy and Leonard leered in the background.

Bierly mumbled something unintelligible, but clearly defiant. Bobby wanted that repeated and started to lean on Bierly for an answer. He expected Bierly to grovel, to show some respect, to cow. Abruptly, Bierly started to laugh. He said something outlandish, something terribly affronting to Bobby. Something like: "You are full of crap, you big jerk – all you jerks! Get out of our way, or we'll beat the shit out of all three of you." By now, committed as he was, Bierly was no longer a cowering little twerp. He was thrashing his arms about, Bierly style, and was screaming at the Big Three.

Stunned silence. Perhaps two or three of the longest seconds in my young life. Bobby stepped up close to a slightly-settled Bierly and said, "What was that?" Some snappy comeback I remember thinking at the time. In fact, I knew we had bested them right there and then. Bierly calmly responded, "I said, 'You are full of crap, you big jerk! Get out of our way or we'll beat the shit out of all you.'" He punctuated this with a solid push with both hands on Bobby's chest.

Unprepared, Bobby fell backwards, bottom first, onto the snow. The fall had hurt him somewhere. We didn't know where, but he winced, and he got up slowly – too slowly. Clearly, Bierly had done damage. "Let's pulverize these two," Bobby said, but without the conviction or authority that usually accompanied his commands, either to us or to his henchmen. Time froze; nothing happened for the next two or three seconds. Billy and Leonard were perplexed. Serious physical assault was not quite the idea of the drill. They certainly knew that the three of them could easily handle us two little shavers. But Bierly's preemptive strike had moved the situation and the relationship to a new level. Real intimidation was one thing; a bloody nose was another. Their hesitation spoke volumes – to all of us.

I don't think Bobby wanted to fight either. At first, I expected him to scramble to his feet and attack Bierly who stood right over him. Instead, Bobby pulled himself to his feet, rearranged his heavy jacket, and glared at us. His scowl didn't really work – just not enough fury or commitment. Mostly he looked bewildered, trapped even. Not much psychological insight was required to realize that Bobby needed a means to diffuse the situation, to save face, and to exit the scene stage left.

I, Huckleberry Finn, had just about that much insight. My problem was that I did not want to lose the momentum or situational control that Bierly had just gained. Close to impasse, I wanted to assure the victory before we let Bobby off the hook. I stepped forward, into Bobby's face full of braces and gave a little speech. I said something like: "We are sick of you guys thinking you can scare us and keep us off this side of the street. You don't scare us. If you want to fight, we'll do it, here and now. If not, leave us alone. Bierly and I are not going to take this shit anymore." We always swore a lot when we were trying to sound tough.

However I phrased it, I was really careful not to challenge them directly. I did not offer those often ill-conceived words, "Do you want to fight or not?" Many a boy has regretted the over-exuberance that led him to utter those words at the wrong time. Boys just have to fight when they find themselves in a box canyon. It is a matter of image over fear. I knew Bierly and I didn't want to fight; the look on those other three faces had already told me that they had serious reservations. It was Bobby's turn to find a graceful way out of this. After all, he was the one who had landed in the snow.

Let it be said that Bobby defused the situation very nicely. "So," he said, "You guys finally get it. We have been waiting for you to get up the guts to fight back. See, now you know you are tougher than you thought. We were starting to wonder if we were going to have to whip you to get you to fight." Bobby was saying this as if he were an older brother dispensing wisdom to a fawning brother. He made it sound as if these guys had a master plan to make men out of us, and that we had just passed some sort of test. And, oh by the way, if they wanted to, the three of them could take us any day. We didn't buy any of that, but we said nothing. "Okay, now you guys are part of this side of the street. Good enough. See you later."

And off they trudged, stage left. So did we, straight to Bierly's basement where we "counted coup," as the American Indian used to say. From then on, we were all friends. I spent many hours in Bobby's house, in his yard, with him at the pool. Later on, we worked together as lifeguards at a state park. Leonard Moyer later became the wheelman and I the organizer for a raiding party that nightly stole sweet corn from all the gardens in town. Billy Solt was also part of that and all the antics at the town swimming pool. It was all just a kid thing.

This story may sound eerily familiar – like some sort of take off of a theme from the popular movie always on television throughout December, *A Christmas Story*. The fact is, it is. I think that is the point of both renditions. Most every boy I ever knew, everywhere, then and now, has had to deal with bullies. There are only so many ways to do that. Each victim has to work out his own salvation. This is how Bierly and I did it. Any other association is not coincidental; it is typical of yet another rite of passage for young men.

***

For all of that, bullying was not a particularly well-practiced ritual in Millheim. There was some temptation for the bigger kids to pick on the smaller ones, but it was more of a tendency than a given. In our small town, all the kids ran together, within some age parameters. There was a time, from about age seven to eleven, when Bierly and I were the youngest in any group of kids rambling about town. We ran with kids as old as his brother Curt, five years our senior, and all the others in his age bracket.

Later on, of course, we became the older kids. Then we ran with "Pudge" Sides, his brother Earl, and others, all were younger than we. Whoever showed up at the old mill was in the group. We investigated the town for adventure, we swam at the pool, and we hung out in front of the restaurant, the post office, and the bank. We didn't really bully each other too much.

Sometimes, however, the older kids did take advantage of the younger ones, usually just for sport. Barry Bonner comes to mind.

Barry Bonner was one of the bigger kids – probably Curt's age. He lived only five or so houses up the street from me, but on Donnie Walker's side of the highway. His dad ran an auto repair business in a white block garage.

Barry Bonner was the toughest kid in town. He was the undisputed leader. He was strong and athletic, although he had slightly bowed legs. Behind his back we younger kids used to joke that he was born over a barrel. But we never said this to his face. Barry Bonner wouldn't like that.

He sort of had that Jimmy Dean look going but without the long hair. He sported a crew cut. But he smoked, and he kept his pack of Lucky Strikes rolled up in the sleeve of his tee shirt just like those tough Hollywood types.

Barry Bonner was not exactly mean or hostile to us younger kids. But he ruled. If he wanted something, he got it. Actually, one of us often got it for him. If he told us to do something, we did it. He didn't need to beat us up. It just always seemed that it was the prudent thing to do. When Henry Winkler's character, Fonzy, appeared years later on *Happy Days,* I recognized him immediately as Milwaukee's version of Barry Bonner. There was this aura of toughness or ruthlessness on the surface that actually hid a decent enough person. At the time, though, Barry Bonner was one of the big kids whom one simply obeyed. It wasn't just the age. There were lots of older kids in town that did not command that kind of respect. But Barry Bonner did.

Anyway, attached to the back of Bonner's Garage was a frame square room that jutted straight back from the main structure. It was a storage shed of sorts with its own external door, high windows, and a doghouse sloped roof covering the dirt floor. The air inside was musty and damp, with the lingering, sweet smell of automotive oil and radiator coolant. The room was lighted by a single bulb suspended from the low ceiling to about the eye level of the bigger kids. The threadbare, black-clothed wire supplying current to the bulb was stapled across the ceiling joists and down the wall next to the exit and into an exposed switch box. When activated, the switch box emitted a bluish spark and the smell of ozone, although we didn't know what that was at the time. I did know, however, that the strange smell of hot electrical wires and scorched insulation did not indicate a safe situation. Naturally, these odors and the general gloomy dankness made the place forbidding to us younger kids. The room had become Barry Bonner's hideaway. We really didn't like going in there, but on at least one occasion we had no choice.

Barry Bonner thought it would be the perfect place to hold some boxing matches.

Barry Bonner took some used clothesline rope and fashioned a two-tiered rope ring in the middle of the square room, centering the hanging bulb. He left lots of room for fight fans. He arranged some old wooden crates into a small, multi-level trophy stand over which he draped a frayed, moth-holed, green army blanket. Beside that sat a wobbly little wash table upon which he laid the two sets of old boxing gloves acquired from somewhere. He added a pitcher of water and a sleeve of Dixie cups to the table. He was just about set.

He only needed two things: some fighters and some prizes for which they should box. He got them both from the younger kids all across town.

Barry Bonner came down to the old mill one day and found Bierly, Donnie Walker, Glenn Blanchard, Johnny Maher, Davey White, Jack Benner, David Stout, his own younger brother, Tony Bonner, and me all lounging on the sloping grass behind the mill. He informed us that we were going to have some contests up at the garage that afternoon. His tone indicated that we had no say in the matter. He told us that he, Curt

Bierly, Ronnie Shawver, and several other older kids would be expecting us. The mention of the bigger kids was all the motivation we needed to attend. There was no use annoying them. Barry Bonner told us that we should find some other kids and tell them to be there also. This was to be a command performance.

"We all will have great fun – tell them that," he said. "Now go home and get all the trophies and plaster statues you have. Get a few stuffed animals from your sisters' rooms — bring them too. Tell the others to do the same."

We followed his directions. After lunch I headed up to the shed with my only two bedroom adornments: my plaster statue of a horse rearing on his back legs, and a snow globe encasing a miniature Empire State Building. I had won the horse at Grange Fair by knocking over three wooden milk bottles with one old, water-sogged baseball. That wasn't easy; it took several attempts and an entire month's allowance before those bottles finally went down. There was a real trick to it. Hitting the little triangle was easy enough. But the contestant had to hit the bottom two exactly in the middle to topple all three and thereby win a prize. The carny worker made it look really easy when he showed us how to do it. Well, I had finally gotten it done.

The snow globe was a gift from my Aunt Mary. She bought it for me on one of her Greyhound bus tours. It and my plaster horse were displayed on the solid metal top of my bedroom radiator.

Now, both the globe and the statue were to be prizes in a boxing competition. I was going to have to fight someone to win a prize that I already owned. If this seemed unfair to me, it was not reason enough to tell Barry Bonner to go pound sand. Barry Bonner was tough. I, as all the others, showed up with certifiable prizes.

Johnny Maher brought the most. His family was one of the best-heeled in town, and Johnny had everything. He brought his prizes in a wagon because there were too many for him to carry. Johnny was younger than I, small for his age, and, perhaps, a bit naive. I guess he just didn't realize that he was putting all these trophies on the line – in a contest that he didn't stand a prayer of winning. But, Barry Bonner told him to bring his best trophies, so he did. He must have had ten of them in that wagon.

So there we all were. The dozen or so pugilists were the smallest people in the room. The audience of perhaps eight was comprised of kids all the age of Barry Bonner.

It quickly became clear that the older boys were not going to do any fighting. They would just organize, referee, and announce the proceedings. Besides, someone had to watch.

It occurred to me that we could have two divisions – say, young and old, or big and little. But the big kids had no real interest in boxing each other. If they had done so, a social structure or power base may be undone or newly established. This could be shattering to those who currently were the alpha leaders – people such as Barry Bonner and Curt Bierly. Barry Bonner was already the kingpin in town. Why would he put all of that on the line? The balance of power had to be maintained.

Better to let the little guys slug it out for the enjoyment of others.

And that is how it transpired. The big kids laced those huge, stinky boxing gloves onto us. With our anemic little arms we looked like we were growing giant Tootsie Pops from our shoulders. They would shoo two of us out to the center of the ring where Barry Bonner served as referee. He would start each match with great fanfare and then blow a whistle. We would come to the center of the ring and begin to flail at each other.

Except for the more timid ones. They would shuffle around, stepping backwards and sideways, trying to avoid having to throw a punch or, worse, take one. This would anger the big kids, and they would threaten these slackers with their own form of bodily harm if the wee warriors didn't get in there and throw punches. A contest went either three rounds or ended in the tears of a dispirited and wounded youth. When a clear winner had been determined, Barry Bonner would reach over the ropes, gather up one of our trophies, and make some sort of presentation. Then we moved to the next match.

I fought about three times. During the proceedings I lost both my horse and my snow globe to winners of other matches. To the victors went my spoils. On the positive side, I got a plaster statue of a parrot that was pretty cool. I had seen it numerous times in Johnny Maher's bedroom, and I had always thought it was almost as neat as my horse.

Johnny went home with an empty wagon.

All of us had bruised ears, lips, and foreheads. Our cheeks were rubbed pink by the dried out, scarred leather of those old gloves. I am not sure what we told our parents about how we looked or about what had happened to our valued trophies.

Barry Bonner and all the big guys seemed to enjoy themselves as we toiled for them.

A year or two later the Bonners sold the garage and moved to Pleasant Gap. I never really missed them.

Chapter 7

Bullies R Us

To be truthful about it, Bierly and I did some bullying too. We were not above inflicting some of the cruelty that kids can dish out. We just tended not to do it to little kids. We did not even bully kids our age. Several of our classmates made fun of, and bullied, Robert Smiley, a large, big-boned, special needs student with a strange growth attached to and behind his right ear.

In third grade, Robert and I shared one of those two-seated, screwed-to-the-floor wooden and ornately-designed metal desks with the hinged tops and inkwell holes used in every classroom at Coburn Elementary School. Naturally, I was assigned the right seat of the two, providing me with a daily up-close and personal view of that strange growth. It terrified me. In fact, it became an obsession that I could hardly abide. As large as a pecan, its pink skin always seemed to be just at the point of explosion. The strange appendage appeared to be hard, very firm rather than soft, yet very swollen – to the point of detonation. The tumor always struck me as ready to expel its innards in the way that fireworks reach a certain point and then fan outward. And who would be sitting in the line of fire? Me. I sat through many a reading class, trying not to look at this time bomb and wondering when it might self-destruct, spraying me in whatever gooey matter or germs it might release. I was less repulsed by it than I was scared of it. It was un-natural, yet life-like. I feared it might be some sort of spore that would pop and envelop me in some terrible green fluid or cover me in powder that would, somehow, destroy my life as I knew it.

As anxious as sitting beside Robert and his extra growth made me, even worse was the necessity to get even closer to the potential geyser when we practiced air raid drills.

In the 1950s, Americans were stricken with the notion that Russia was about to attack us with one of its newest, most powerful bombs, either an atomic bomb or the even newer and deadlier hydrogen bomb. This was all part of the "Red Scare" that had all of us trying to learn how "to live with the bomb." Drastic measures were necessary. Bomb shelters were designated in all populated areas. In Millheim a yellow and black triangular sign hung beside the door of the firehouse. Supposedly, the firehouse had been retro-fitted with anti-nuclear devices and procedures. Public service messages told everyone to look for this harbor of safety if the Russians hit the button.

Schools needed to be prepared also. Because of our country's extreme concern for its children during the Cold War, precautionary measures were instituted in case of just such an attack. Time zone differences made the U.S. especially vulnerable during school hours. So, students across our country were taught basic defense from a hydrogen bomb. We were instructed to climb under our desks and keep our heads down. The exercise was called "Duck and Cover." We practiced this procedure more frequently than we rehearsed fire drills. Looking back on this nationwide undertaking, I have wondered just how effectively my half-inch desktop would have saved me from nuclear destruction. But I didn't think like that at the time.

I lived in fear of nuclear holocaust. I thought the Russians – the Chinese, too — were evil. I figured bomb shelters were a good idea. But, I had an even greater concern then. I cringed at the thought of practicing, or participating in, air raid drills in school.

I did not want to survive a nuclear attack with Robert Smiley's ear growth, to which I had developed an almost fatal attraction. Much as I loathed it, I was fascinated by it, consumed by it, and worried about what it might do next.

That growth had taken on a life of its own. I tried to give Robert the disassociated distance of someone who has to share close confines with another very much unlike himself. That worked pretty well on a day-to-day basis. As Americans learned to live with "The Bomb," I was learning to live with Robert and his ghastly anomaly. But air raid drills were asking just too much.

Here's how they worked. Some sort of siren, installed throughout the country, would sound. People were instructed to go to their air raid shelters, just for practice. I have no idea how many actually did.

I do know that we kids, trapped in schools, like Coburn Elementary, crawled under our desks assuming the most fetal-like position we could muster. Because there were two students to a desk, Miss Cunningham told us that the bigger child should assume the position first, while the second should sort of cup ourselves around that twisted body. So, during these drills, Robert retreated to a comfortable position under our shared desk. Then I filled in the blanks.

In doing so, I was head to head with Robert, with him lying curled up on his left side. I had to lie somewhat entwined with him – and stare at that large, explosive-looking growth on Robert's right ear. My face and Robert's tumor were only inches apart. While we waited for the drill to end, I looked at the grisly growth from a distance of about two inches. I could see it for what it was: a skin-straining volcano in the making. I could see the blue veins – a few reddish ones too – snaking across the abomination as illustrations of a road map. My face was so close to that growth and Robert's ear that I sensed a tiny pulsating in the pinkish glow of this appendage, what appeared to be a beating heart. I could see earwax. It was traumatic. Having such a close encounter on one occasion was bad enough, but I knew, even during the first drill, that I would have to endure this scene more than once in the future.

Every American was hoping we would reach some détente with the Russians. I surely did. I wanted the Cold War and the Red Scare to end, for reasons different, I expect, from anyone else on the planet. I didn't want to be that close, ever again, to Robert's strange right ear.

Still, Bierly and I never bullied Robert Smiley. Just too consumed with other matters, I guess. Other kids would approach Robert on the playground and insult him with names and epithets, ridiculing his odd tendencies, learning disabilities, and behaviors. They had a heyday when Robert decided to collect all his spit for a week in a mayonnaise jar. He wanted to see how much he actually produced. The answer is one jar, if the product is compressed now and again. I did not participate in the flight of jokes that accompanied that effort, even though it was I who sat beside him while he opened and added to that jar during class. I had my own problems with Robert.

So, Robert's case aside, we mostly besieged old and infirm people.

Rae McNair was our favorite target.

Rae McNair had several disabilities – "feebleminded" was the kindest term they used in those days. We were kids, and we never really knew what or cared much about her mental or emotional deficiencies. She was just strange, and we loved to rile her.

Rae lived in one of the apartments that honeycombed the second floors above the downtown stores. If one wanted to find her on a cold day, the post office was the best option. On a warm day, Rae wandered about the diamond. On the day of anyone's funeral, she could be found at Reiff Funeral Home and then in the basement of the church where they served the post-burial ham dinner.

Not that anyone ever went looking for her. She was somewhat of an omnipresent pest. Rae ambled about town, mumbling to herself or vociferously upbraiding others for perceived shortcomings or any ill treatment or rudeness toward her. As Harry S Truman would have said, she was "a small pot, and soon hot."

Rae was between sixty and eighty years old. It was impossible to tell. She surely looked older than she was, but none of us kids knew even an approximate age to assign her.

She stood only about five feet tall – maybe shorter. She was squat of build. She wore thick glasses – "coke bottles" we called them. If she had any teeth, they were not in the front of her mouth. She kept her lips clenched in permanent defiance of the world, forming a sort of toothless pucker. The folds of her sallow skin sagged down her face behind her glasses, almost obliterating any definition between her cheeks, her nose, and her mouth.

She owned only black and brown clothing — tattered dresses, shoddy shawls, black boots or shoes, a black coat in winter, and usually, a brown hat with netting that stuck out in no particular direction. She wore those heavy brown stockings that were practically leggings, rolled up just below the knee, creating a most distasteful sight. She always, no matter the temperature, the season, nor the day, carried an umbrella. Her clothing hung on and around her in layers and shards. Disheveled is a natural adjective one would reach for to describe her, but it is not quite robust enough. When she was shuffling down the street, she looked like a large bird's nest that had blown loose from its moorings, tumbling over itself and rolling erratically over its own parts.

That sight alone was cause for kids to bait her, to get her chasing us with her umbrella raised in threat. This became the challenge of many a town kid. Bierly and I made it an art form. We used to torment the poor soul to distraction.

Like the bank, the post office was a place that town kids, even young ones, had reason to frequent. Millheim did not offer mail delivery services to street addresses; in fact, there were no street addresses. All the address needed was Millheim, Penna. Later they added zip codes. Later still, authorities changed Pennsylvania's official abbreviation to PA. But then, everything was sent to the post office, and, if families wanted to get it, that's where they went. So, kids were often dispatched to the post office to pick up the family mail.

We accomplished that by opening a little metal door on the ornately designed box assigned to us. Row upon row of these boxes formed the entire side wall of the ante-room. There was a little caged and slatted window in the middle of this bank of mailboxes behind which the postmaster and his assistant worked. That's where citizens reported if they needed stamps or special handling services.

Claude Musser was the postmaster at the time. He ran a tight operation, typical of branch offices that conducted the official business of the day. Mr. Musser was a severe, little fellow who would busily flit about the back room of the post office with that officious air of doing the work of the government. That left him little time to deal with the problems and complications of us poor mortals who either asked for service or demeaned his building with impish behavior. He seldom was seen outside the work area portion of the room. When he was, it usually was to dispense a lecture or a sanction to someone for some lack of respect for government property, services, or the institution of the U.S. mail service itself.

The left wall featured a bulletin board with all those notices of services and announcements that the U.S. Postal Service offered or demanded. There also, of course, were those wanted posters that Bierly and I perused with such great enthusiasm. The floor was oiled wooden tongue-in-groove boards, the kind of floor used in all the old buildings of town – the hardware, Bierly's heating and plumbing, the 5 and 10 cent store, and Bricker's market. That kind of floor had a peculiar and individual smell to it that, when mixed with the hot air of the coal-fired furnaces in the basements, created an aroma of yesteryear and a step back in time. These were darkly stained and noisy floors. They didn't add charm to the rooms so much as personality. There were the sounds of paper being sorted and a stamp canceling machine bopping each hand-fed letter. In the post office people spoke in somewhat hushed tones – not as quiet as the bank, but almost.

Except for being a little too hot, the post office was a good place to loaf. Everybody came in there at some time each day, and there were lots of official documents to read and to ridicule. Not that Mr. Musser allowed loafing in the building. He wanted people to come in, attend to their business, and get out. If Bierly and I lingered too long, Mr. Musser was sure to tell us to get moving; our business was done in the post office for the day. His disemboweled voice, coming from behind that wall, was intimidating. We did as he demanded.

Unless we chose to prey on Rae. She was the single person that Mr. Musser allowed to loiter in the ante-room. I suppose he knew that she had no other place to go. She was a fixture inside the glass windows that formed the front of the post office. A railing supporting a heavy curtain about three feet high ran along the edge of the raised display floor in front of the window. This was just the right height for Rae to lean on as she looked out onto the street from the warm, dry interior of the post office. She would watch people come and go at the post office and speak to those she liked. With others, she would just mumble under her breath.

She didn't speak much to Bierly and me. We were not her favorites. We'd enter, and there she'd be, mumbling something to herself about kids today or whatever. Then we would start in on her.

"Hey, Rae, are you warm enough? It's eighty degrees out there, and you have on your winter coat. Hey, Rae, have you had a bath since Easter? You smell a little rancid (we liked "rancid"). Hey, Rae, been to any good funerals lately? Hey, Rae, are those new shoes or did you just walk in a mud puddle?"

Bierly always found false teeth and wigs to be two of the funnier things in his world. He loved to joke about them. He often blamed people who were not wearing wigs of sporting one. He referred to false teeth as "choppers" and liked to talk about old people who, when they got excited and animated in a conversation, would inadvertently spit out their "choppers" to the delight or horror of all those assembled.

Well, Rae McNair did not wear a wig, nor did she have "choppers". She needed choppers, of course, but she wasn't planning that purchase any time soon. But Bierly would start right in, "Hey, Rae, forget your "choppers" today?"

Usually Rae could withstand this verbal assault from two young ruffians. She would mumble a bit, and turn away from us, hoping that Mr. Musser was about to toss us from the post office. He would sometimes hear us assailing her and give us the heave-ho. He probably wished he could just toss her. But that would be cruel, whether or not the post office was to be a site for government business only. It was just better to let her stay, with all of her annoyances to postal customers, than to shoo her out into the cold or heat.

Sometimes, however, before he could intervene, we would get the best of her, and she would step toward us brandishing that tattered umbrella. That was about what we hoped for, and we usually quit tormenting her if we could get her to commit to this demonstration of exasperation. Usually, we could get her going in about one minute or less. Bierly was better at it than I, although I did get in my own best shots. I tended to focus on her leggings and legs. I used to tell her that I had seen better legs on a piano. That usually got her going.

One day, however, we took her too far. We were teasing her as usual, and she was muttering as usual. We had started right in on her when we entered, not even going over to the window to take care of whatever business we had. Anyway, we got her all hyped up and muttering. That was a victory for us, so we declared the game over and went to the caged window. In doing so we turned our backs on her.

When we turned to leave, she was coming at us. She had moved from her favorite spot, over by the curtain in the front window on the left side. She was now between us and the door. We were trapped.

Suddenly, Rae had become this maddened, whirling dervish who struck with a fury we had never seen. She was swinging that old umbrella around and then up and down. She was shooting for the very tops of our heads and our rear ends.

And connecting. We were surprised and cornered. We retreated under her attack to the rear wall, to the corner with all the mail boxes. Now we were really trapped. Rae kept flailing away and mumbling. She never broke into shouts or loud rage. But her eyes, now looking huge behind those thick lenses, were no longer foggy and glazed. They were focused like big black marbles on her two targets. I wanted to raise my hands in submission, but I was afraid to. I had them positioned to protect my groin.

I couldn't even cower very well because Bierly was trying to share the same corner with me. We were trying to cover up and retreat into the woodwork. Every time that I got a little bit protected from her, actually by burrowing in underneath Bierly's body a bit, he would move away and try to do the same thing to me. While we were trying to out-position each other, Rae rained down a constant barrage of blunt and pointed attacks with what must have been the best made umbrella in the world. I remember thinking that this was all Bierly's fault. And where was that postmaster when one really needed him?

The only way to get away was to attack her – to push her back so we could get around her and out the door. But both of us knew that was just beyond the limit. Boys did not strike women, especially old and deranged women. Besides, we would have been really vulnerable to her blows if we tried to escape. Better it was to put up with the shelling we were taking.

So, we took our beating. Soon we were hollering, "Okay, okay, Rae, settle down. We were just kidding. Easy, Rae, that hurts. Now, Rae, quit that."

Finally, Mr. Musser heard the commotion or, at least, attended to it. He certainly seemed to take his good old time, wandering around the bank of mailboxes and out the door in the back wall that led into the anteroom. He told Rae to stop it. She did. He looked at us with the expression that adults save for children. Its essence is "Don't look to me for sympathy. You had this coming." He told us to get moving. We did – sore and sorely beaten.

Rae had finally won a battle – perhaps the war. Bierly and I never really tried to regain the upper hand in efforts to provoke Rae McNair to action. We had seen it. It wasn't pretty.

One of my mother's old sayings was, "The boys throw rocks in jest, but the frogs die in earnest." She was correct. Bierly and I were just fooling around. Our torments were just kid stuff to us. We toyed with Rae because she was different. When she had finally had enough, when we finally caught her on the right day, when the figurative frog died in earnest over our taunts, she reacted the way most of us finally would. One had to respect that. We left Rae pretty much alone after that.

We still had Barley Braner to torment.

Barley lived somewhere in Coburn but spent lots of time in Millheim. He was a relatively young man, probably in his early thirties during these years of my youth. He was crippled from a bout with polio. His left arm, hand, and fingers were terribly contorted, almost useless to him. He had a severe limp although I cannot remember which leg exactly (I suspect it was his right one.) He spoke in the slurred tongue of a stroke victim; he did not seem very bright or well educated.

Barley drove an old green Chevy pick-up truck that he steered with the assistance of a "knob", a wooden handgrip that was bolted onto the steering wheel. These were all the rage in the 1950s. Many teenagers equipped their cars with designer models of these devices, originally created for steering big tractors and trucks. Young drivers favored knobs featuring pearl tops, nude women, or the U.S. flag. Sometime in the '50s these knobs were outlawed for all but handicapped drivers, so Barley was able to maintain his.

Barley used his truck to do light hauling for the local citizenry. If someone had garbage to haul, brush to truck away, or dirt to move from the footer of a room addition, they called Barley. He was a hard worker who compensated well for his physical afflictions as he labored for others and carted away their offal.

His affliction should have kept all of us kids from tormenting him. His diligence as a worker should have earned him our respect. Unfortunately, neither did. We teased him mercilessly. Right to his face we would say mean and vicious things, mocking his walk and talk. When he drove up or down the alley or when he entered or exited the restaurant, we had a little song we would squeal at him, in sing-song, jeering fashion: "For a nickel or a dime, Barley'll take you to Millheim!"

The song sprung from the common knowledge that if a kid in Coburn wanted to get up to Millheim, just about two miles away, Barley would take him or her. He would charge a nickel or a dime for gas. For that act of kindness we derided him. I think we were less occupied by his physical deformity than we were with our perception that he was not quite all there intellectually. His social skills, his diction, his general appearance were all feeble. Not too unexpected for someone who has been ravaged by polio.

His self-esteem could not have been high. We kids did nothing to help him in that department.

I am ashamed of my participation in the mocking and derision of Barley Braner – more ashamed of it than of any other illegal or immoral transgression I committed in my youth. I should have identified more with him. In fact, there but for the grace of God, would have been I.

I had polio too.

I was six years old when I contracted infantile paralysis — poliomyelitis. I lived in State College at the time. The year was 1951, nearly the end of the national epidemic of this famous child crippler. I contracted it from a little girl, Patsy Folk, who lived across the street from us on West Beaver Avenue. One day I made it to the landing on our broken stairway to the second floor of our little house when I seemed just too tired and mired to move. Before Mom called the doctor, she knew what was wrong. When Dr. Stuart arrived, he looked at me momentarily, drank a glass of water, called the hospital in Danville, and gave my sister a shot. Hours later I was in Geisinger Memorial Hospital, unable to move my arms and legs.

In the 1940s and '50s the polio epidemic swept this country with devastating effects on thousands of young people from pre-adolescent age through their early twenties. Carried by a virus, the disease paralyzed and then crippled both the fine and gross motor skills of body extremities. Skeletal muscles would atrophy, reducing victims to crutches or wheel chairs. Worse, if the disease migrated to the lungs, death was likely. The famous iron lung, a huge tube-like machine, would be needed to provide artificial respiration to the afflicted. Sometimes that was only a stop-gap measure; people died from the worst of several strands of the disease. Polio was both a crippler and a killer. Until Jonas Salk developed his life-saving vaccine and got it to market, parents lived in a constant panic that their child could be next. My mother saw her worst fears realized.

I was struck toward the end of the epidemic. In fact, I was actually used in some experiments with the new vaccine. Perhaps that increased my degree of recovery. I had so much of the vaccine that, when I finally returned to school, it was deemed unnecessary for me to take either the shot of the first year or the two or three sugar cube dose later supplied to the entire nation's schools.

I was in the hospital thirteen days. For most of them I was unable to move my arms and legs. Twice a day nurses would put hot, steamy wool towels on my back, supposedly to keep the muscles flexible. As they cooled, these woolen blankets itched my skin. Due to my paralysis, I could not reach back and simply pull the cloth off my back. I would call loudly for a nurse who would then chastise me for making so much noise in the hospital.

Doctors would come in and prod and poke at me. They would try to make me laugh. My parents would visit and bring me little games or puzzles that they bought at a little market halfway between State College and Danville. I would share these with the other kids in the polio ward. There were about eight of us in a large room with glass walls behind my bed and a window at the end of the room. Some were in better shape than I was. Some, like Patsy, were doing worse.

Thankfully, the disease did not gravitate to my lungs – I never had to enter the dreaded iron lung. Luckily, the disease did not center in just one or two limbs, making it a crippler. Instead, it attacked all my limbs and my back, and in doing so, dissipated to the point where permanent damage of muscles and tissue was somewhat minimal.

But in the main, I survived with little consequence. But I can remember the others in the polio ward at Geisinger. There was Patsy who had arrived just a few days before me. Her growth would be permanently stunted. There were little kids there who would never walk without those heavy metal and leather leg braces. There were children whose arms were already twisting into the same grotesque configuration as Barley's.

I remember all of that. I remember the needles every day, so many and so frequent that I came home with a black and blue rear end. I remember the older kids on West Beaver Avenue building a little wagon to pull me around the neighborhood so I could be with them while they played. I remember the physical therapy that my father was taught to give me to keep my legs from stiffening. I remember my mother calling me off the street for a rest while everyone else got to stay out and play in the sun. I remember my mother talking on the local radio station about our trials, carefully thanking The March of Dimes for the financial assistance it provided.

But I didn't seem to remember that Barley Braner must have gone through all that too. Now there is a lesson in peer pressure.

I knew what Erin Major had endured. Erin was the daughter of Ken Major, the meat man in Bricker's Grocery. Erin had polio too.

One year younger than I, Erin was a pretty girl of alabaster skin and black, black hair. But thin, reed thin. Poor Erin had been ravaged by the disease. She was typical, I think, of the polio victim. She could have been the poster child. One of her arms was permanently bent at the elbow in a slightly elevated and forward-thrusting angle. Her opposite leg – the disease tended to cripple cross-laterally – was stiff as a board and angled outward from her body. Walking was difficult for Erin; doors and steps were a real challenge. This was long before any disabilities legislation eased the way for such victims, so movement presented constant struggles for her.

But Erin was always smiling. I remember watching her battle the steps on the school bus. I remember her school books hanging off her arm on a strap, bumping into her as she fitfully negotiated the hallways. I remember how tiny she always seemed, brittle and emaciated. But mostly, I remember her smiling. She never complained. She loved when we would pay attention to her. She talked clearly and cleverly, if a bit shyly.

It was easy to be nice to Erin Major. She was tiny and frail, younger than I, and she was a girl. Barley Braner was none of those things. So I joined the chorus of "For a nickel or a dime, Barley will take you to Millheim."

Later on, my dad hired Barley to do a few hauling jobs for the school district. This was during the time of school consolidation when Dad was closing down one small elementary school after another. Because I also was working for Dad, Barley and I ended up doing some trash hauling together. He wasn't a bad guy at all. He never mentioned to me that he knew I was one of his tormentors. We just started out on our work together as if we had no history at all.

***

There is one more little snippet that must be told about the post office. This one had nothing to do with Rae McNair, although she was probably present when it occurred. For me it is an enduring memory of the Millheim Post Office.

It was one of those days between Christmas and New Years Day. The afterglow of Christmas was all about town as Bierly and I wandered about the diamond. For one reason or another we ended up in the post office. We were about eleven at the time. While we loafed, this little kid entered. He was so little we didn't know who he was; we only knew kids closer our own age, give or take two or three years. So, this kid could not have been more than six or seven years old. He had to stand on his toes so he could see over the ledge of the little window.

Well, it turned out that Mr. Musser was not there that day. His assistant, a pleasant, heavyset lady named Myrtle, was on duty. She came over to the window and looked down at the little fellow. She asked the boy how his Christmas had gone. "Did you have a nice Christmas, Billy (or whatever his name was)?"

"Yes."

"Did you have a big turkey dinner?"

"Yes," the boy answered, this time a bit bored or annoyed by the small talk.

"Well, did Santa Claus bring you everything you asked for?" Myrtle continued.

Little Billy (or whatever his name was) jerked his head up to stare at the assistant postmaster. A look of disbelief and condescension came over him and he said, "My God, Ma'am, do you still believe in Santa Claus?"

127

It was a great moment. Bierly and I rolled out of the post office doubled over in laughter.

***

The bank and the post office played big and significant parts in my childhood. They were epicenters of important adult business. We kids of the town were peripherally involved in that world. We had our own savings accounts; we retrieved the family mail, purchased stamps, weighed and sent packages, and what not. We did business, just like adults.

These chores brought everyone, regardless of station, to one or two places on a regular basis. People got to know each other at the bank and at the post office. That helped to forge a shared bond and culture.

While we hung out in or in front of the bank or the post office, town persona would stream by in pursuit of their own daily routines. Each mid-morning Hustie Forengast, one of our town's more notable drinkers, would shuffle in for his mail. He would read it, right there in the post office and deposit most of it in the waist high trash barrel that sat under the little shelf by the wanted posters. He'd usually acknowledge our presence with a toothless hello that was sort of expelled from the left side of his mouth like a puff of stale air from a whoopee cushion. Then he would amble out of the building and cross directly over to the restaurant, and sit on his favorite counter stool. He'd order a Texas hot dog – a wiener smothered in a hamburger-based chili sauce served in a bun – and a cup of tea. He would wait for his meal and scratch his four-day growth of whiskers, seldom chatting with anyone else in the place. After lunch, he'd go next door to the tavern and begin his afternoon the same way he would spend his evening — drinking and becoming much more conversational. The only thing that seemed ever to upset his routine was a job now and then. Someone might die and Hustie would be needed to dig the grave up at Fairview Cemetery. Or his long-suffering wife, sitting alone in their ramshackle home up Texas, might come and fetch him because a widow somewhere wanted some shrubbery trimmed or a tree chopped down. That was Hustie's life, and Bierly and I shared one little sliver of it with him.

The town fathers came by too, of course. Frosty Conners, before all his trouble, would stroll in and give us a man-to-men nod and say, "Good day, Gentlemen." He made us feel like grown-ups. Johnny DeSoto would be about the same with us whenever he left his service station briefly to hurry up to the post office.

Russell Bressler came into the post office one day, struggling with the door as he manipulated his aluminum crutches. Mr. Bressler would talk about the war rarely and only then in historical more than personal terms. Sometimes though, we could get him engaged in a conversation about his experiences. He had great and heroic tales to tell. Almost all of them involved other soldiers. His own story was difficult to elicit. This day, however, he was feeling more forthcoming, and he described to us how he was wounded in two separate incidents. The one that crippled him occurred during the St. Lo Campaign in France during the D-Day invasion. He was in a half-track that drove over a land mine. He was launched right over the front of the vehicle, both legs mangled and rendered useless. He and my neighbor Keith Hartel were heroes to us. Both were quiet, unassuming men of great personal faith and fortitude. Both had struggled with the concept of war and killing; without any bravado for their own acts of courage. Both were much more self-reliant than their injuries should have allowed.

All the merchants made daily deposits at the bank. If we were standing around there (for example, when we were casing the joint for the stick-up), we'd chat with Albert Stover, Boyd Blazer, who ran the restaurant, Johnny Mench, the jeweler, and all the other downtown businessmen. Numerous farmers, some of whom we knew, perhaps from church or playing ball with their kids in little league, would drive in, park on the diamond, do some banking, get the mail, and maybe catch a tall, cold one at the hotel or tavern before heading back out to work. We'd chat with all of them. We knew them, and they knew us.

The regal Bobby Musser would often grace us with his distinguished presence, an encounter we always enjoyed. Bobby was the retired jeweler – he had sold his business to Johnny Manick.

He was healthy, but old. He was sharp as a tack mentally and took great pride in his personal appearance. He was a little, fit-as-a-fiddle, trim man who could not have weighed more than 110 lbs. His thin, gray hair was always carefully combed and parted very near the middle of his head in sort of a 1880s look. He dressed formally to walk from his house, about five buildings down from the post office on Main Street. He had a penchant for black, three-piece suits, with a gold watch fob, of course, hanging from his vest pocket. He'd amble down the street with an air of genteel graciousness.

Bierly and I loved the curious old gentleman. We'd cross the street if we had to just to be sure he would notice us. He took time, every time, to chat. Often he had a story to tell.

One day, Bierly and I were finishing off a four-pack of those little paraffin bottles that enclosed a miniscule amount of sweet Kool-Aid-tasting liquid. Shaped like classic coke bottles, but only about three inches in length, the little containers had two salable-to-kids things going on. First, one bit off the top and sucked the juice from the inside. Then one could chew the empty little vial as if it were chewing gum. Inserting two of these guys into one's mouth formed a wad that made understandable speech just about impossible.

We had just completed this operation and were chewing down our wads when Bobby Musser strolled up to us. He smiled and took from his pocket a thin, flat piece of copper.

"Do you boys know what this is?" he asked.

"No."

"This is a penny that I put on the tracks of President McKinley's funeral train. The president was assassinated in Buffalo, you know, in '01 (Bobby pronounced it "aught one") while he was attending the Pan American Exposition up there. Well, we heard that the train carrying his body back to Washington would be going through Coburn – that was the regular route for that trip, you know. So, all of us kids went down there. I laid this penny on the tracks when I heard the train coming through the tunnel at the far end of the mountain. I carry it for good luck. Do you want to feel it?"

"Yes."

Anyway, that was the kind of stuff one got from hanging around downtown, especially near the post office or the bank.

Sometimes we fumbled the ball. One day my mother commissioned me to get the mail. Usually, my dad would stop and get it on his way home from work. This procedure protected those vitally important documents. But on this day my mother must have been expecting something she wanted before 4:30 p.m.

I had all day to get the mail. Mom knew Bierly and I would be downtown and could bring the day's communications home when we got hungry.

My intentions were good. Bierly and I extracted the mail from our designated box, collected Queeny at the front door, and started right off home. We made it to the bridge. We decided to crawl down the bank and under the bridge to see the size of the catfish and occasional trout that often lay in the deep, shaded water. We spent some time there and then waded right across the dam, through six inches or so of summer water and clamored up the other side of the bank. We went on home.

Leaving the pile of mail lie up on the metal bridge rail where I put it so it would not get wet or lost when we climbed down to the water. There were about five pieces of mail. Whether or not the pack included the important missive Mom awaited is not important to the story.

All I know is that Bierly and I walked into my house and my mother said, "Where is the mail?" I must have looked like the proverbial deer in the headlights.

"I forgot to get it. I'll go back and do that right now." I was just hoping that the wind, either natural or that stirred by cars and trucks crossing the bridge, had not carried away the letters.

Mom looked at me hard and said, "No reason to go back to the post office. Mrs. Breon just called. She found our mail lying on the bridge, so she took it to her house. Now how do you suppose our mail got to the bridge?"

At that point Bierly excused himself with some story about having to change the batteries in his flashlight or something. I had to stay for the rest of the lecture about personal responsibility. Then I had to retrieve the mail from the helpful Mrs. Breon, thanking her profusely for her thoughtfulness. Finally, I got to recount the entire adventure for my dad that evening, receiving the expected lecture from a slightly more animated point of view.

***

Two recent events cement for me the importance of the bank and the post office experiences we had as youth. The first is the incident reported in the preface of this book. After years and years of absence, I stepped into the modernized version of Millheim's post office only to discover that someone still knows me there. The second involves my suddenly-widowed sister who recently moved back to the Millheim area for her retirement years. She built a new house in Aaronsburg. She had a choice of home delivery or a post office box for her mail service. She chose a post office box because she likes dropping by the post office every day. She thinks it just makes her more a part of the community.

Chapter 8

Down On The Farm

"I've sold the house."

One day in the spring of 1956 Old Man Brindle dropped by to drop that bombshell on my mother. He said we would have to move by the summer. I was in the living room playing and replaying our 45 rpm record of *Don't Be Cruel* by Elvis Presley. Even at the time I recognized the irony of the situation even though I did not know what "irony" was then. I probably just thought that it was appropriate to the situation. When Old Man Brindle turned to leave, I offered him a disdainful look. I hoped he interpreted it to mean: "I don't like you, and I am going to steal more of your plums." He was always upset about Bierly and me picking a few of his prized plums from a tree that hung out over the alleyway. Once, he came over to complain about it to Mom. To soften the blow, he offered her a bag of plums. They were groundfall, all of them, wet, cloyed, and muddy. I took them over to his fence and threw them back on the ground. Let him pick them up again.

Old Man Brindle's visit threw my mother into a tizzy, of course. She took time to compose herself, and then she made one of her rare calls to my dad at his office. She didn't very often do that. Dad's office was sacred ground. For only the greatest of family emergencies should he be interrupted. That was more Mom's rule than Dad's. I don't think he ever really cared if we called him at work. But Mom was from the old school. Dad was at work. Calling for non-essential business was misuse of the telephone at best and a form of stealing from Dad's employer at worst.

There was at least one other occasion when Mom simply had to break her own rule. And that did not work out for her as well as she had hoped.

About a year prior to our eviction Bierly and I were throwing a baseball around our small front yard. Queeny loved pitch and catch. She would sit expectantly between us and to one side of our game. When one of us threw the ball errantly or failed to catch it, she would retrieve it for us. Dutifully, she would deliver the saliva-covered, broken-stitched ball to whichever of us was supposed to catch it in the first place. She'd wait for us to take it from her mouth with a sly look in her eye that seemed to be teasing us for our ineptitude.

Normally, we did not throw toward the house. For some reason, however, Bierly got his back to the front porch with me facing it. I unleashed a throw that cleared his head, and his outstretched glove hand. It did not clear a living room window. First we heard crashing glass, then tinkling glass, and then Mom yelling at us even before she appeared in the frame of her former window.

There was good news and bad news associated with that window. The living room featured a large window – a picture window we called it. The huge pane was at least five by seven feet. Down each side were three or four smaller windows, extending our panoramic view of the alleyway; very scenic. Luckily, it was one of these smaller windows that I shattered.

Still, Mom was really ticked. Breaking a window was bad enough. Being so stupid as to be tossing a baseball directly at it was additional cause for rage. Somewhere in there, too, was her deep-seated fear and loathing of Old Man Brindle with whom she wanted to avoid all negative contact. So, she was angry. Still framed in that now-aerated space, she ordered me inside immediately. Bierly and Queeny were dismissed with a simple wave of her hand. The dog caught on before Bierly did. She scooted off for home without even looking back to see if Bierly was following.

Even after giving me a tongue-lashing, Mom was dissatisfied with my level of punishment. She had already told me that I'd have to pay for the window (we both knew that was impossible given my paltry fifty cents-a-week plus Christmas Club allowance). She had already commissioned me to tell Old Man Brindle (he didn't scare me any, and she knew that.) She had already informed me that I would be "grounded" for the rest of my life (we both knew that just didn't work in our family – it just wasn't part of our culture).

I had absorbed this brow-beating and sentencing pretty contritely, I thought. But, jeez, it wasn't like I had shot the president or anything. Privately, of course, I was really wondering how one went about replacing a window like that. Seemed tricky and complicated.

Still, she wasn't done. Just too upset, I guess. So, she pulled out the big gun. "You can just call your father and tell him what you have done," she decided out loud. "Call him up and see what he says about this."

Now that was cause for alarm. Here we were, about to invade Dad's sanctuary with some late-breaking bad news. We were going to interrupt Dad – at work – with a crime of the century story. This scenario had a dismal future written all over it. This was not a good thing. It was going to call for some Yankee ingenuity, and I knew it.

Mom made the call. Mom dialed the number with such fury that I thought she might break one of the little circles on the rotary dial of our newly-upgraded phone system. She asked for Dad. When he came on the line, she said, "I want your son to tell you what he just did." All of a sudden, I was *his* son. She jammed the phone into my sweaty, little hand, with a glare of expectation: "Now you are going to get it."

"Hey, Dad," I started hesitantly. I had thought this through pretty carefully. "You know that big picture window in the living room?"

"Yesssss," he replied, his voice rising in preparation of the sonic boom that we all expected.

"Well, I broke one of those little windows beside it."

I could hear the tension seep out of him. "Oh, thank goodness," he said. "Just a little one, huh?'

"Yep."

"Well, don't worry about it. I'll take care of it when I get home."

"Okay, Dad. You want to talk to Mom? Okay, see ya."

I handed the disconnected phone back to Mom who had already begun to realize that I had dodged a bullet. "Well?"

"He said he would take care of it when he gets home."

And that was it. No more talk about Eddie paying for the window. No more fear about Old Man Brindle finding out. No more discussion of grounding me for the rest of my life. I was home free.

It's all in the delivery.

Anyway, Mom called Dad about our being evicted. They had an animated conversation, but they both were finally resigned to the fact that the inevitable had just happened. It wouldn't be the end of the world.

Dad knew Old Man Brindle would want to sell sometime. He also knew he did not want to buy the house as it just would not suit our needs much longer. After all, my sister and I could not share a bedroom forever. He and Mom had been looking all over town for a suitable place, but there was little available and appropriate. So, my parents had been planning to build a home. Still, the suddenness of the decision forced my folks to accelerate their plans. First and forthwith, however, they needed to find a place for us to live while our new home could be built.

The upshot of Old Man Brindle's bombshell was a family move to Aaronsburg for the summer months.

It is not as if there were multitudinous choices. Penns Valley was not exactly dotted with apartment dwellings, rental properties, or empty and habitable houses. In Penns Valley most people owned what they lived in; there was little real estate speculation or development. So, finding suitable and temporary quarters in Millheim turned out to be impossible for us.

Actually, Aaronsburg was much the same story. However, Dad finally found us a most interesting set-up. Right in the middle of the town stood the old Aaronsburg Hotel. Built in the 1800s, the old hotel had been a travelers' way station for more than a hundred years. Such rooms/eats/bath establishments were numerous across 1800 – 1920 America, usually located about twenty miles from the one preceding them in one direction or another. That was about the distance a horse or horse-drawn conveyance could manage in a day. The wooden frame building was simple in its architecture but long on old-world craftsmanship and materials. It had long since ceased hotel operation.

Charley Snyder, a prosperous grocer and car tire businessman, now operated his store out of most of the first floor. Only a wraparound porch and a wide hall with a stairway leading to the second floor rooms were unused by that enterprise. Charley was willing to rent out the second floor space for a short time, but he wanted Dad to know two things. First, the second floor did not exactly look like an apartment. This was an old hotel. It featured a long hallway broken in the middle with steps. Down the right side of the hallway were rooms, all in a row, each with its own heavy door. Some of the rooms were locked, full of God knows what. Unfortunately, the only bathroom/toilet was located in the middle of this line of rooms that ran back through the building. Up front, in sort of an alcove, were three or four rooms that could serve as living quarters. There was a kitchen, somewhat primitive but adequate. There was a sitting room adjacent to it and in the very front of the hotel. Off to the left of the steps were three rooms, possible bedrooms for the family. It was sort of an odd and old world arrangement, and Charley was concerned that a professional man like my father may find it beneath the dignity of his family.

The second problem was worse. There was no heat on the entire second floor. We would be living there from May to about September while our house was being constructed. Heat would certainly be necessary. There was a hot water heater alright, but the old hotel never had heated rooms.

Stanley C. Bierly Plumbing, Heating, and Wiring solved that problem by installing an old pot-bellied stove, complete with a stovepipe right up through the hotel roof.

That shortcoming solved, we moved in.

Bari and I had no problem moving. For us, this was like camping out. We only moved about a mile; we'd still see our friends at the pool, and we would be back to Millheim in no time. And the old hotel was slightly mysterious what with those locked doors and long halls. It creaked and moaned under foot, and the inadequate lighting made nighttime shadows, real or imagined, a mind-bending experience. Sure the toilet was inconvenient and we had to wear shoes or slippers because of the big splinters in the wooden floor. But mostly, living there was fun – at least for a summer.

And we got to know the Aaronsburg group of kids. Foremost among these were Larry Rossman and Spit Unger.

Larry Rossman was Bari's age, three years older than I. He lived on a farm at the far edge of Aaronsburg, right at the top of the hill leading out of town. From our suite of rooms at the old hotel in the middle of town, at the bottom of that hill, it was about a five-minute walk up to Larry's. Spit Unger, a.k.a. William Unger, lived approximately ten houses away from me in the opposite direction, but that didn't matter. Spit was always at the farm. Spit was my age.

Almost immediately, I hooked up with those two. We met just about every morning up at the farm. We either went down the back lane that snaked between the barn and the house to play in the fields or woods, or we headed back to town where we were sure to get in trouble with someone.

Larry and Spit were the defining archetypes of country boys raised in the '50s. They ran unfettered through the farm fields and the back alleys of Aaronsburg. Running with them was literally life on the edge. They were mischievous. They were the usual suspects when there were pranks or incidents involving some minor destruction of property, gardens, or outhouses. Residents always kept a watchful eye for these two lightening rods of mayhem. It was a reputation they had earned. Wherever they were, something was different when they left.

One just doesn't join up with such miscreants. There are various rites of initiation. These two taught me how to shoot guns, ride horses, and drive tractors. However, my introduction to these new pursuits was in no way typical, instructive, or traditional. Their style was to immerse a newcomer in the activity first, scaring the hell out of the victim. Only then did they provide the subtleties of the skill.

They both loved guns. They often carried rifles – powerful ones like .30-.30s or 30.06s — out to the fields when we played. They'd shoot at anything, living or dead just for target practice.

That included me.

One morning I trotted up to the farm and asked Larry's mother about their whereabouts. Down the back lane she informed me. So down the winding hillside I went, taking the sharp left turn that led to the back forty.

Suddenly, I heard a gunshot and the pop of a bullet hitting the clay path just beside me, making a little arrow of dust. Instantly another shot, another pop, another arrow. Then another. These guys were shooting at me! Where were they? I couldn't see them. Actually, I could hear them laughing and hollering taunts at me, but I could not find them. A few more shots, close enough that I decided this was enough. I headed back up the lane. Only then did they show themselves. They had been lying in the ditch that ran along the lane on down the hill in the middle of a soft curve. They were perfectly concealed. They stood up and called for me to come on down, promising that they wouldn't shoot at me anymore. "Don't worry," one of them said. "If we had meant to hit you, we would have already done it."

The Rossman farm lane. Horses, cows, and guns.

That is how they defined fun. Nothing too mean, but always with a dangerous or serious consequence in the mix.

They had .22 rifles that day. They wanted smaller caliber guns because of the game they were playing before I arrived. They had been down in the pasture where the family dairy herd grazed on uncut field grasses. Each took a position beside a pile of fresh cow dung, about thirty yards from each other. Then they shot at each other's pile, the object being to try to spray cow dung on the other's leg. These two good shot adolescents made the contest possible with a smaller degree of danger than one might first imagine. Both of these kids could cleanly shoot the eye out a newt. They were accurate and confident marksmen. More than that, they recognized those skills in the other. It was a game they never asked me to play.

But they did teach me that day to shoot a .22 rifle. Later, I was instructed on larger caliber weaponry, Larry's prized Winchester .30-.30. The trick to that was to overcome both the fear and the reality of the recoil impact on one's bony shoulder when firing the heavy gun. Before my first shot, Larry told me it wouldn't hurt. Just let the gun rise in the air after squeezing the trigger. Well, that was a lie – pretty much like all the lies these two told me when I first tried something.

Like riding one of the two old draft horses that worked the farmland.

It may have been the mid-1950s, but many a farm in the area still had draft horses. Of course there were lots of tractors around, but there still existed some farmers and farm hands who used horses for plowing, hauling, and the like.

Larry's dad had tractors. He used big yellow Minneapolis Molines and a small gray 1954 Ford tractor to do most of his work. But he had a hired hand who lived and worked on the farm. Paul Coover never learned, or wanted to learn, how to drive a tractor. The old and odd fellow did his share of the plowing, harrowing, and raking with two Morgans that boarded in the same barn as the tractors. These old draft horses, Dick and Harry, were crotchety old plugs with huge feet – feet that had already plowed more fields than the horses must have thought necessary. They were perpetually in a bad mood.

Harry was in such a bad mood one day that he took off from the farm and headed for the mountain across the road. The trouble was that he had to cross Route 45 first to get to the promised land. He forgot to look both ways before he headed out. The poor dumb animal galloped out across the road only to stick his head right through the driver's window of a passing flatbed truck. He lived, the driver lived; the window was shattered. The glass from that window, however, did blind Harry in one eye. He always seemed to be in snit about that from then on. We never rode Harry. He was just too mean and unpredictable.

Dick was somewhat mellower. He wasn't as mean or aggressive. He was just tired all of time. Paul Coover would take the two of them out in the morning and work them all day in the fields. At milking time, he would bring them in and feed and water them. Then the three of us kids would decide to ride Dick.

That was a lot to ask of Dick. We'd all three jump up on his broad back and head down the lane, bareback, of course, with only a bit in Dick's mouth to guide him. When we would get down the hillside and onto the flat part of the lane beside the same fields Dick had worked in all day, we would order him to gallop. Dick would oblige us by starting a slow trot – after all, he was a draft horse, not a Tennessee Walker.

Then, because he was tired and/or not too coordinated of foot, he would either stumble or just plain stop, lowering his head to the gravel lane. That would launch all three of us out over his head directly in front of him. We'd hit the lane hard, tumbling into each other or rolling toward the ditch. The second was the preferred course of action because, if he stumbled, Dick would still be moving, albeit it slowly. Now we fallen riders had to be sure he did not trample us. This horse was huge, and his tufted feet had heavy metal shoes that could rip holes in body parts.

More than once that is exactly what happened. That possibility, for Larry and Spit, is what made the ride truly exciting. Usually though, we landed safely and just crawled back up on and urged the poor old plug to continue out the lane.

Well, Larry and Spit never explained those possibilities to me the first time they asked me if I wanted to ride a horse. I had this picture in my head of me sitting atop a fine steed, with silver-buckled reins controlling his every move. I saw myself like Albert Stover atop his fine mount. Instead, my first ride began with me holding onto Larry's shirt for dear life and digging my legs into the bowed sides of the horse under me, trying to get a purchase on something that would keep me up-right. That wasn't to be. My first ride, like almost all those that followed, ended with me rolling down Malcolm Rossman's farm lane trying to avoid one-half a ton of horse flesh about to pummel me.

It worked pretty much the same way when they taught me how to drive a tractor. First, they decided to take me for a ride. One evening we were standing about the dooryard of the farm just as dusk was giving way to dark. Larry suggested that we take the Ford tractor out to the woods where we could spotlight some coons, maybe a deer. He grabbed the big nine-volt powered flashlight and climbed up onto the driver's seat. Spit stepped up behind him to stand on the axle housing and held onto the rear of the seat. That left me with a heavy gauge steel, rear-facing scoop attached to the tractor's power take-off. With controls at his side the driver could maneuver the scoop to move grain, to transport feed and chop near and around the barn, and to clear out the cow stalls. This four-foot wide contraption was not the cleanest piece of machinery on the farm, but it was my seat for my first tractor ride.

We headed out the lane in darkness. Larry had headlights out front, but I saw precious little of that. I was inside the scoop and facing where we had last been. Larry drove that old split-wheel tractor the same way he rode Dick – as fast as it would go. The trip out the lane was bumpy and rough. I had to hang on for fear of either falling off or hitting my head on the rear slope of the scoop.

It turned out that the ride out the lane was the quiet part of the trip. Once we entered the woods at the edge of the farm, Larry stepped the whole ride up a notch. The thick woods had only one cut path that overlapped itself as it carved big scars in the dense, lush undergrowth. The path was actually just the result of repeated trips that Larry had already made out there with various pieces of machinery or horses. He opened up the hand throttle on the old Ford, and off we went, up and down the slopes of the woods with Larry adding hard left or right turns just to jostle me around that steel scoop. He could make some of the turns very, very sharply by using the regular brake and other foot-operated levers that allowed each of the huge rear wheels to brake independently from the other.

I was in total darkness back there. I had no idea when we would turn next, when we would head uphill or downhill. There was really no place on the scoop to hold onto to steady myself. Mostly, I was just a little ball being tossed from side to side, front to rear, and up and down. Staying inside the scoop was full time employment. The only way it could get any worse was for Larry to start manipulating the scoop itself with those controls he had at his right side.

So he did that. Now, in addition to the two-dimensional tossing and turning of the tractor on the path, I had to endure the up and down and left to right movements of the scoop itself. All this amid Larry and Spit's hoots and howls. They were really enjoying this. There I was, being caromed about like a pinball, and they loved it. I tried to tell Larry to slow down, but I was careening off the backside of the scoop toward the open end. Our speed seemed supersonic. I did not want to exit the craft onto who knows what on the floor of the woods.

So, I just had to ride it out. We stopped when they had had enough. I was bruised and sore for a week.

The next day Larry showed me how to operate the Ford. I adopted it and ran it all over the farm that summer. I liked being alone on this engine-powered big toy. I enjoyed the power under my control with the use of the hand throttle, the range of usable gears, and both sets of brakes. That Ford and I were bonded. The Ford just didn't know it.

But I liked riding cows, too, probably more than the unpredictable draft horse. Riding a cow is an almost serene and contemplative use of time. Cows mosey along, they don't stumble, and they sit better than a horse for the bare-backed rider. Somehow, they seem happy to make a rider happy. So, a young boy has very little to do except enjoy the scenery, get in touch with his own consciousness, chat with others, and consider great and wonderful thoughts or fantasies. It is an exquisite experience.

We did that often on the farm. Larry's dad would send us out the lane to herd the cows from the furthermost pasture for the evening milking or feeding. The three of us would amble out the lane in the summer sun and heat and find the thirty or so cows in that field. We'd locate the "bell cow" – the one with a brass bell hanging around her neck — and head her toward the open gate to the lane. Usually, I would just jump up on the old girl and point her in the right direction with my toes. The bell would shake, the other cows would look up, and then they would follow her out of the pasture. Larry and Spit would herd any stranglers, jump up on two of them, and our parade back to the barn was underway. Once everyone was moving, following the leisurely pace of my bell cow, Larry and Spit would make great sport of jumping from one cow to another until they were near the front with me. Then we would spend the rest of the ride to chat, joke, and consider the way things were. This quality experience, I think, represents one of the defining moments of a country boy's future outlook on life. The self-fulfillness, the self-awareness, and the self-possession that results from piloting cows, horses, and tractors are character-making experiences. I enjoyed an entire summer with two just such characters.

Spit Unger acquired his nickname exactly as someone might expect. Being able to spit further than any other kid in Aaronsburg did not result in a trophy, but it did cement a nickname. He was especially adept at this questionable skill when he was chewing plug tobacco, a habit he acquired at a very early age. He was the youngest of three siblings and certainly the most adventurous. William Unger was a large-boned, gangly, big-eared kid who loved the great outdoors. Even as a child he was a great hunter and fisherman. He knew the fields and mountains around Aaronsburg better than an adult ten times his senior.

Spit tried to make a fisherman out of me, but he just couldn't get that done. My only talent was snagging my hook on the rocks on the creek bottom or in the trees behind us as I tried to cast. Now and again, especially when Larry was unavailable, Spit would make me go anyway. At first I borrowed one of his rods, but after a while I just tagged along.

What was more fun than fishing was going to catch minnows for Spit to use as bait. These little fish were to be found in all the little streams and brooks that sliced across the valley on all those farms outside of town. Spit knew just where to go. We would take his minnow net, called a seine, and hike back into the valley where the Amish lived on farms without electricity or running water. We would find a shallow, narrow brook and stretch our net across it. Then we would drag it a distance across the bottom before lifting it quickly to trap the minnows. Often we did this under the watchful eyes of Amish children peering out their open windows at us "English" boys more or less trespassing on their property.

But that summer was mostly about guns. Most mornings the three of us would take off out the back lane, each carrying some sort of weapon. I liked that .22. Larry favored his Winchester 30.06; Spit always had his Stevens. Amazingly, we never shot each other. We'd fire at squirrels (a .30-.30 is no way for a squirrel to die), we'd shoot a crow, or we'd set up old cans or bottles and shoot at them. Usually we were pretty careful. Larry had already had two bad experiences with rifles. Unintentionally, he had shot one of the Vonada boys through the hand before I moved to town. The two of them had been shooting bottles and cans off a fence, and the kid held up his hand to tell Larry to quit shooting for a moment. Unfortunately, he put his hand in front of Larry's barrel just as Larry had sighted in on an old Pennzoil can. Luckily, Larry only had the .22 that day, so the wound was small even though it went cleanly through the boy's palm. His hand healed with just a small round scar on both sides of his palm. He regained almost full use of the extremity.

The news wasn't so good for one of Larry's favorite dogs, Shep. That retriever loved to run in the fields with us, flushing up birds and rabbits for our shooting pleasure. One day Larry raised his rifle to shoot at rabbit in a new wheat field. At that moment Shep, chasing after the rabbit, bounded into the line of fire and was struck in the head with a bullet that killed him instantly. Larry felt badly about that dog for a long, long time. I'm glad to this day that I was not present for this little tragedy.

So, we tried to be careful. But three boys and three guns constitute a lethal mix. I wonder how it was that we didn't maim each other.

We used Spit's pellet gun to capture a pigeon. This gun shot a BB or a regular pellet without the benefit of gunpowder. The gun used compressed air that we built up by pumping a small lever on the underside of the rifle. The more one pumped it, the more powerful the shot.

Spit and I went into the barn that sat opposite our old hotel. We had pumped the gun to a low level because we were not out to kill anything. We only wanted to stun a pigeon. We wanted to drop it to the ground with just enough force that it could not elude capture. Then we'd have me a bird to domesticate and make into a family pet.

That is just how I got Ace. He was a beautiful white pigeon with a gray head and gray-tipped wings. He was sitting majestically on a rafter in the unused barn. He looked down at us quizzically even while Spit took aim and dropped him like a target in a shooting gallery.

I scooped up Ace and put him in a birdcage that Spit had purloined from his attic. I took him up to the second floor porch that ran out the back of our suite of rooms. I showed him to my mother and told her I had a new pet. She said we would see.

I nursed Ace back to health. He wasn't badly injured, but it took him a few days to recover from the traumatic incident and to get used to his new confines. All the while I assumed he would be grateful for this.

It turns out that he wasn't. He stayed several weeks with us. We could hold him outside the cage; he would eat from my hand. He liked my sister and would sit on her shoulder, just like those parrots in the pirate movies. He would fly off and come back in just a minute or so. He actually went into his cage without insistence or assistance from us. I thought he would stay forever. I called him my bird. My mother told me that if he stayed, he was my bird. If he did not, he never was.

He never was. One day he flew off and never came back. I went over to the barn to look for him, but I suspect he knew better than to go back there again.

***

One of my more notable adventures with Larry Rossman actually unfolded after my family had returned to Millheim, all established in our new house. It involved Halloween.

All of us kids in Millheim thought we knew how to celebrate Halloween. We were good at it. In those days Halloween was a season, not an evening. Over three or four nights we engaged in mischief. We saved "trick or treating," the actual candy-begging activity, for Halloween Eve itself.

We would arm ourselves with bars of soap and bags of corn. Then we raided houses – Penn Street was a target-rich environment – soaping windows and pelting the panes with pinging kernels of corn.

We climbed the huge maple trees that overhung Penn Street and dropped water balloons on passing cars below. That activity often ended with us scurrying on up the tree limbs to avoid capture by some irate motorist who would stop to identify us. That never happened though, because the thick canopy overhanging that section of the roadway allowed us to scurry from one tree to another.

We once made a dummy out of old clothing with straw stuffing and laid it in a small dip in the road, near the Lutheran church. Motorists would drive over the dip, see the body lying there too late, and pass right over it, sometimes hitting it with a wheel. Expecting the worst, they would stop and run back to the scene to see if they had killed someone. We'd stand in the shadows, shaking with gleeful mirth.

We would topple outhouses – vestiges of years gone by – and hope that someone was actually in them. There never was. We draped toilet paper in trees in front yards; we scratched softly on kitchen window panes where some wife was cleaning up the dishes. We thought we were very clever and imaginative.

The whole season reflected an odd irony. For days we would terrorize homeowners with behavior that was just not condoned during the rest of the year. Then, on the last night, we would politely appear at the same doorways, and hold out bags for free candy. Everyone paid up. I think residents were just glad the assault season had passed.

But Larry Rossman brought an entirely new perspective to our Halloween endeavors. He joined me on the first Halloween my family observed in our new house. Larry came to town, prepared to show me how it was done.

Larry took no delight in preying on strangers. His twist on Halloween involved terrorizing the Halloweeners themselves. He targeted the ruffians, not the adults.

He arrived at my house on his bicycle. Strapped to handlebars were his double-barreled shotgun and a cloth sack full of birdshot shells. Off the crossbar hung a plastic bucket half filled with fresh, sloppy cow dung. Covering the goo were several inches of corn. In his pocket were a dozen cherry bombs. We set out.

We reported to Penn Street as darkness fell. We parked our bikes and carried the tools of our deceit down the alley. We concealed ourselves in the shadows of the homes that sat right on the sidewalk and waited for a small group of my friends who were organizing themselves for the evening's assault. They never saw us. We waited until they had selected the house they were going to attack with soap and corn. Larry and I positioned ourselves between them and the escape route we knew they would use at the first sign of trouble. We waited.

They attacked the house. Predictably, lights came on, doors flew open, homeowners appeared, and the chase was on. Now Larry sprung into action.

He waited for the kids to turn and start running our way. Then he took the loaded shotgun and fired both barrels into the ground about ten feet in front of us.

Everything stopped. The kids stopped; their pursuers stopped; time stopped. The kids thought they were outflanked by a madman. They were trapped by someone angry enough to shoot them. Meanwhile, the homeowners behind them wondered what the hell was going on. Were these kids armed? They decided they better get back inside. They bolted. The kids turned to run off in another direction. Larry had reloaded and fired two more shots in that general direction, although well out in front of where the kids were headed.

That did it. Everyone stopped. One at a time, each boy started to raise his hands in surrender. Cries of "Don't shoot, we give up," reached us. There was real fear in the voices.

"Get on your hands and knees," Larry ordered in a rough, disguised, adult-like voice. Everyone did. "Now shut your eyes until I get to you," Larry yelled. Everyone complied. Tickled pink, Larry and I walked out of the shadows and over to four or five of my good friends. "So, you boys think you are pretty smart, do you?" Larry asked.

"No, no," the shaking heads indicated.

"Well, stand up and look at me," Larry finished, unable to do anything else without laughing at the pitiful group.

The looks of relief on the faces of my friends were priceless. It took a few moments of recounting their terror, but they finally forgave us. They were feeling lucky to be alive and still free.

We chatted with them for a few minutes and then joined up with them. Larry promised not to fire the shotgun again. He told them he had corn with him, showing them the disguised bucket of cow crap. That settled them a bit. We selected the next house for attack.

There is something about human nature, related to either greed or over-indulgence that causes us to overdo a good thing. Larry knew that about people. He knew that if he offered up a bucket of corn for everyone to use, every Halloweener would reach for it in the same way. Forgoing the corn on the top, they would jam their hands all the way to the bottom of the bucket, as if only the stuff on the bottom would work.

Well, the bottom of this bucket of corn was not corn at all. Our friends found this out too late. Four or five hands dove into the bucket for the ammunition. All of them came out covered almost to the elbow in cow dung – wet, sloppy cow dung. On their fingers, hands, and jacket sleeves.

Larry and I were the only two who saw any humor in this. Everyone else released vitriolic oaths and loathing. They had to quit their pursuits for a while so they could go home and clean up.

Larry and I found another group a bit later. This time we climbed those huge maples (leaving the shotgun on the ground, of course) and moved out on the limbs over-hanging the sidewalk. When the band of rascals came down the walk, we dropped lighted cherry bombs into their midst. Cherry bombs make a lot of noise. They explode in small balls of fire. Just the results we were seeking.

More scared kids. They could not identify from where the explosives were coming, let alone who was doing it. They didn't wait to find out. They scattered. Someone out there had more fire power and gall than they. That slowed them down for a while.

It was the best night of Halloweening that I ever had.

***

Farming is a dangerous way to make a living. Shuffling around big animals, operating huge tractors and heavy pieces of equipment – balers, corn-pickers, combines, cutters, wagons, and such – can really become a contest of odds. Sooner or later someone is going to get careless, just for a moment, or the equipment will malfunction or move unpredictably, and a serious injury occurs.

Numerous farm accidents throughout my youth became part of the valley's history. Bobby Winchel's knee injury on his dad's farm was the first. Soon after that, Mallie Rossman ran over Larry with a disc, a long row of semi-sharp blades used to break up the clods of dirt in a newly-plowed field. Luckily, Larry was wearing a coat; that spared him many cuts. However, he received a compression of most of the organs in his body. He decided perhaps he ought to tell his dad if he was going to jump from a moving tractor. Other accidents happened to the most experienced farmers, hard-boiled men who just happened to do a dangerous thing at the wrong time.

Perhaps the most feared and widely-spread accidents involved corn-pickers. This piece of machinery is a particularly nasty-looking hunk of metal, sharp blades, and thick chain. The front of the corn-picker consists of two pointed and tapering shoots that funnel the corn stalks into the stripping bin. Inside, the cobs of corn are ripped from the stalks and released out the back of the machine. Meanwhile, the stalks are ground into a fodder and forcibly shot out a long rear-facing snout.

The dangerous part is the front. While designed to handle even the thickest of stalks and the heaviest of yield, corn-pickers still often become clogged. The correct procedure for clearing the increasingly narrow opening is to disengage the power take-off on the tractor that runs the picker before clearing it. Everyone knows that. Yet, every so often, some valley farmer would, in haste, jump off his tractor and try to free the opening without shutting the machine off first. Sometimes clearing the opening meant reaching into it to untangle the stalks. That is where the sharp cutters are. More than one farmer simply reached in too far. Others did not reach in but grabbed a stalk and tried to pull it out end first. The machine, just as the opening began to clear, would grab that stalk again, and in doing so, would drag the farmer's hand in with it.

Evan Beard lost his hand this way. So did Bill Vonada.

Mallie Rossman had his own run-in with a corn-picker. Fortunately, he did not lose his hand, but he cut himself up rather rudely. Mallie, like most of the valley farmers, was a tough guy who seldom let adversity get him down. Once, when he was working alone in the fields, he somehow trapped his leg in either a moving tractor part or a piece of machinery. His left ankle was crushed. He pondered his predicament out there in that field, watching his leg bleed profusely. Seeing no other option, he climbed back onto his tractor and drove back to the farmhouse. This seems obvious enough until one considers the pain that must have been involved. Mallie needed that left foot, now dangling by tendons, to engage the heavy clutch on that tractor. The agony he endured to get that tractor back to the farmhouse would have been excruciating.

During one of my visits to the farm, Mallie came up the lane holding a badly bleeding hand. The barbed wire he was installing along a fence row with his wire-stretching tool had slipped, allowing about three feet of barbed wire, under tension provided by the tool, to rip through his hand. Raw, torn flesh was hanging in all directions. He was white and sweating, but he brushed it off as no big deal and headed off to Doc Henninger's office to get himself stitched up.

Kenny Dutrow, whose daughter I was later to marry, once stood under a grain elevator as it moved combined wheat to the bin on the second level of his barn. For some unknown reason, the elevator fell from its supports and landed on Kenny's head. He sustained neck injuries and recurring headaches that lasted a lifetime. Dick Huber was clearing his pasture one day with his tractor and mower attachment that hooked just below the tractor itself. On a steep hillside the tractor tipped sideways and Dick fell off, in front of the three-foot mowing deck. It is said that they gathered him up in pieces. Death in the prime of his life. A tipped tractor later claimed the life of a classmate of mine, Earl Valory.

Some of these occupational hazards associated with rural living may help to explain why farm kids tended to be risk-takers – why they may have had a more cavalier attitude about dubious undertakings. Life was a gamble. Farming was a real gamble, what with the vicissitudes of nature, the erratic market prices of cash crops, and the danger in working with mercurial animals and power equipment. Using guns, driving cars and tractors, learning safe procedures for implement use were underpinnings of the society. That kids should be involved in these things at an early age was a given. The family farm required all members of the family. Relieving kids from any potential threat was not going to be either a short—or a long-term solution. Being an issue, safety was always discussed; it was expected. Farm kids knew danger from an early age. They really could not avoid it. Most were simply fortunate enough to escape it successfully.

One might have thought that parents would have been very, very watchful of small boys and their guns. But, on a farm, using a rifle and operating dangerous farm implements are not only rites of passage, they are necessities. The day would inevitably arrive when parents just had to assume that the children were ready and able to handle equipment and guns without supervision. Whatever the kids lacked in judgement or skill, they would just have to make up with luck or divine intervention.

Chapter 9

Millheim — Again

The summer of 1956 was my time of living dangerously. Two miscreants taught me the subtleties of youthful recklessness. I had been shot at, thrown off horses, and tossed about that tractor scoop. I had begun to develop an enhanced level of self-reliance – a higher, albeit foolish, sense of invincibility. Coupled with my earlier escapes from danger, those adventures in Aaronsburg were making me more fearless than wise. Experienced, to be sure, but a bit blase' about my own well-being, I returned, upon the completion of our new home, to "the home of the mills."

I did so with the swagger and brashness of a seasoned sixth grader, one of the oldest kids who would be attending a different school. I was to land in Mrs. Pearle Deever's classroom. She made it her mission to dispel me, and all my classmates for that matter, of any delusions of grandeur we may have harbored. Spit Unger and Herb Bierly were both in the same class with me, and so were the two most beautiful girls in the world, Nancy Fox and Peggy Moore. Life was good. How we all got there is a story of its own.

My dad had been systematically closing down many of the tiny, often one-room, elementary school houses that sprinkled Penns Valley. From a total of seventeen in 1951 he had reduced the number of schools to five. That meant that students from wider geographic areas began to attend those schools still in use. Consolidation was also taking place at the secondary level as plans were completed to combine the four small high schools into one facility housing grades seven to twelve. Actually, this was occurring all over the country, this consolidation and modernization of the nation's local school systems.

Dad closed the small school in Aaronsburg. Students in grades four to six, along with those from Coburn Elementary, joined us Millheim kids in our new elementary school, the former East Penn High School, just four lots out Main Street from my new house.

My dad had two problems with the sixth grade class scheduled to attend this building for the first time. The first was a numbers problem, the second a political problem. I helped him solve both.

The numbers problem was obvious enough: There were too many fifth and sixth graders for just one class of each. There weren't enough of either to justify a second single-grade section. There were no extra classrooms to put in a second class of both anyway. The new Millheim elementary school had just four classrooms, enough for one class of each grade, four, five, and six, plus one extra class. Baby boomers had struck their first blow to Millheim and America, generally. Where do we all go?

That overflow class was going to have to be a combination of fifth and sixth graders. That was not an option Dad liked educationally, but he was trapped by the number of students and the limited number of rooms. Now he faced the unpopular decisions he would have to make about who was going into this "split class." Such classes had been done before. They were never very popular with teachers or parents; they were difficult to justify educationally. I had already been in one or two down at Coburn.

But it got worse. This numbers scenario was accompanied by a political one. Just as students from other schools such as Aaronsburg, Woodward, and Plum Grove were being reassigned, so were the teachers who taught there. The venerable and mild-tempered Maude Mailer and the archetypal schoolmarm, Eleanor Banner, would come up from Coburn to teach fifth and fourth grades respectively. Ray Faluth would be assigned to teach sixth grade and would serve as head teacher, the on-site boss when my dad was at other schools in the valley. So far — no problem.

155

But Pearl Deever was coming to Millheim also. She had been teaching in Woodward, and now she would be assigned to teach that extra, mixed-grade class.

That fact didn't make this class any more attractive to the parents whose children were going to be in a mixed grade class. Pearl Deever had a reputation.

Pearl was not the average schoolmarm. She was a brassy, big-bosomed, wide-hipped gal who dressed more colorfully than any teacher we had ever seen. She wore big, dangling earrings, often color-coordinated with her dresses, sweaters, shoes, and fingernail polish. Her favorite hues were fire engine red, Easter egg purple, and lemon-lime green. Her dresses were bold fashion statements. Her taste ran to polka dots and wide, contrasting stripes, usually horizontal, the wrong way to flatter her plump, short stature. Her dresses often started at the same point as her cleavage and fell provocatively only to the knee. More than one hoop skirt pushed her dresses out into tent-shaped affairs. These undergarments swished when she walked and showed when she made sudden turns on her scandalously high pumps. She looked, and bustled about, like a square dancer. Pearl wore large jewelry, sporting rings on several fingers, and multiple bracelets on both wrists. Simply put, she was showy.

And she smelled good. Most teachers of the day, as our mothers, augmented their personal, feminine essence with dusting powder. Every student of the times must certainly remember leaning over the teacher only to get a whiff of some heavy rose or lilac fragrance emanating from the fine powder these ladies sifted onto themselves. I always have associated that smell and that powdery face and neck with both my mother and most of my female teachers. I actually helped to perpetuate this ground stone dusting of female skin – continued, I'll bet, from some ancient culture, like the Aztecs or Incas. For Christmas, more than once, I bought my mother some alluring scent of this fine talc. It was not expensive, and I could obtain it right down at the 5 and 10,

Daily application of this powder, over time, seemed to create a permanent thin shade of gray, or pinkish-gray on those schoolmarms' skin, gently masking any natural, human color. This scent and its visual effects both stick in my memory as "the funeral look," the pallor of a corpse at a public viewing. "Oh, my, doesn't she look natural?"

Pearl Deever did not coat herself with dusting powder. That was obvious because her skin, face, neck, and ample bosom were always deep, shiny, clear, and almost luminescent. She wore perfume, different perfumes all the time. She exuded an aroma that was exotic, thin, but fetching. Because Pearl taught hard, physically moving about the room, quickly and adroitly changing direction in those high heels, waving her slightly saggy upper arms about the room, she was capable of working up a "glow," a slight sheen to her exposed skin that was at once attractive and sexy. Chubby or not, Pearl had sex appeal even while she swished about, dictating everything that happened in that room. Wherever she was, Pearl ruled.

From all that and her public persona came her reputation. Pearl was assertive and noisy. She was opinionated and confident. She made no effort to play the conservative schoolteacher. She did nothing to dispel any rumor that she could drink and swear, or shout and argue as well as any man in town. There was talk that she and husband, Abel, drank beer. They lived in the second-floor apartment in a narrow building right next to Penns Tavern, and they were said to slip next door, late in the evening, for a few brews before bed. People talked about Pearl; nothing particularly derogatory or nasty, but that raised eyebrow stuff. She just seemed to be notorious, not exactly the quality for which small town elementary teachers were known in those days. She was a bit mysterious to us kids, and probably to some of the townsfolk also. There was just this aura about her. She seemed like a lady with a past, a story that few knew in much detail, but one that simply hung over her.

She was the kind of employee who gave supervisors fits. One had to run interference for her, and hope that she did not cause a stir in the community that would somehow involve the classroom. With Pearl, Dad always had to engage in damage control.

But she was a great teacher. Dad already knew that, and I was going to experience that. Dad always supported Pearl's teaching, which, like her fashion statements, was a bit off-beat and eccentric. Pearl never mailed it in. She worked hard in the classroom, although she sometimes ran afoul of parents because of her unorthodox style and discipline procedures. Dad knew she was creative and solid with the basics. He knew she did her job well. I never heard Dad criticize Pearl Deever's teaching ability. He liked her, and I believe she liked him.

But for now, Dad had a problem. Because of her self-inflicted reputation, Pearl was not easy to sell to parents as the best teacher placement for their children. She was just too controversial. Given the choice, most parents were going to ask for either Maude or Ray, not Pearl the Girl.

Nevertheless, someone had to go. And Dad thought I ought to be one of those so assigned. His reasoning was that if he put his own son there, no one could argue that he was playing favorites in the assignment process or selecting kids that he cared little for as he threw them to this modern day she-devil. That would ameliorate his political problem.

He sat me down and gingerly asked what I thought. He was expecting me to say that I wanted to go to Ray Faluth's class with all my other sixth grade friends. As it worked out, there would only be six sixth graders in this new, mixed class of about twenty-five kids. So, how was that going to suit me, he wondered.

I surprised him. I told him I would gladly take this assignment under one condition. I wanted to select both the fifth and sixth graders who were going into that room. How many kids get that option?

Well, Dad jumped at the deal. He saw an improved state of affairs with regard to his political problem. If I were choosing the kids, most of them would not be complaining to their parents because they would be grouped with lots of close friends – like me – in this class. They would be trading preferred teacher for preferred classmates. That is an easy choice for a kid.

So, that is what we did. I sat down with the entire lists of both fifth and sixth graders newly assigned to Millheim Elementary School. I exercised the first twenty-five draft picks and formed the perfect classroom – two dozen of my closest and dearest friends. It was the best year of school I ever had.

I selected Bierly, of course, Spit Unger, and Kermit Riley, a kid I met while living in Aaronsburg. The two loves in my life at the time were Nancy Fox and Peg Moore, in no particular order. These two girls ended up sitting right in front of me as the six of us older kids formed a little postage stamp in the right rear corner of a room dominated by fifth graders.

I selected some great fifth graders too. Most of the boys demonstrated formidable baseball prowess. Jimmy Brown from Aaronsburg was there along with Jake Reber, Jack Konrad, Mike Snavet, Jimmy Winchel, and a few others.

The girls included Susie Fox (good for me in case my deal with her sister Nancy didn't work out), Brenda Breon (really bright and could help me with my spelling, younger or not), Diane McClintic (already wore a bra), Darlene Wolfe (cute, her dad worked in the bank we were still trying to rob), and some others with distinct possibilities.

I knew before the first day of school that this year was going to be special. There was Mrs. Deever up there smiling (her reputation among former students was that she was mean and insulting). Having used my plan, Dad faced no controversy. Everyone was going to give Mrs. Deever a chance. Meanwhile, here I was with all my friends.

Pearl Deever ran an imaginative classroom. We wrote stories, creations of our own that were really great personal challenges. This was the year of the Russian invasion of Hungary. We read news stories of these and other current events and wrote stories related to them. Mine was a short story of a Hungarian boy my age named Jan (I found out that Jan was a typical Hungarian name) who became a freedom fighter during those awful days for the Hungarians. Typical of Mrs. Deever's' flair for color, she had about ten different colors of inks that we could use to write our final copies. I choose purple for this one. I also wrote a tale about Ace, my erstwhile pigeon. Purple prose from a sixth-grader. Cool.

We made special art projects for our parents in Christmas season. Pearl taught us to parse sentences and to do really complex math problems. She wove in a bit of sex education, which we needed, approved by the Board of Education or not, and taught us the difference between blue birds and blue jays. We put on class plays. Every child's birthday warranted a day of no homework.

She stood up front and asked all sorts of questions – expecting us to start thinking on our own. She treated us as young adults, requiring us to rise to one occasion after another, educationally, socially, and morally. She expected us to work independently much of the time. This, of course, was necessary because she had to work with the other grade as she split her instructional time between us.

While Pearl worked with one grade level, she kept close watch on the other group. She was a strict disciplinarian, and she could get snippy if we were not "on task" as educators say. Her big brown eyes bugged out of her head a bit so that we could always see an inordinate amount of the white part. Those huge orbs were in constant motion, not only about the room but just in general. They seemed to be in constant vibration, sort of wobbling or quivering at parade rest, poised to focus on some scoundrel wasting a moment of school time.

Then, through that deep red lipstick, Pearle would sarcastically intone, "Eddie, are you going to talk or work? I need to know before I decide on homework for this evening."

"Oh, Mrs. Deever, I'm here to work. Don't you worry about me."

I loved sixth grade – at least until Memorial Day.

Larry Witherite drowned on Memorial Day weekend at Poe Valley State Park. Larry was one of the fifth graders in our room. He was a nice kid and a good baseball player. Just before the weekend he had helped our team beat Faluth's class in an historic softball game that pitted mostly fifth-graders against mostly sixth-graders. I forget how. I just remember that he was one of the heroes of the game.

Larry came from a large family in Aaronsburg. His dad, Kenny Witherite, drove a delivery truck for Frame's Dry Cleaners, over in Lock Haven. He'd stop, chat amicably to everyone, and haul off our woolens and silks. So, we all knew Kenny and his kids. They were a close and friendly family.

They embarked on a picnic to the mountain park over the holiday weekend. Poe Valley State Park is one of those government projects from the depression days, a product of the Civilian Conservation Corps. Poe Valley was just about ten miles of dirt road from Millheim. It featured a twenty-acre lake for boating, fishing, and swimming.

Every few years, park officials drained the lake by opening the gates at the dam. This allowed maintenance to the swimming area and removal of unwanted undergrowth in or near the lake. This year the lake had been drained.

It required about a week to bring the lake back to normal level again. Authorities had started the process before Memorial Day, but the lake was not full by the holiday weekend. That meant that the swimming area, at the edge of the lake, had not yet filled. So, pre-season swimmers had to walk out much further, out to the ledge that formed the original banks of the stream that fed the lake.

That's what Larry did. He walked out to the ledge and stepped off into water that was significantly over his head. Apparently his family wasn't nearby. He drowned, and they had to use a grappling hook to recover his body. It was ghastly.

We returned to school for the last few days before summer to find all this out. It was a sobering experience. In those days there was no such thing as grief counseling for kids who have lost a chum. We simply went on with it. It was sad. A hero one day, dead the next. It was a poor ending to that sixth grade year.

***

Around this time, Bierly and I were involved in our rather dismal efforts at being scouts. There had already been a few fitful attempts at maintaining a Boy Scout troop in Millheim. They failed. Actually, the real originators of the new scout troop were Curt Bierly and Lee Bartges. These two highly-principled, civic-minded lads wanted to be Boy Scouts. They decided the town needed an organized, official troop, complete with uniforms, merit badges, and levels of attainment. They convinced Elwood

Bressler, Sheldon's father, to serve as scoutmaster, and they organized the whole start-up for him.

Now Bierly and I were too young to be Boy Scouts – there were national guidelines that separated boys of specific ages into Boy Scout troops and Cub Scout packs. Well, we had no Cub Scout pack at the time, so Bierly and I, because we knew the organizers so well, were allowed to join the bigger boys in the Boy Scouts. This was clearly a violation of what seemed like a very important national rule, but who was watching, and who cared?

That went well enough for a year or so. We would meet down at the old, mostly-abandoned elementary school beside the ball field and tie knots, conduct municipal improvements, and plan camping outings. We conducted monthly "paper drives." Scouts would ride in the back of someone's old, green pick-up truck, usually with the legs of the two or three "runners" hanging over the open tailgate, so we could collect the little bundles of old newspapers and magazines homeowners left on the curb. Nobody seemed to consider this a dangerous activity, even though we would slide off a still-moving truck in front of vehicles directly behind us and stumble toward our bounty beside the roadway. We'd unload these parcels at a shed near Ward Gramley's big house, minus the few girlie magazines we often spirited away from a particular residence, so a bigger truck could later carry all this paper to some recycling plant far away. Residents rid themselves of this offal, the scouts were paid something for our efforts, and the world was a greener place. Bierly and I were integral parts of all this.

But then some citizen got the idea to form a Cub Scout troop. After all, there were many kids our age in town who were not enjoying the rich experiences Bierly and I were having.

When that plan came to fruition, Bierly and I were demoted. We both had already met all the requirements for Second Class Scout, even though we could not receive the recognition from the national organization. Pretty heady stuff for two little shavers. But now, we were to become Webelos in Pack 88. It was like starting all over again – at a level well beneath our proven skills. This was crushing to our self-esteem.

The unfairness of it all made us angry. Our protestations fell on deaf ears. Down to the minor leagues we must go.

But not without first making our statement. We planned some apt revenge.

Soon after we were established in the new Cub Scout pack, the Boy Scouts planned one of their overnight camping trips to the Honiheis – their first outing without us. The Honiheis is a Pennsylvania Dutch-named field back in a swale in the mountains north of town. This huge, sloping hillside was really just a ten-acre clearing in the otherwise thickly-wooded mountain. It featured tall grass and sparse, young pine trees that accidentally grew from wind-tossed cones from the trees surrounding the field. The land caved in on both sides to form a gully that traversed the field. In the gully ran a little mountain brook.

Bierly and I had camped there with the scouts before our demotion. We knew the hiking path to the enclosed and remote mountain field. In fact, one or our favorite "private places" was just off that trail, about half way up to the Honeheis. Just where the trail turned hard right and headed up to the top of the mountain was a sharp bank that fell off to the left. Down over that bank was a small stream meandering through a shaded glen. The pine trees there were mature enough that there were no branches from the base of their trunks to a level of ten feet or so. The ground underneath them was soft, moist, and covered with pine needles. Often Bierly and I would wonder up to this little dell to smoke cigarettes, eat snacks, and catch tadpoles, which he referred to as "mulliegrubbers." We would catch slews of the little swimmers and put them in a coffee can. Then we would lie on our backs on the soft, natural carpet and stare up through the trees to the sky. We would share our secret thoughts, enjoy our smokes, and fiddle with our catch. We'd look for snakes, raccoons, and squirrels. We'd build little dams in the stream and wade about the water for hours.

So, we certainly knew where the troop pitched tents in one corner of the high hillside. We knew the camp routine of dinner followed by a rousing game of Capture The Flag that would go on until dark.

That is when we planned to strike.

After our dinner on this summer evening, we hiked up to the Honiheis. We crouched in the tree line and spied on the kind, loyal, and brave scouts as they prepared their vittles and then cleaned up their Boy Scout Approved mess kits. We waited until they descended the hill to the brook to begin their game of Capture The Flag. The flags were always put by the little stream.

While they were all down there, engaged in a mock epic battle, Bierly and I pillaged their tents. We were armed with jars of peanut butter and jelly for the villainous deed we had concocted.

Like good Boy Scouts, all the older boys had unfurled their sleeping bags and arranged them inside their pup tents, two to a tent. Bierly and I unzipped the upper side of more than a half dozen sleeping bags and slathered the insulated insides with the gooey mixture we had brought. We had wonderful and devious visions of the kids sliding into their bags by lantern light and feeling a sticky, slick substance on their legs. We had decided they deserved this for expelling us from the scouts.

Then to indicate our presence, we searched for the camp water supply. Drinking water was transported in a five-gallon can originally used to store some sort of industrial fluid. We used that to douse the two camp fires left burning by the battling scouts below.

That, of course, changed the thin, wispy smoke that each fire was producing into a heavy steaming flume. It did not take the scouts long to notice the change. They roared up the hill to see what the problem was with the fires.

Bierly and I hastily exited the area. We could hear their decidedly non-scout oaths as we moved through the tree line, back to our escape path. Surely, all the tents and bags were checked. Probably no one actually did crawl into a vandalized sack. We hiked down the mountain basking in our success. We giggled and cackled over our cleverness.

We weren't fingered for the deed for about three days. There were suspicions, of course, but not until Curt finally put Bierly in his dreaded headlock maneuver – "The Crusher," he called it — was a confession forthcoming.

For a while, it appeared that we were going to have to replace six sleeping bags at our own expense. But no one threatened to sue, and mothers about town just set to cleaning out the fouled sleeping bags.

We were tossed out of the Cub Scouts. All our contributions and merit badges as faithful Webelos didn't seem to carry much weight. We received the extreme sanction. It didn't matter much though. The Cub Scouts – and the Boy Scouts, for that matter – disbanded for lack of leadership not long thereafter. Bierly and I always believed that our absence from both hindered any designs of longevity.

Oh, yeah, our parents were really angry and embarrassed. We had apologies to make all over town. I lost swimming pool privileges for a week. And two of the tougher scouts promised revenge that I still await today.

***

Curt finally got his horse. Older than us by five years, Bierly's brother had reached that age where he could prove the personal responsibility for a life other than his own. He had been trying to tell his parents this for several years as he angled every which way he could to acquire his own horse. He wanted to ride, and there was serious talk in Millheim about forming what later became the Black Panther Riding Club. Curt wanted to join that. Obviously, the entrance requirements included having a horse. His folks fought him off for a few years, but sometime around 1956 or so, Curt got the lucky confluence of breaks that made the deal possible.

Bill James, one of the richest and most influential businessmen in the whole valley, purchased a grand Arabian mare from some important horse trader far, far away from our town. Bill, too, planned to be in the new riding club. It turned out that the dealer had another horse for sale that, seemingly, no one wanted.

She was a feisty, black and beautiful animal totally lacking any signs of domestication. She was wild and obstreperous, moody, and aggressive. She was mean-spirited and was almost impossible to ride. That mare would paw the ground at the approach of any human, known or unknown. She would rise up on her hind legs and lash out with her front hooves at any perceived threat, and everything seemed to threaten her. She'd try to bite anyone who reached in to stroke or nuzzle her. Simply put, she was such a bitch that the dealer was very anxious to unload her, whether he made any money on her or not.

Well, Curt bought her. Bill James knew of the boy's interest in owning a horse and felt compelled to bring this offer back from his buying trip. He did try to explain to Curt and his parents the problems this particular horse would present. But that was of no matter to Curt. His boyhood zeal and his firm conviction in his own skills and patience were matched with the very enticing price tag. The horse dealer even agreed to deliver her free to Curt at the same time Bill was to get his fine horse. Curt convinced his folks that he could tame the savage beast.

Having received his parents' tacit and guarded approval, Curt made arrangements to rent a stall for her in a barn down on the alley that ran behind Penn Street. He read up on horse care, secured the necessary hay, straw, grooming implements, buckets, shovels, and so forth to care for his horse. Not long thereafter, Curt Bierly was a horse owner and a charter member of the fledgling Black Panther Riding Club.

Curt named his new acquisition "Flicka." The name was not a particularly creative selection. He took it from the currently-running television show *My Friend Flicka* that featured a horse with a disposition about 180 degrees from Curt's mount. The famous Flicka was a docile, smart, and almost human mare, stalled on the Goose Bar Ranch. She helped Ken, her twelve-year owner, achieve all sorts of miraculous feats and family harmony on that mid-1950s Saturday classic. For Curt to name his horse Flicka was a flight of fancy.

To his credit, it must be said that Curt was somewhat successful in cultivating his new possession. He made her almost civil. Almost. It took lots of his time and all of his patience. Flicka threw him several times, bit him often, and caused consternation among the other Black Panther members. But Curt stuck with her, and after a while Flicka began to act no worse than a troubled kindergartner. She remained constantly nervous, wary, fidgety, and unpredictable. She was never to be truly trusted. She certainly never won the Miss Congeniality Award from the Black Panther

Riding Club. But Curt often received compliments for just how far along he had brought her.

So, after some time, Curt had tamed Flicka to the point where he could actually saddle her, mount her, and take her on a ride.

I had been on Flicka on more than one occasion, but always under Curt's watchful eye. But one summer day Bierly and I decided to take Flicka out for some exercise without Curt's presence or knowledge. What the hell, we were already in the neighborhood, and the poor horse had been cooped up for some time. What was the harm in giving the old gal a workout? Curt would probably be happy that we helped him out with Flicka's exercise program.

We turned off Penn Street and went back to the barn. We entered and chatted Flicka up for awhile to assure her of our good intentions. We knew her feeding, watering, and grooming routines because we had often helped Curt with all of these. We knew lots more by this time about horses. My own experience with Albert Stover's Tony had taught me not to scare them with sudden movements or bad positioning. My forays with Larry Rossman's draft horse had taught me the foolishness of making excessive demands of a stubborn animal and how to take a tumble without breaking a bone. I thought I was getting pretty good around horses. And, I was ready to ride.

Bierly and I put the saddle and bridle on Flicka without incident and led her from the barn out into the alley. Bierly would ride first of course. He'd take her up and down the alleyway just to get her warmed up and loose. Then I would take over. I'd get her used to me, and then we would both hop aboard for a ride all over town.

Bierly's short ride went well enough. Flicka cantered effortlessly up and down the alley. She was amicable if somewhat fretful. Finally, it was my turn. Bierly dismounted, and I climbed up on the tall mare. I wheeled her in a tight circle and headed down the alley. We walked a bit, and then we trotted. For a moment or two we broke into a comfortable cantor. I reined her in to head back to Bierly. That was the last moment I was in charge.

Once turned, Flicka decided that the ride was over; she was going back to her stall. From a dead standstill she reached a Mach I gallop in two seconds. She sped up from there, heading straight for the barn. She charged forward even though I was pulling like hell on her reins. My resistance didn't faze her – Flicka and E.T. were headed home.

There was none of that poetic, synchronized blending of man and steed that we had seen in horse shows. We were definitely working at cross purposes. I was trying mightily to stop her; Flicka just kept gaining speed. I tried turning her to our right, up a narrow path that led to a narrow field by the creek behind the barn. But Flicka would have none of that. She stayed right on the alleyway even as I was pulling her head hard to the side.

Bierly realized what was happening and quickly figured out how this was going to end. He jumped behind the open barn door and pulled it against him, effectively shielding himself from our approach. This was fortuitous for me because God only knows what that horse would have done if she could not have entered the barn.

Flicka and I stormed the barn at about ten miles per hour and her stall at about five miles per hour. Now the barn door was not quite high enough to accommodate the height of both horse and rider. Realizing that I was headed in there, like it or not, I had squished down as far as I could. I almost made it. The very top of my head hit the lintel above the door as we passed through. Hard. Additionally, I hit the left side of the doorway with my elbow and knee. That doorway would have been wide enough for us had Flicka gone in straight. But of course she figured on just enough clearance for herself; she did not much care whether or not I got through the door. We were too far to the left of the opening for me to get through unscathed. I had the same experience with the doorway to the stall, only on the right side. So, I had matching sides of scraped discomfort.

We stopped abruptly with her facing the rear of the stall. That catapulted me over her head (I could see that coming – I had had that experience before at Rossman's.) I flew over her head, face first, into the rear wall of the stall, and hung here for a second because my left foot was twisted in the stirrup. In slow motion, like a scene in a Roadrunner cartoon, I slid down over Flicka's neck and nose to the stinky, damp straw on the stall floor.

I lay there long enough for Flicka to look down at me and snort. She followed this with one small kick of her hoof that caught me flush on my ribs. She might have done more damage, but Bierly had arrived by then and, grabbing her reins, pulled her in circle away from me to face the front. In the process, she stepped on my left calf with one of her hind legs.

I was finally able to stagger from the barn to take inventory of my wounds. I had a goose-egg on the very top of my head that was already throbbing. Skin was ripped away on a half dozen brush burns on both of my bare elbows and knees. They all immediately began to seep blood and sting. I had a cut on my forehead and splinters the size of toothpicks stuck in my nose and cheeks from sliding down the rough wall of the stall. I had chipped a lower front tooth. My calf felt as though a horse had stepped on it. I smelled like horse urine.

Flicka looked no worse for the trip. In fact, she looked so content to be back home again that I wanted to smack her. But I didn't. She wasn't my horse.

Flicka and I did make a pact that day, however. I promised that I would never try to ride her again. She promised not to bolt with me on her back again. We both fulfilled those pledges.

Only once did I receive some pleasure from that horse. One beautiful winter day following a huge snowfall, Curt came gliding out to our house with Flicka attached to an old sleigh acquired from somewhere. Flicka seemed to like pulling the sleigh much more than having someone on her back. She accepted the trailing contraption well and actually seemed really pleased to be out frolicking in the deep snow. I jumped in with Curt, and off we went. He had supplied the old green and red rig with a warm blanket and a hot water bottle for our feet. He had cleaned the sleigh up some and had bells hanging from the traces leading up to Flicka.

We trotted all over Millheim. The heavy snow had made motorized transportation just about impossible, so the streets and alleys were devoid of traffic. We headed down the alley past Sheep Hill and turned onto Main Street at the bridge. We steered Flicka right up the street, through the red light at the diamond, and then into the alley system and across the ball field. We crossed the footbridge to the swimming pool and rode about the park.

The fresh, white blanket of snow was pristine. Flicka's black coat stood out in stark relief as we looked out over her rear quarters. The bells jangled as we went, creating, except for the horse's periodic snorting of steamy breath, almost the only sound in the otherwise eerily silent landscape. Curt and I sat swathed in the heavy blanket, each with a foot on the hot water bottle. We spoke little as we rode all over the burg. People shoveling snow stopped to look at us and wave as we slid by. It was simply a moment from a Currier and Ives painting. Flicka and I had finally made our peace.

I do not remember whatever became of her.

***

"Donnie, it's pea season — now is the time to get 'em. The trucks are running. Where's your dad's pitchfork?"

I planned on heisting some raw peas from the trucks carrying them through town. Donnie was all in, and we headed to the road, armed and resolute.

Up Route 45, near Centre Hall, was a canning factory. All types of fresh produce were processed there and came out with various labels on the cans. During the summer months the place was always hopping with big trucks delivering peas, corn, potatoes, and other produce to the plant.

Somewhere down Route 45 many farmers were growing peas and selling them to the cannery. Truck after truck, loaded as high as possible with pea-filled vines drooping over the edges, were going by our houses on their way to the cannery. These were huge flatbed trucks with pea vines sort of slung over them by whatever equipment picked the crop in the field.

The pile was high, higher by far, than the height of the truck cab. From a distance, they looked like great big turtles coming at us.

So when these trucks started their annual pageant through town this summer day, I decided Donnie and I ought to have some raw peas. We knew a truck would be coming by about every fifteen minutes. Planning on that, all we needed was a system for getting the peas off the truck.

At that time there was no concrete curb along Main Street/Route 45 through Millheim. The highway just tapered down from its crown in the middle to a wide, crushed stone berm. Where the berm stopped, Donnie's yard began. We would work from that berm.

The trucks seemed to be travelling awfully fast when we stood and watched them. But in fact, they were sort of rumbling through town and they certainly did not have anything near highway speed when they went by us. Besides, if most drivers saw kids playing near the road, they were going to let off the gas for a moment. Faith in that response formed the basis of our ruse.

I sat with Mr. Walker's pitchfork across my legs on the small rise that was the front boundary of Donnie's yard. When a truck started down the hill, Donnie walked out near the berm, head down, as if he were looking for a lost coin. That would slow the driver down just a bit and distract him just a little. When the truck got within a house or so of us, Donnie would step back onto his driveway. I would rush forward with the pitchfork outstretched and scrap off some pea vines from the right side of the truck. The driver never knew what hit him.

The trick was to scrape the vines rather lightly with the pitchfork. The only place the vines hung loosely was at the very edge of the pile. The weight of all that vinery and peas made the mass of the load very heavy and secure. But, if one could just snare the ends of a few vines, the momentum of the truck would fill the pitchfork with a wad of vines.

I had a knack for this kind of thievery. Several times this day we scored big. A truck would come by, Donnie would wander out in its path, it would slow just a bit, I would dash out and snare us a snack. We would sit there for the next fifteen minutes shelling and eating raw peas. Another truck would appear on the horizon and we would repeat our trick. I missed once or twice, but we had lots of peas.

But then Donnie just had to try it. I had some reservations. I really feared that he would run out too far and get clipped by the truck. But he assured me he could do this. Well, what the heck, I thought, it was his pitchfork.

"Look, Donnie, there are tricks to this. First, the depth of the "plunge." If you don't stick the pitchfork in deeply enough, we get nothing. However, if you stick the pitchfork in too deeply, you'll wedge it into the load. Off it goes. Also, don't run onto the road so far that you get hit by the truck."

"I got it, I got it," Donnie reassured me.

"Donnie, just watch me. See, I put the pitchfork out to the side, but I don't stand behind it." I showed him my successful technique of sticking the fork directly out from my shoulders to my right and moving left as I did so. I showed him exactly how far into the pile the fork head had to go.

"I got it, I got it," Donnie kept saying. He was ready. He kept saying that too.

Well, he didn't. So, what happened next was pretty predictable.

The truck came over the hill; I assumed the position of distracter. The truck rumbled up to us, and Donnie made his move. He ran out to the truck at the proper angle to set the fork. But when he raised the pitchfork, he kept it out in front of him with the prongs headed for the peas but with the horizontal wooden handle level with, and in front of, his neck. He plunged the fork into the passing vines – too deeply. He didn't scrape at them as he had been instructed.

The fork stuck. That meant that in a millisecond the fork and its handle were travelling west, and Donnie was travelling east. Donnie quit travelling in a hurry when the pitchfork, now extending at a right angle from the vines, knocked him off his feet. The handle hit him just below the throat and set him rolling backwards, head over heels. That actually was a stroke of luck. Had it connected with his face or throat he would be working in a circus side show.

As it was, it pretty much shook him up. He wanted to cry, but he also wanted to laugh. I was having trouble not laughing even though I could see scrapes on his knees, elbows, and legs. He was wearing a lot of berm.

Looking at Donnie, I started to realize just how dangerous this little trick was. He could have rolled under that truck's rear wheels. That fork handle could have injured him seriously. Then it occurred to both of us at the same moment that not only had Donnie lost his dad's pitchfork, that thing was still in a position to do damage.

The last we saw that fork it was sticking out from the pea vines at a nearly ninety degree angle. The truck was headed right through downtown Millheim. The road through the diamond was narrow; there was just enough room for cars to pass each other in opposite directions and for cars to be parked on each side of the street. Call it a four-car-wide street. But a narrow four-car-wide street. If that wide load met oncoming traffic and moved over just a bit, a parked car or anyone between the truck and a parked car was going to get clobbered by the handle of that pitchfork.

It dawned on us that we were going to be on the hook for that. That driver, when he crawled out of his truck at the scene of some devastation on the diamond, was going to wonder how in the hell that pitchfork got there. Then he was going to remember those two fool kids out on East Main Street. Then we were in for it.

"Oh, shit," Donnie said. "Oh, shit. Oh, man, oh, shit. Man!" He was walking in little circles around the driveway. "We lost the fork – that sucker will hit someone – my dad will hear about this – he'll ask where the pitchfork is. Oh, man, oh, shit."

"Now Donnie, calm down. We need a plan. Look, we can't just stay here. We'll be caught red-handed. Let's go see what happened."

So, we headed for the alley.

We crossed over to my side of the street and took the back alley downtown. We slipped across the bridge and walked down the alley by the race, looking up the connecting alleys for signs of trouble on the diamond. We finally turned up to the square at the bank and peered around the corner. We fully expected to see a crowd of people surrounding a huge pea truck with a pitchfork sticking out.

Nothing. Business as usual.

Relieved, Donnie and I went back to his yard and watched pea trucks go by for a while. We tossed a baseball. I don't know what Donnie ever said when his dad couldn't find his pitchfork.

Donnie Walker and I had become good friends, what with him living just up the street from me now. A year younger than I, Donnie was a good little baseball player, and he had lots of athletic equipment, left over I suppose, from the salad days of his brother Jake who was quite a bit older and already living away from home. That made Donnie a good playmate because he had the apparel that I never had, plus a pool table in his basement. I wasted quite a bit of my youth there.

Donnie was a sensitive child. He was blonde and fair-skinned. He was thin and gangly even though he wasn't tall for his age. He could be a little spastic.

But mostly, he was just sensitive – maybe squeamish. He had this little brown and white dog that was some mix of beagle and terrier by the look of it. It was a friendly dog named Theo, who had the habits of an alley cat. Once, Donnie and I were in his basement playing pool when we detected the distinct smell of dog excrement. We looked over to the side of the basement where Donnie's mother did her laundry and, sure enough, Theo had just pooped. That grossed Donnie out, but before he could react to that or even make a move to clean up the mess, Theo, typical of some poorly-bred dogs, turned and began to eat his own mess. That was it for Donnie. He promptly threw up on the gray basement floor and ran upstairs. I followed him, a bit upset because I was winning the pool game and wanted to finish it. I got him calmed down, and he agreed to go back down there.

We discovered that Donnie's damn dog had eaten the puke. Well, that set Donnie off again. He puked again. He ran upstairs again. Pool game over.

Still, Donnie was an adventurer. Looking back, I regret putting him into situations like the pea truck episode which almost killed him.

Chapter 10

It's Just Sinful

Many of life's lessons are learned outside the home, of course. Kids from "good homes," and that would be most of us in Millheim, had to learn about the sins of the world and how to commit them on the street. Our family lifestyles offered little in the ways of excessive materialism, violence, and swearing. Our parents were true-to-the-bone middle class citizens. Any one of them might have a weakness or indiscretion here or there, but mostly, we valley kids came from the kind of homes that made America great. Parents were of only limited assistance in regard to life's sins, things like swearing, drinking, smoking, and sexuality. Because most parents addressed such problems mainly by ignoring them, we had to acquire our knowledge, experiences, and attitudes about them from other sources. Thank heavens we had television.

We children of the '50s grew up with television. Television and the Baby Boomers were infants at the same time. We became toddlers, adolescents, and adults together. Our stories were simultaneously told. It was a story of simplicity and naivete, and it was told in black and white.

By the time I moved to Millheim, television had begun to lose the novelty that it had enjoyed in its infancy. I can remember the first television set in our end of West Beaver Avenue in State College. Garen Barrett's parents had purchased a Zenith, and all the neighbors would congregate at their house to watch snowy episodes of *I Remember Mama*, *The Big Top*, and *I Love Lucy*. In those days the phenomenon of pictures through the air was just about as impressive as the shows themselves. We marveled at the new technology, even as little kids, and we watched whatever was on – the news shows, the local station's early efforts at studio programming, and the westerns that were the staple of the limited-day schedule. I would show up at Garen's so early in the morning to watch television that the test pattern still hummed quietly before the day's programming was aired.

We purchased our first set when we moved to Millheim in that winter of 1952. Dad bought a nineteen-inch Philco from Stan Bierly. I believe he did it, in part, to mollify my misgivings and foul mood when we moved in the first place. Just like the basketball hoop.

Early on the broadcasters realized the tremendous advantage of television to reach and market mainstream American culture. Long before Marshall McLuhan opined that "the medium was the message," television executives were using the box to move more product than ever before possible. Mostly, producers and advertisers played it safe. The "sitcom" was born early on, and the earliest efforts centered on the everyday events of lovable, white, American families: *Father Knows Best, The Adventures of Ozzie and Harriet, Lassie, Rin Tin Tin*, and *Leave It To Beaver*. Even the cowboy shows, the cartoons, and the fifteen-minute news reports reflected more than changed current American values. The difference between right and wrong was easy to identify. The contrast between them was not filled with shades of gray. Bad guys lose, and justice can be swift.

Advertisers were exploiting the new medium and the new materialism that it offered. Swanson's offered its TV Brand Frozen Dinner so that moms everywhere would not miss the action on the tube. The foil-encased full meal included an entrée, potato, and vegetable all neatly compartmentalized so that dinner preparation was reduced to slipping the pasty components into the oven for a while. This relieved moms from the kitchen duties early enough to enjoy both the afternoon soap operas and the evening spectaculars. Similar to these was someone's version of a chicken pie: one meal, one dish. Heat and serve; now that was a new idea for homemakers. Never mind that both were terrible. I was subjected to both at the Toomis house when invited to stay for dinner. We did get to eat them on TV trays in the living room so that we did not miss those important offerings from the three networks that programmed all our options.

Marketers were showing us that there were some really neat things out there, and that we could have them for $3.99. All we had to do was call or mail in our order today. The '50s became a transitional era between the self-sacrificing days of the depression and World War II and the coming days of conspicuous consumption of the next three decades.

The kids of Spock had been discovered by television marketers as a lucrative consumer group, so they pandered to us. And many kids were buying a lot of stuff from television. Bari and I were not. Our parents just never sprang for all those modern toys and gizmos being touted on the airwaves. We were always told that we simply did not use our meager discretionary money on such things. Dad was not open to requests for funds to purchase the latest gadgetry or "tom-foolery." Our family just did not collect "stuff." We couldn't have had a garage sale if our lives depended on it. There just weren't extra or novelty things in the house.

In contrast, Bierly bought whatever was being hawked. He was the intended target for all those child-oriented marketing blitzes. He ordered any and all of proffered promotional items and gimmicks. He racked up an entire bedroom of this week's special valuables as shown on whatever kids' show we watched.

He bought the "original" Declaration of Independence for one dollar. It was printed on parchment paper, all the proof that Bierly needed that it was the only one – the original. And he had it. "For one dollar? Your mom paid more than that for that picture on the wall," I'd argue. Bierly would assure me that this was the genuine article. I could never talk him out of that. Bierly never let reality get in the way of a romantic notion. That, simply, was the Tom Sawyer in him.

He also bought one square foot of Alaska from *Sergeant Preston of The Yukon*. To prove he owned it, the purveyors sent him a deed and one square inch of soil from his exact plot of ground. Bierly made this purchase before Alaska achieved statehood. But worse, he bought it from a show that ostensibly took place in Canada – It was the *Canadian* Mounted Police, after all.

That didn't matter to Bierly. He started making plans to move up there and build a home, just as soon as he was old enough. He knew there was gold in "them thar hills," and he was convinced that some of it was on his property. I tried to tell him how small his property was, but he just never seemed to think that was an issue.

Bierly was a charter member of Captain Strombecker's Model Maker Club. This prestigious affiliation allowed him to place orders for kits of model airplanes, cars, and ships in bottles from the club at prices "way lower than those found in stores." Captain Strombecker advertised his wares on the tube during all those Saturday morning cartoon and cowboy shows that we watched so faithfully. Bierly had his own membership card, complete with his personalized club number. Every week or so he would jump out of his seat to record the order number of that month's offering, fill out his personalized order form, and have it ready to carry off to the post office on Monday. The window seat of the bedroom he shared with his brother featured a stack of opened but unassembled boxes of model kits of the Titanic, the Hindenburg, a B-17 bomber, and Model T Fords.

During those glorious early days of TV Bierly also bought toothbrushes, science kits, piggy banks, Swiss Army knives, and assorted gadgets. I played with them all. But I could never match the enthusiasm that he had for everything he acquired. He believed in the authenticity, the importance, the quality of everything he collected. I saw them as toys; he saw them as artifacts, jewels, and prized possessions. He loved his stuff – for brief times. Then he would move on, and, like the first aid kit, a thing would disappear from sight and mind.

In our early Millheim years Bari and I watched hours of television at Bierly's house with Curt and him. On Saturday mornings the television offered great shows for kids. Sealtest Ice Cream sponsored the *Big Top*, a weekly circus. There were cowboy shows such as *Roy Rogers, Gene Autry, The Lone Ranger,* and *The Cisco Kid.* There was a science show called *Mr. Wizard* and cartoons like *Mighty Mouse*. While Bari and I were watching the shows, I believe Bierly was watching the advertisements, looking for something to own. This was especially true of all the new interactive stuff that so was prevalent in those days.

An early example was the first attempt at "color" TV. Even from the earliest days of television viewers wanted color. We knew that color television was coming. CBS actually broadcast its first color program in 1951, but no one had color sets to receive it. They did not hit the market until very late in the decade.

Some entrepreneur offered a solution to this desire for "color." It ended up in many American homes. The item was a thin piece of colored acetate – a plastic film that would adhere by static electricity directly onto the television screen. One just pressed this film against the screen and smoothed it out. It stuck like Saran Wrap – it probably was Saran Wrap, now that I think about it, only slightly thicker. It had three horizontal bars of color: blue, red, and yellow. Now the folks on the screen could be viewed "in color." They would have blue faces, yellow ties and red hands – unless they moved, then they could have any combination of the above. Yep, this stuff sold.

And Bierly had that. He told his parents that he and Curt needed that, and they got it. This was a short-lived innovation, however.

A better example of interactive television was one of our favorite shows, *Winky Dink*. The producers of *Winky Dink* attempted to make us youthful viewers part of the action via a little kit they just happened to sell for the purpose. Any kid who could cajole his/her parents into accepting how much this package maximized viewing pleasure ordered one. Bari and I did not even try to accomplish this feat. But, of course Bierly could do that.

The kit consisted of another acetate sheet, four crayons — red, brown, green, and yellow – and a special cleaning eraser-shaped do-dad. Kids fortunate enough to have the kit could actually help our hero, Winky Dink, extricate himself from the precarious situations into which he fell every week. For example, Winky Dink might be chased by the bad guys to the edge of a canyon. The announcer would say, "Quick, whoever has the brown crayon, run up to the screen and draw Winky Dink a bridge to the other side of the canyon." At that point, kids all across America would rush to the screen and draw a bridge right on that clear, plastic film. Later on that bridge would need to be erased so that we could add another means of escape for the hapless Winky Dink. Before the show ended, all the various crayon holders were called into action.

Well, Bierly owned that system. So Bari and I would go to his house every Saturday morning to help Bierly and Curt save Winky Dink. We had great fun with this. Bari and Curt, being older than Bierly and I, were very serious about their responsibilities. If Bari had the red crayon, she never failed to respond to her opportunity to serve our hero. Same with Curt. But Bierly and I had to be forced. Early on we decided it would add much more drama to the plot if we let the little guy hanging on that canyon ledge, or floating in the ocean, or dangling from a vine. We wanted to see what would happen if the person with the green crayon sat on it instead of responding. That would drive Curt and Bari wild. Every Saturday there would be a big discussion about who was getting which crayon. Our siblings were convinced that this crayon or that would be more important in the show, and they wanted to ensure that neither Bierly nor I had responsibility for using or not using it.

***

Materialism was one thing. But television was also providing lessons about violence, smoking, and drinking.

I think that my tendency to view death and violence in black and white is a by-product of television. That is where and how it was portrayed. Before my encounters with the deceased Mr. Homark and others in town and my own several brushes with death, I saw death and violence vicariously, on the small screen. Perhaps that explained why my mind failed to register tints and hues in situations involving misery, mayhem, danger, and death.

Early television featured a plethora of violence. In comparison to today's unblinking, technical standards and the vivid up close and gruesome special effects, the gore of these early days was very tame. Some of it was almost laughable. Still, there it was, and it was the state of the art at the time.

Westerns were the rage in the era. Shows such *as Cheyenne, Rawhide, Wanted Dead* or *Alive* – even *Roy Rogers, The Cisco Kid*, and *Hopalong*

Cassidy – featured fisticuffs and at least one gunfight in every episode. And several of these were kid shows, aired Saturday mornings to maximize our patronage. There were guns everywhere, many of them six-shooters which, somehow, could deliver fifteen shots during a four-minute gunfight. Our heroes knew how to bring down a foe with just a single shot, often from horseback at the speed of Man Of War. Even we kids ridiculed this obvious breech of verisimilitude. The ham-handed fistfights, the lack of blood resulting from some intense beatings, and the neatness of the hero's wardrobe following the skirmish were simply unbelievable. Roy Rogers could get off dozens of shots without ever having to reload. He could leap off Trigger at thirty miles an hour and tackle another rider, beat him senseless, and never lose his hat or free his shirt-tail. Violence was a neat, almost clean thing on television.

They were killing a lot of people on the tube in those days. The act was swift and sure. One bullet would do it. The hero seldom worked up a sweat. It was the beginning of our acceptance of death as a spectator sport.

But all the television death we were offered was somehow different than what we were beginning to witness in our town. Television murder was committed for the high principles being furthered by our heroes. On television, death was choreographed and stylized. TV deaths were simply the wages of sin, payments to no-goods, or foes of *The Lawman*. Main characters weren't dying on television. Sure, nameless Indians and cavalrymen died in droves. Enemies of the United States died. But our heroes did not.

By contrast, death in Millheim was messy. It involved people we knew, and had the sense of tragedy that was missing from television. It was personal. The only thing the two portrayals shared was the coloring.

We held a similar naiveté about tobacco and alcohol. It seemed everyone, both on television and in real life, smoked. Heck, Lucille Ball smoked on *I Love Lucy,* and guys like James Cagney smoked in all the movies. Our heroes smoked; our parents smoked – Bierly's mom and my dad certainly did. Even the urbane Edward R. Murrow smoked on air, as he analyzed world events. Tobacco companies advertised freely in all media. While there was a general and wide-known knowledge of the hazards, tobacco was an accepted part of adulthood in America.

For children, smoking was a forbidden pleasure that had to be taken on the sly. Certainly our parents' concerns were health-related, but there also was a sense at the time that smoking was an adult vice, reserved for older people. Actually, I believe folks were just as concerned about young kids with matches as they were about the cigarettes we would be lighting. Of course we were told that smoking would stunt our growth, make us cough, and take away "our wind" for sports. Of course our parents did not want us to acquire this unhealthy, addictive, and dirty habit.

Of course we smoked a lot. We weren't worried about health. We planned on living a long time. People in Millheim were not dying of cancer. They were having heart attacks, drowning, and committing suicide. How bad could smoking really be? Besides, our advice was coming from those who were smoking anyway. Besides, it was cool.

Getting cigarettes was not difficult. We simply went to Johnny DeSoto's Atlantic station and waited for him to go out to gas up a car. Then we slipped thirty cents into the cigarette vending machine and got our Lucky Strikes or Camels. At one time cigarettes sold this way for twenty-seven cents. We would put a quarter and a nickel into the slot and receive our treasure with three shiny pennies wrapped inside the outer layer of cellophane covering the pack.

We would take our trove and head to the creek, the old mill, or the back alleys where we would puff away at three or four "cancer sticks," as we called them. Then we hid the pack in a gaping crack in the stone wall of the old mill for the next time. Often someone else would have already stashed some of the contraband in there. We could always "borrow" one or two cigarettes if we were lacking the financial resources to purchase our own.

Bigger kids often provided our smokes. One day at the pool Harry Winger gave Bierly and me each a Kent, the cigarette with the Micronite Filter. We were probably about ten years old at the time. We decided to save them for later, so we stuck them behind our ears as was the fashion for tough-looking kids in those days and headed for the bridge. We planned to climb under the bridge by the water's edge and enjoy our good fortune. We were right at the bridge with these "weeds" sticking out from our behind our ears when we encountered Mrs. Stover, Albert's wife, heading up to the hardware. She noticed those cigarettes and gave us what for. We got a big lecture about the perils of smoking. Then she threatened to call our parents. With great fanfare, we pitched the smokes into Elk Creek, making sure she had witnessed our contriteness, and woefully asked her to rethink her earlier position about our parents. She relented.

Alcohol was a somewhat different story. The same general cultural guidelines applied. Beer – "Mabel, oh Mabel, Black Label," — Seagram's, and Mogen David were advertised on television and present in many homes. But fooling around with alcohol was one of the deadly sins that a kid could commit. It was much more frowned upon than smoking, and punishment was decidedly more drastic. Pre-teens just didn't do it. Alcohol was harder to come by than smokes, and the whole aura of its results served as some deterrent.

"Strong drink" was not really a part of our early youth. This changed of course when we reached our teenage years, but as adolescents, we had very limited experience with the perils of alcohol.

We certainly tried it. Curt once pried the cap off a bottle of his dad's Ballantine from a case in the basement. The three of us tasted that and wondered what the thrill was. We found out. Bierly's parents returned home and smelled stale beer in their tiny kitchen. That cost us a few days confined to our bedrooms reading various adventures of The Hardy Boys.

Swearing was something we couldn't learn from television. Roy Rogers, "The Beave," and Chuck Conners didn't swear in those days. We had to get that from our home, our friends, or a trained professional.

We did not swear in my house. My mother simply never swore. My father swore rarely. He did it so seldom that he was no good at it; he was no role model at all for the craft. Even during one of his angry tirades, any oath he might insert lacked any tone of naturalness or conviction. He just could not use swear words effectively. The standard in our family was that swearing was just plain offensive and unnecessary.

Lots of my friends came from families in which swearing was a more accepted practice. These kids tended to be good at it. It is an acquired skill, like a taste for martinis. Still, the norm of the town was that kids should not swear, and it was not looked upon favorably. If one swore in front of almost any adult in town, he/she could expect to be called on it.

The one exception to this norm was at The Right Deal Garage. Not only was swearing accepted there, it was graded. Vic Stoler, his two grown sons, Johnny and Delbert, and all the workers there were the best swearers in the world. If a kid wanted to learn how to use profanity, The Right Deal Garage housed the instructors.

Vic's garage was just up the street from my new home, directly across the street from Dot and Jake's soda shop. Vic and his sons sold and repaired farm equipment – specifically, red farm equipment.

In those days, manufacturers of farm equipment – tractors, combines, balers, harvesters – painted all their machinery in one color. To see the color was to know the brand. John Deere equipment was always green, Case always golden yellow, Alas-Chambers orange, and so on. Farmall/International Harvester machines were fire engine red. Vic Stoler worked with red stuff – only and exclusively. Don't call Vic if a Minneapolis-Moline tractor died; that was a job for someone else. He'd tell the farmer to take it back to where he bought it. Vic dealt in red only.

Vic was one of the town's most colorful and eccentric citizens. He was old from the time I first saw him, at least sixty. He worked at that business well into his eighties. He was a tall, rangy, thin man with long arms and huge hands. He sported a stark gray goatee beard that matched his wispy hair. Minus the horns, of course, he appeared to me about like what the devil would look like in street clothes.

Vic always wore a pin-striped railroader's cap with an IH insignia. He wore long john underwear – the one-piece, trapdoor model — until the Fourth of July. He'd put it back on for Labor Day. On the warmest days in June Vic strode about in his long-sleeved shirt rolled up to the elbows with his long johns sticking out beneath them.

He carried a flask in his hip pocket from which he would nip constantly. He'd flit about the big repair shop in long strides and a brisk gait, castigating everyone in the place, employee or customers.

But mostly, Vic swore. At the top of his lungs.

The irascible, ill-tempered old guy was always arguing with someone. He'd holler at his two sons about something they did or should have done. He'd scream directions to his wife who served as the cashier, working in a little glass enclosure in the show room. He'd upbraid a customer for bringing him a perfectly fine piece of equipment that had no business needing repair. "Why don't you just take care of the #%^&*# thing!" he'd roar.

And he did it all with the most amazing string of swear words ever produced. His sons were great swearers. But no one could match the endless oaths that emanated from Vic Stoler. He was the supreme master. He could put profanity together in sequences that did not seem to fit. He could get nine oaths into a ten-word sentence. Only a master can use the same vulgarity as a noun, verb, and adjective in the same utterance. Vic could also make it an adverb. He was the best.

Bierly and I would go up there just to learn how it was done. Our parents didn't want us hanging out up there, but the goings-on were just too good to miss. We'd go in and buy a Coke from the machine (red machine, of course) and watch the show of the day. More than once the recipient of Vic's wrath would retaliate in kind, and then the war would begin. There would be a shouting match of epic proportion. Once, an employee got so mad that he just quit and walked out of the place, greasy hands and all.

Actually, that happened en masse about every hunting season. Every fall Vic would declare that the shop would be open the first day of deer season. Every fall his employees would tell him that they were going hunting. Vic would tell them, punctuating his thoughts with profanity, that he would fire anybody who didn't show up for work that day. Nobody would report to work. He would fire them all. The shop would then be closed for about three days because there was no one else in Millheim to fix tractors for Vic. Finally, he would realize how much business he was losing and hire them all back. It was an annual ritual.

Vic Stoler stories were legion. Once he produced an expensive part – from his advertised "million parts inventory" – for a customer who had been told by another employee that the store did not have one in stock. Grateful that the part was indeed available, the customer asked how much the item would cost. Vic, mad that his staff had overlooked the part in the first place, said, "How can I #%&*@ charge you for a %^&$*+ part I don't have? Harold ^%$&* said we didn't have it, so I can't %$##$$ charge you for it. By God, you can just %%$^&& take this %$$%$^& part I didn't $%$^&^* have for #@#$%^ free." And he turned, walked away, and dumped a five-minute profanity-laced harangue on poor Harold.

Once, an out-of-towner, doing some work near town for the state highway department, visited The Right Deal to replace a broken part. Luckily he was using a red backhoe for his task. He showed Vic the broken part and asked if Vic had a replacement. Vic went into his million-part inventory and returned with the new article in hand. "Yep," he said, "I have one – my last one."

"Great! How much will that be?"

"Fifteen dollars, but I can't sell it to you."

"Why not?"

"Because," Vic explained, "this is my last $%$^&^* one of these. If I sell it to you, I won't $#%^&^ have one if someone comes in and needs one."

"What? I need one! I'm that guy. You have to sell it to me!" exclaimed the incredulous backhoe operator.

"No I don't. I $#@%^&* don't know you. I'm keeping this $%$^&* part in case one of my regular customers needs it."

That ended that. The backhoe operator had to wait around town until someone from Harrisburg could find the part ninety miles away and drive it up to him.

Anyway, people like Vic Stoler helped us kids to learn the finer points of swearing. We swore often, but not much around adults. I did try it a few times up at The Right Deal just to see if I could run with the big dogs. I was a failure. There is no use competing with a legend. He just scoffs at you.

For any of that, Vic Stoler was a boon to Millheim. For all that swearing, for all that buffoonery, Vic had a heart of gold. In addition to that flask he carried, he also had a pocketful of wrapped candy, mints, chocolates, or taffy that he handed out freely to any kid he encountered on the street. He'd give us a ride anywhere we needed to go. Unbeknown to most folks, Vic gave money to several families in the community who were facing hard times. At Christmas time he would assure that folks down on their luck would have a turkey or access to a turkey dinner. He carried bills for hard-strapped farmers for years; his garage contributed to every local cause that was afoot. He simply was an icon in our valley, and I always liked him.

Street drugs were not an issue in our childhood. There was no drug abuse in Millheim. Illicit drugs just had not hit the scene. Our parents had no experience with them except what they heard from the big city. My mother told me never to accept drugs or needles from anyone except Doc Henninger. That was an easy rule to follow because I never faced such an opportunity. She told me horror stories that she had read. They were so extreme and represented such stupidity to me that I never considered that the experience would be any fun at all. I knew people who smoked and drank. They didn't seem so bad – hell, they were our friends, family, and neighbors. But drugs? That culture was far removed from us. I never knew one kid in Millheim who would have needlessly subjected himself or herself to the pain of a needle not wielded by Doc Henninger.

Chapter 11

Endless Days of Summer

Sheldon Bressler and Billy Solt were both known to be a few bricks shy of a load in the common sense department. These two kids, who lived "up Texas," were three and two years older than I, respectively. They required more oversight from townsfolk than Bierly and Frye. As all the kids in Millheim, they weren't really bent on devilment or troublemaking. Their antics, however, often caused bewilderment about town. How could two otherwise normal kids get themselves in such fixes?

Usually, I think, because they were oblivious to the unintended consequences of the comical situations into which they hurled themselves. As Bierly and I were, these two were part of any round up of "usual suspects" whenever some mischief occurred around town. I know that their names kept popping up during the Penn Street flooding affair. An incident at the Millheim swimming pool is illustrative of their spur of the moment creativity.

One summer afternoon they became enamored with a two-foot length of wood that they decided to use in a daring diving maneuver. They were going to perform a double dive that would involve a risky display of timing acumen.

The lifeguard wisely cleared the pool for this wizardry. We all sat on the asphalt apron and watched Gaston and Alphonse prepare. They climbed the metal ladder and edged to the end of the ten-foot high springboard. Sheldon placed the wooden board on the springboard, extending about half of it over the water. Billy stepped on the back half to hold it in place while Sheldon gingerly made his way past Billy onto the extension. There he sat down, balanced by Billy's weight on the back of the slat.

So far, so good. It was a coordinated trick of maneuvering just to get them in this position. But, sitting there, we all knew this was all going to hell in a hand-basket any second.

Now the idea was – and we could hear them plotting it out and arguing over the procedures – that both would leave the springboard at precisely the same moment. Billy would dive out and over Sheldon. Sheldon would simultaneously tuck his body into a neat little pike position and fall into a straight dive directly below where he was perched. None of this required the board extension, of course. It was just there to add difficulty to the trick.

Well, it didn't work. Actually, it didn't work at all. Just watching them get ready for this was funny enough. But what happened next would have been a laugh riot had there not been blood involved.

The appointed moment for the execution of this stunt came and went several times as the performers kept stopping the countdown for one reason or another. Suddenly, Billy shouted "Now!" and dove from the board. But it wasn't a clean dive. His objective was to clear Sheldon's head. He didn't. He clipped his partner with his knee, bending his own dive sideways toward the water instead of head first. He hit the surface on his side with his arms still extended instead of covering his head. We could call it a side-flop. It knocked the wind out of him, and he rolled onto his back to gasp for breath. Cary Myers swam out to pull him to the nearby ladder.

Sheldon did not make out so well. He had already taken a blow to the head from Billy's knee. When Billy catapulted over Sheldon, without giving his partner an adequate and precisely-timed warning, the board naturally tipped with Sheldon still just sitting there. Now Sheldon was behind the timing curve required by the endeavor. He was supposed to have tucked forward to form a head-first dive. Now he couldn't. Beginning to fall, he rockered back to gain some momentum to get into his tuck. That brought his head to the edge of the diving board.

Hard. We heard his skull hit the board. We knew there would be blood. Sheldon passed beneath the springboard and was falling feet first toward the water. On the way down, he met up with that two-foot piece of wood. It hit him lengthwise, butt-end first, on the bridge of his nose and worked its way down from there. It scraped Sheldon's nose raw and then caught his lips and chin. When boy and board hit the water, the wooden piece somehow flattened out and smacked him right on the head as he entered the water. We counted at least four hits from that length of wood.

When Sheldon emerged from that plunge, he was already swearing at Billy. Sheldon was an accomplished source of profanity. He was so angry he couldn't even get himself organized to swim to the side of the pool. Cary Myers, already in the water to help Billy, had to pull Sheldon out also. By the time Cary was pushing Sheldon up out of the water, Billy was already trying to get enough breath to explain what had happened up there. The only adult there, Tomkins, prevented fisticuffs between these two closest of cronies.

We got out the first aid kit and ministered to the barking on Sheldon's face and the nasty cut on the top of his head that was bleeding the way head wounds do. We had that stopped in ten minutes. Sheldon sat on the asphalt the rest of the day.

***

Summers in Millheim were all about the town swimming pool and little league baseball. Summers in Millheim were not of wild and exciting times. They were of meandering days that lasted forever. They were of hot summer days that mellowed into cool evenings, when our pursuits followed the route of the sun. We spent the high and hot sun hours of the day at the pool and the increasing twilight on the baseball diamond. Between the two we ambled home, eating blackberries along the creek, to dinner and the prospect of evening adventures.

Soldiers and Sailors Park was a large square of mostly open space located up the paved alley that formed the right field border of the baseball field. If one were going to the park by that route, he walked across a sturdy wooden bridge that crossed Elk Creek. Car and driver used a dirt road that cut directly left off Main Street at the bridge and headed up around the creek to come in on the park's back side. Had Albert Stover's Tennessee Walker crossed the road instead of turning left on it to head downtown, he could have run harmlessly up to the park. But no, he couldn't be that cooperative.

Anyway, Soldiers and Sailors Park was developed and dedicated after World War II, actually in 1949. Nestled into a small draw between the hills behind it and Elk Creek in front of it, the park was dotted with several buildings that were used for community events, most notably the annual Millheim carnival. But the major feature of the park was the swimming pool.

Calling it a swimming pool may invoke a picture of a neatly-tiled tank with a concrete apron and shiny stainless steel diving boards. One may think of crystal clear water lined by multi-colored floats that formed perfect swimming lanes. Perhaps near the main body of water there would be a child's pool or a diving area, perhaps even a spa. There would naturally be modern dressing rooms, complete with hot showers, and a full-service refreshment stand.

Such images would not capture the Millheim swimming pool. In fact, to call it a pool at all may be to overly flatter it. The word "pool" indicates that water can be held there, against its will, for long periods of time. Our pool was more of a water detention system. It held water up for a while, but released it quickly back to the creek from which it had been pumped.

Our pool was one of those asphalt, slanted-sided holes in the ground. Many of these were built around the country in the 1950s. I assume that they are all closed now. I do not think that this represented one of the better uses of asphalt.

At the pool's shallow, ankle-deep end was an old, dilapidated sliding board that someone installed to maim small children. No mother I ever saw subjected her tyke to a slide down the hot, dry, scarred chrome shoot with splintery, paint-peeling wooden rails only to land in three inches of cold water underneath which was slippery, algae-coated asphalt.

From that depth the bottom gradually tapered downward for twenty-five yards to create a deep end of nine feet. That would be nine feet in the very center of the pit. Along the edges of the pool the water varied in depth as it came up those slanted sides. The sides of the pool dropped off quickly to deeper water. However, it was a fool's mission to dive straight down into the water from the three-foot asphalt apron that surrounded the pool. We veterans knew to make long, shallow dives into the water. Many a newcomer, usually rookies from surrounding towns, dove too deep and too close to the edge. The injuries ranged from scraped palms to brush-burned cheeks, to ravaged kneecaps, depending on the size of the error in judgement.

Swimmers could not see the sloping bottom of the pool from a depth of one foot on down to the diving boards. It was the same with the sloping sides. The water was deep, deep green/black. The pool surface was black. The chlorine that was supposed to clear and purify the water was as transitory as the creek water itself. It exited the area before it could have any real effect on the water or serving its primary purpose of neutralizing unwanted contaminants such as the algae on the bottom.

The pool was just creek water pumped over from Elk Creek. Cold water. The Millheim pool never registered a water temperature above sixty-seven degrees. Elk Creek was a fast-flowing stream of water fifteen minutes from the draws and valleys of Brush Mountain. A single, underground, lead pipe sucked up some of the torrent and fed it to the pool, pushing it through myriad little holes that poked through the asphalt in the shallow end. An automatic chlorinator was attached to the pipe so that the chemical was mixed in proper ratio to the water as it began its forty-yard journey across the park to the pool.

That never worked very long or very well.

Every year the town elders responsible for the park would try to improve the chlorinator's function. Sometimes it would work for a while; usually it did not. It seemed that they could always get water into the pool all right, but they just could not improve it along the way.

So the lifeguards, schoolteachers in the valley and great friends to all us kids, had to take water samples constantly to see if enough chlorine was present. There never was enough. They would haul out huge, five or ten-gallon jugs of chlorine and pour it into the pool. Meanwhile, we all just kept swimming, sometimes in water that just reeked of chlorine. Sometimes it burned our eyes. No matter. It just never occurred to anyone to get us out of there until the chemical had dissipated a bit.

The guards could have poured chlorine in that hole all day. The pool was not going to retain either the water or the chlorine for very long. It leaked like a sieve. The asphalt was not water tight. Even if it were, the ravages of the seasons caused such upheaval and depression of the soil underneath the asphalt that gaping cracks and holes formed every spring. Try as they might to fill these, the town fathers were fighting a losing battle. The detained water simply leeched back into the ground and found its way back to Elk Creek about a hundred yards downstream from where it was pumped in the first place.

This problem was to cause state government officials to close the pool when I was a seventh grader. For years little officious men wearing white shirts, clip-on ties, and straw hats lugged large, black instrument cases into the pool. They collected water samples in little vials from various corners of the pool. Then they held the finger-sized tubes up to the sun like little sacrifices, peered at them intently, and then shook their heads in obvious scorn. Through pursed lips, they would tell Tomkins or Faluth that more chlorine was needed in that pool or they would close it down. Tomkins told them about the leaks, the quirky pump system, and that this was creek water to begin with. That had no impact on the inspectors. They were from the government, and they were here to help us. Their job was to see that no kid was stricken with some exotic, foul disease from untreated creek water.

They didn't know it, but that ship had already sailed. Virtually every kid in town had at least one seasonal bout with "swimmer's ear." This affliction is one of the most painful human inconveniences available. It is an ear infection, caused by some bacteria. It seldom has visual manifestations; the ear does not beal, bleed, or change color.

But it hurts like hell. A kid with swimmer's ear can't abide being touched anywhere near the ear. The ear itself is extremely sensitive even though the infection is deep in the ear canal. It was an act of savagery to taunt someone with the problem, and a capital offense to wittingly touch the ear of the afflicted.

The problem usually lasted about three days to a week. The best treatment was to stay out of the water, put a few drops of alcohol in the ear twice a day, and live with it.

Swimmer's ear or not, virtually every kid in Millheim spent afternoons at the swimming pool in Soldiers and Sailors Park. Big kids and small kids all laughed and played together there. There was no fighting, no bullying, no nasty tricks. Just water tag, and diving contests in which we competed to find sunken coins, stones, or bolts from the black depths of the pool.

Most of us were in the water so much that our bathing suits never dried. We would swim until our lips turned blue. Then we would sit and shiver on that macadam apron and work on our tans. Every year Diana Albright would fashion her initials from white adhesive tape and place them on her back, between the straps of her suit. After a few weeks in the sun, she would have someone strip off the dirty tape and parade around with the only visible spots of non-tanned skin at the pool.

There weren't many rules at the Millheim pool. If there had been, Sheldon and Billy would never had been allowed to try their gravity-defying feat. We were permitted to run around the apron. Two or more people were allowed on the diving boards at once, even the ten foot one. We could have "chicken fights." We could throw balls and use water toys, preservers, inner tubes, and wooden or inflatable floats. These floats were all for games because no kid in Millheim needed assistance to swim. We were water rats.

The guards, being teachers in the schools, knew and liked all of us. They really did not need to discipline us very often. They unlocked the gate, met the obligatory insurance requirements, tended the pump, and poured in the chlorine. They provided some adult supervision so things did not get out of hand. They often participated in our antics.

The guards never worried about lawsuits or parent complaints. Neither the Bresslers nor the Solts ever came to the pool or the town council to complain about the lifeguards. These men were pillars of the community. They watched out for everyone's children. It just didn't seem strange that they would condone great freedom at the pool.

Few adults, other than the guards, came to the pool. It was our place. Now and then the svelte June DeSoto would come down with her very young children. She would stay up at the shallow end, playing with her babies or sunbathing in the small sandlot. We didn't mind her presence; she was a friendly lady, and she looked great in a swimsuit.

Bud Roddle used to come by now and then. Bud was a huge guy, at least two hundred and forty pounds of bald head and beer belly. Always smoking and always laughing, this traveling salesman would be eagerly greeted. He was a cannonball expert. He would climb the ladder up the springboard and wait for all the kids to get into the water right below him. Then he would run and jump off that board, aiming to get as close to one of us as he could. By close I mean that he could come within inches of a kid who never moved, trusting Bud to land just where he wanted. He would wrap his arms around his folded legs just before he hit the water, making a perfect cannonball.

The tidal wave he could produce was enormous. It engulfed those in the water. He would do that over and over. On a really good one he could actually make water come up to or over the banked sides of the pool. We loved that. Probably another bad idea.

Parents all over town loved that pool. They knew where the kids were, and they were rid of us.

During the last year or so of the pool's operation Bari and I opened the tiny but unused concession stand that connected the two primitive dressing rooms in the concrete building at the pool's entrance. Jim Tomkins had suggested this to us and had talked with Dad about how and where we could get our supplies. We sold candy and soda – pop – in vast quantities. We worked in shifts. Bari worked for about an hour, I worked for about an hour, and then anyone who wanted to worked for about an hour or two. We never had any problem with that. Nobody was going to steal nickels and dimes from us. It would have been bad form.

Most town kids were at the pool every day. Bierly was there perhaps two days a week. So I was spending lots of time with other kids — Ivan Rendell, Ed Zommoris, Mike Geyers, Dean Fendorf, Davey White, and Cary Myers. After forming my new friendship with Larry Rossman and Spit Ungar, they began to come more often. They would ride their bikes in from Aaronsburg as often as Larry could get away from the farm. This was true also for a few kids from both Rebersburg and Spring Mills. I got to know the three Corman brothers and the Gentzel boys at the pool. When Barry Gates moved to town and knew no one, he shyly showed up one day at the fence. We sent him home for his suit. He was a member of the group by the end of the day.

To find us on a summer afternoon, one needed only to go to the Millheim pool. Any afternoon.

***

Evenings were about baseball – Little League Baseball.

I played three years of little league baseball. For Millheim. Just Millheim. Not the Millheim Tigers, or Yankees, or Braves, or Red Sox. Just Millheim. In our league we didn't have nicknames for the teams. We were just known as Millheim, Centre Hall, Rebersburg, Spring Mills, Pleasant Gap, and Boalsburg. In fact, that was the entire league, right there.

There was no reason to have team nicknames until Ronald Toomis, Mike's older brother by a good ten years, created the second team in Millheim.

When a man has one watch, he always knows what time it is. When he has two watches, he never knows what time it is. Well, when Millheim had one team, we all knew who we were. We were Millheim's little league team. We wore heavy, itchy, hot, commercial-grade wool and flannel uniforms, gray with red piping. We knew they were at least ten years old because some of the businesses that sponsored the team by purchasing a uniform had gone out of business or changed names. Each uniform was unique because the name of the sponsor was sewn right on the back, running from shoulder to shoulder – where they put the player's name today. My uniform was from R.E. Breon's and Sons. Only the B was long gone, leaving only its unweathered shadow. So, I was really playing for R.E. reon.

Anyway, Millheim only had the one team until I grew too old and moved up to the newly-formed Centre County Junior League. Then Ronald started that second team. He had looked around town and noticed that there were lots of boys (boys only in those days) who wanted to play baseball but couldn't. There were just so many spots on the team, so only the best players were selected. With Millheim, Coburn, and Aaronsburg growing, there were simply more kids who wanted to play baseball, "best" or not.

So, Ronald Toomis started a second team comprised of all those castoffs. It wasn't easy. He had to face the league officials from all the towns and plead his case for changing the way things had always been done. Heretofore, it was one town, one team. This troublemaker wanted to change all that.

It wasn't even easy in Millheim. Now families in town were divided, for the first time. Some of their kids were going to play on one team and some on the other. Best friends might be parted. How good could this new team be anyway? The players couldn't make the "first team."

Ronald's team was to be awful for several years. Somehow, the original team maintained the authority to select the best kids first. That left Ronald's team with mostly young players or those who had come to baseball late in their young lives.

The point is that Millheim now had two little league teams. Now nicknames became necessary. Now, Millheimers, the fans, the merchants, the parents, had to choose the team they would support. The original team handed down those old gray and red uniforms to the upstarts and bought new ones, switching their colors to black and white. They became known as the Yankees. Ronald's laughable little rogues put on those moth-eaten uniforms and called themselves the Cardinals. It took about three seasons, but I umpired the game in which the Cardinals beat the Yankees for the first time.

Anyway, I played for Millheim. Boyd Blazer, owner/operator of Blazer's Restaurant and Jake's dad, was the manager. Early on I was a right fielder. I now owned that black leather, Clem Labine Signature Edition baseball glove. I didn't need it much in right field. But later, when it became apparent that we needed Spit Unger pitching instead of catching, I moved behind the plate.

That was no mean feat. It took some adaptability. Not to the position, but to which arm I was going to use to throw the ball.

I was born a left-hander, just like my dad. But my bout with polio severely weakened my upper left side, and I learned during my resultant therapy to do many things from the right side. That included handwriting in first and second grades and throwing a baseball. Actually, for a while, I could throw a baseball with either hand – equally ineffectively. A natural left-hander, I could throw harder and more accurately from the port side. As I got older, I played left-handed, although I always batted from the right side, the side I was using when I was first learning the game.

But for Spit to pitch, someone else had to don "the tools of ignorance." Boyd looked at me. I was eleven then, one of the older kids on the team, stocky of build, and a team leader. It was time to move me in from right field.

Of course there was only one catcher's mitt in all of Millheim. Of course it was a right-handed mitt – we would have had to order a special left-handed model. I guess one could do that today. But, when I played, the possibility, and the funds necessary to acquire one, was not even discussed. So, I switched over to the right side, again.

I did okay. I hit well enough to make the all-star team. My catching and pitcher management skills were good. My throwing skills were suspect. Even in little league, hurling the ball to second base to gun down an attempted base thief was a challenge. That distance was the limit of my range. Once other teams learned that, they stole on me often.

When I graduated to the junior league, I had to contend with what we called big league bases and diamond measurements. The throw from home plate to second base was just too much for my weak right arm. My catching days were doomed. I switched back to my left hand and played a little bit of first base. But I was short and stocky, not a big target. Pretty soon I was back in right field from whence I had come.

But I always identified with catchers. Of course we followed the big leagues. Millheim folk, located as centrally in the state as we were, generally had allegiance to the Phillies or the Pirates. I was a Pirate fan. So, I idolized Smokey Burgess and Hal Smith, two Pittsburgh catchers. I remember when Roy Campanella had his paralyzing car crash and was lost to the Brooklyn Dodgers. I respected Yogi Berra even though I hated those damn Yankees.

We had a good team. Jake Blazer at third base, Cary Myers at second, Benny Zerby at first, Spit Ungar, Kermit Riley, and Dale Brewer rotating on the mound and filling in around the infield – these were all good ballplayers. Our problem was that Centre Hall, with Joe Rimmey, Whitey Searfoss, and that crowd, was really good. In fact, Whitey Searfoss was so good that we knew he was going to get a shot at the big leagues. And he did just that with the New York Yankees, after we all graduated from high school. Now there was a catcher. A rifle arm and a terrific bat. Centre Hall usually won the league championship. We would come in second or third, depending how good Rebersburg was that year.

Bierly did not enjoy baseball nearly as much as I. While he would join a pick-up game from time to time, he never signed up for little league. He was a talented athlete and was good at baseball. He just did not like it enough to play as often as the rest of us. He seldom came to our games.

Three things of note remain from my little league experience. The first is how much a guy will do to impress a woman.

Louise Lords kept the official score book for Millheim. Mrs. Lords loved baseball. She had two boys of her own, both too young to play during my stint. But she was at every game. She would keep the lineup, score the game, tally our batting averages and errors, and generally run the bench during a game. She cheered for us heartily and shamelessly.

She was beautiful. Probably in her late twenties, Mrs. Lords was petite and lithesome. She was thin without being bony; she was proportioned like a high school track star. She usually dressed in summer shorts and tube tops, something most young Millheim mothers were not wearing in those days. She was wonderful, kind, and sensual in an understated way. I loved her.

In the middle of my last season as a twelve-year-old, she thought I should be hitting better. Hell, we all did. I was in a slump. We were playing twice a week in those days, and for about three weeks, I had come up with just one hit. Boyd Blazer kept dropping me down the batting order until I was batting eighth, just in front of – who else – our right fielder.

Then Boyd had to miss a game for one reason or another. He asked Mrs. Lords to run the team. Wearing that shameless, form-fitting tube top above her red shorts, she called me to her before the game. Her midriff was bare, and her straw-colored hair was pulled back into a ponytail, the way she wore it only when baseball was involved. Her skin, as usual, was clear, flawless, and slightly suntanned. She smelled good, like vanilla or something.

She told me that she was going to try an experiment. She thought that I might hit better if I were moved up in the lineup instead of down any further – as if there were any place for me to go in that direction. How about leadoff she wanted to know.

I agreed. I had no expectation that it would help, but if that was what she wanted, well . . .

I went four for four that game. I never looked back. I, the catcher of all things, led off the rest of the season. Ah, Louise Lords and I shared a special bond.

The second thing I remember about little league was Boyd Blazer's passion and dedication to the game and to us kids. He was a good coach, even if it didn't occur to him to have me try the leadoff position.

He took the job seriously. He held practices. He taught the mechanics of the game. Not just how to field grounders, but fancy things like throwing to the right base, hitting the correct relay man from right field, and how to run the base paths.

Boyd did not holler or scream at us. He did not argue with umpires. He was serious about our efforts and tried to improve the game each of us was playing. He bought us ice cream cones if we won. Sometimes he'd buy even if we lost – if we had played Centre Hall well, for instance.

The third thing I remember is how little league changed during and right after my years in it. Herein lies a comment on what happens when adults take over an activity meant for children.

When I first began to play "organized" baseball, the entire activity was conducted at the old East Penns Valley High School schoolyard, right up the street from my new house.

I liked that field and knew that field. After all, we East Main Street kids played pick-up baseball games there on many a summer morning before heading to the pool.

Looking back, I now realize how important that simple, unadulterated field was to the little league program in which I was engaged. The venue, I believe, kept the game simple for everyone. When adults started to change that, they changed little league in Millheim.

The field at East Penn was pretty basic. Home plate was placed not far out from the most distant corner of the field with only enough room behind it for a wire mesh backstop that had an overhanging lid on it. Home plate faced due west, so that in the early evening a batter had to contend with the setting sun right in his eyes.

The base paths and the pitcher's mound were worn bare. The rest of the infield was spotty grass except for a few bare spots where repeated use had just shorn off any hope of turf. This uneven surface caused unpredictable bounces of ground balls.

There was no fence defining the outfield. It was just the rest of the entire schoolyard, and the schoolyard was about two acres. If one got a ball into the gap, it could roll for one hundred yards if it were hit hard enough. There was no such thing as an official home run. Much more prevalent was what Bob Prince, the famous announcer for the Pittsburgh Pirates, would call "a bug on the rug."

There were no seats for the fans. Moms and dads had to stand, sit on the grass up the first base line, or bring folding chairs. That is what most did. There was no concession stand, so parents brought their own coolers filled with whatever refreshment they wished. (By the way, we players drank from a communal bucket, extracting water by the single, long-handled dipper we all shared.)

Ostensibly, parents were there to give support to their "boys of summer." But mostly they just socialized. They formed little rows or semi-circles, little social cliques really, with their folding chairs and blankets, sharing their squatter's territory with friends and relatives. They "visited" — the Pennsylvania Dutch term for conversation. After all, everyone was from the valley, and everyone there was related to someone else also present. They talked, they shared snacks, and they laughed along the sidelines. They didn't watch the game too closely.

If they heard an authoritative crack of the bat, they would suspend their discussion to see the play, maybe call out a cheer or a groan for it. But then they would return to their adult chatter. I saw several parents get plunked with foul balls because they weren't paying attention to the game right in front of them.

And that was probably good. When we played on our field, John Maher Jr., Esq. often umpired. His son, John III, played in the outfield for us. In many places, that would have created a conflict that would need to be reconciled by league officials. But not in our league. This was John Maher, Jr., Esq. He was a former district attorney for the county. He was now one of the richest, well-known, and fairest attorneys in Centre County. He belonged to the country club up in State College, he was the lawyer for all the schools in the area, and he was a friendly and engaging person whom people were proud to know. He was respected, the most favorable attribute in the valley. No one would have ever accused him of being a "homer."

If John Maher Jr., Esq. said it was a strike, it was a strike. No one argued, not parents, not coaches, and certainly not us kids.

John Maher Jr., Esq. didn't even need to be behind home plate to make his calls. He wasn't going to risk getting beaned with a foul tip for that. No, he just stood out behind the pitcher and did it from there. That also allowed him to umpire the bases. He could just spin toward any base from his position in the middle of the diamond and make the call. A call impervious to dissent.

Who would dissent? Parents? They weren't even watching; they were chatting in those little circles of lawn chairs and blankets spread on the ground. They didn't care. The coaches? Umpires were hard to get. One didn't argue with the only guy who was willing to help. The kids? Forget that. We were cheeky, but we weren't stupid.

That was a good system. Except for the sun in our eyes, we liked that arrangement. Little league was then about the kids. It never really occurred to us that we could expect some improvement in our playing conditions. After all, stadiums were for the big leaguers.

But someone decided that we should play some of our games down on the big field beside the American Legion. That is where the town team played. The field had no official name, just as we had no mascot or nickname. It was simply the Millheim field, home of such local baseball legends as "Dump" Surplee, Carl Vitell, and Rich Blue.

It was a smallish field by adult standards. There was a road running behind the entire outfield, clearing defining the home run boundary. But that distance down right field couldn't have been more than two hundred feet, maybe two hundred and twenty-five to dead center. Many an outfielder had to dig a long drive out of the creek bank across the road to continue a game. But the infield was dirt, and the backstop behind the plate was further back and larger. There were benches for the teams on either side of the diamond.

And there were bleachers.

We liked playing there of course. First, home plate faced northeast – no sun factor. Second, we liked the benches. Third, the field was right downtown, so we got more foot traffic, more casual fans attending the games. Some of them came right from the Legion, and that could lead to trouble, but more people meant more money when they passed the hat. That meant new bats, balls and other equipment.

But those bleachers changed the game forever in Millheim.

Three sides of the field were bordered by asphalt roads, and the fourth had bleachers carved out of a hillside directly behind home plate. There was no picnic area, no folding chairs, and no inattentive pods of chatterers at the Millheim field.

Now our parents and those revelers from the Legion sat on bleachers facing the game. There was no where else to look. So, they started watching the game. Too bad.

Instead of seeing the children do something good – responding to that crack of the bat or the slap of a line drive being captured by a new leather mitt — our fans were treated to the other elements of little league baseball: botched grounders, dropped pop flies, strike outs, bad base running, and the rest of it.

Including questionable calls by the umpires.

For the first time, a dad is watching as the umpire rings out his son on a called third strike. And the pitch looks high to the dad. So, he tells the umpire. Loudly. Perhaps someone else's kid strikes out with the bases loaded, and a dad just can't contain himself: "Put someone in there who can hit!"

The coaches heard this, the umpires heard this, and the kids heard this. The dynamic of the setting changed. Pressure to produce was introduced to the performance of all the participants. That pressure was brought by those who weren't even involved in the game. The adults in the stands started to influence the game, how it was played, who played it, and where it was played.

The camel now had his nose under the tent. Soon the game would become the purview of the adults.

That is what happened in Millheim.

Parents became too interested in the game, or better said, in winning the game. Suddenly, conditions of the field mattered. Quality uniforms mattered. Coaching and umpiring mattered. Equipment mattered.

I was playing when all of this took wing. I remember games when the adults were a bit carried away with the action. They insulted the umpire, they belittled the efforts of kids, argued among themselves about a close call at the plate. The adults started talking about the improvements that could be made for the town's little leaguers.

Not long after I outgrew little league, all that began in earnest. First, they moved the games back out to East Penn. The town team didn't like sharing the scheduling and maintenance of the downtown field with our league. Our base paths had to be measured off inside their regulation, adult league ones. That caused holes and ruts in their infield. Their raised pitcher's mound was a land mine for us little folk. It stuck up behind our pitcher and changed the roll of balls or tripped our infielders trying to capture a pop-up!

East Penn field, it was decided, would be better. All that was necessary were a few improvements. These were forthcoming. Some local heavy equipment operator had young sons ready to play little league. He said he would peel the grass off the infield at no charge to the team. And, while they were at it, why didn't they just turn the field around so batters wouldn't be facing the sun? After all, there was lots of room out there. As a matter of fact, why not build two fields on the grounds, in case we decided to have a little league tournament. That would also provide space for the really young kids to have a place to play too.

Well, if there were to be two fields, then there ought to be fences in the outfields, which were now contiguous, to define home runs and to keep balls in the right ballpark. Some resident who was somehow involved in the fencing business said he could do that job at cost, provided that he could attach a sign to his new chain link construction advertising his business. Other merchants became interested in that space. So now the field sported two new attributes – fences and advertising. That allowed sponsors to take their names off the uniforms and put them on the fences.

Soon a local mason said he would build roofed, concrete block dugouts on both sides of both fields, at cost of course, provided he could put a sign up somewhere indicating his support. The little buildings weren't really dug outs; they were at ground level. But they featured nice new pine seating, protective screens in front, and a bat rack.

Later on it was decided that there ought to be a loudspeaker system so that all these people watching from the newly-constructed bleachers (donated by a planing mill that advertised that fact on the back of the erection) would know who was batting, and so on. Kids would love to hear their names over such an amplified system. That meant, of course, running electricity to both fields, which offered the future prospect of holding night games, in case we held a tournament or some such thing.

All that would take more money than the little league had. Several fundraisers were needed. Naturally, parents could be asked to pony up more for their kids to enroll. Then, the price for advertising could be raised. Why not? More kids were involved and, therefore, more parents and relatives were attending the games. Thus, more people would see the advertising. Meanwhile, mothers could hold a bake sale.

And little leaguers could sell candy.

Before and during the season the league could hold each player responsible for selling, say, twenty-five boxes of assorted chocolates or family-sized Hershey bars, or whatever. They could do that. After all, the teams always had "Poppy Day." We players would stand about the downtown businesses on a Saturday morning and sell little red fabric poppies on green sticks to townspeople for a quarter. We also used to appear in the annual Halloween parade, wearing our gray and red uniforms so that everyone could see that R.E. reon and Sons was highly committed to little league baseball. That was pretty much our contribution to financing our fun.

But kids could do more. Who could turn down a kid in uniform? The sales – and the money raised – would be guaranteed, too. If a kid didn't sell twenty-five boxes, he'd be responsible for the money anyway. In other words, his family would literally eat the loss.

All of this was so successful that enough money was raised not only to run electricity to the fields, but also to build a press box behind home plate on the premier field. Now the neat thing about having a press box was that it could be a two story affair with the top being used by coaches, scouts, and media who could be expected to join the announcer up there. Meanwhile, the bottom level could house a concession stand.

A new rule prohibited people from bringing coolers to the field. The intent of this edict was two-fold. First, it was apparent to the officers of the league that some fans were bringing alcoholic beverages onto the grounds. This was not good for the children and could not be tolerated. Also, it occurred to these officials that food and drink were untapped sources of revenue. They wished to encourage snack purchases from the newly-formed Little League Boosters Association so that profits could be plowed back into continued field improvements.

The new association took great pains to ensure that all parents had the opportunity/responsibility to make the Millheim Little League be all that it could be. (By the way, Millheim had long ago left that other league and now had multiple teams from lower Penns Valley of multiple ages playing each other.) Parents had to sign up for dates that they would work in the new concession stand. People were needed to boil hotdogs, grill burgers, draw sodas, replenish the paper supplies, and take the money. No longer could parents expect to spend the evening watching their progeny play ball. Now they had assignments to keep in the concession stand, or the recently-organized grounds crew, umpires' training program, or fund-raising committee.

The good news: more kids got to play organized baseball. Certainly organized. I remember, from just a few years ago, sitting on my mother's back porch, four lots away from those two fields, and hearing that loudspeaker system working the day's games. I could hear player names, parental lineage, pitching records, batting averages, and today's special at the concession stand. For some reason I was just not tempted to stroll up there and watch a little league game.

Chapter 12

Hormones Rage, Are You Listening?

And then along came Jones – slow walkin', slow talkin', lean, lanky Jones. Actually, his name was Elvis. He was the undisputed king of the rock and rollers. Kids across the nation, and certainly all of us in Millheim, were abandoning *This Old House* and *The Happy Wanderer*. We were rocking around the clock with Bill Haley and the Comets. We were buying Connie Francis songs and going *Down the Aisle of Love* with The Quinn-Tones. We loved Fats Domino, The Everly Brothers, and The Coasters. This was not music inherited from our parents, but our own.

But foremost, we loved Elvis. His on-stage antics were novel and iconoclastic. His songs became our anthems. The fact that he was controversial and revolting to many adults only added to his appeal. We emulated his singing style, his wardrobe, his public persona. When he made his first foray from our radios and records to our televisions, we were all glued to the sets.

The night Elvis appeared for the first time on *The Ed Sullivan Show* I doubt that there was a single person on the diamond in Millheim. Elvis' performance on the hugely popular variety show in the fall of 1956 caused national controversy, what with his gyrating hips and provocative movements. Later that same fall the scandalous performer did it again, causing even more outrage from the keepers of decency across the land. Ed Sullivan was both vilified and admired for allowing this wild man to display such suggestive and wanton sexuality on national television. Again, the performance had emptied the streets of town.

Elvis appeared for the third time on the Sullivan show in January of 1957. The anticipation of what The King would do for an encore had reached a crescendo by the time the show aired on that cold winter night.

It turned out to be a bust, both literally and figuratively. Sullivan's cameramen showed Elvis from the waist up only. Millions of girls across America went to bed utterly frustrated. We had no way of anticipating this anti-climactic ending, of course, so the event had once more made Millheim a ghost town. People had hunkered down for the last of Elvis' three mini-concerts with Mr. Sullivan. Of course all the stores and three of the four bars were closed anyway, it being a Sunday night, but, still, there wasn't anyone walking a dog, standing in the street, or even driving through. Except for Bierly and me. Just before 7:00 p.m. we were hurrying home to catch the show as well.

We had been peeking in windows.

Bierly and I realized that everyone who had a television or could be near one would be in front of it that night. Especially all the girls. We set our plan accordingly.

We were sixth graders at the time, probably twelve years old. Sex was really beginning to make itself known to us. Over the last few years Bierly had become more accepting of the method used in his own conception and his dad's role in the matter. Our hormones were coming alive. Nancy, Peggy, Carol, Suzie, and Betty were starting to look different all right, and we liked what we were seeing. We wanted to see more.

The way to do that was to do a little peeping. We decided to cruise the backyards of town to catch some of our female classmates – or their sisters or mothers, for all we cared – taking a bath or getting ready for the Elvis appearance first and bed later.

Just as there was a lack of real concern about security and the absence of locked doors or dog-guarded properties about town, there was a certain laxness toward such privacy issues as pulling window blinds. We had discovered this by accident one night when we happened to come up the alley behind Penns Street and had an encounter of the second kind. The second floor bedroom window of one of the street's more striking women cast both a shaft of light down to the alley and the non-shaded view of this woman donning her nightclothes. It was an illuminating experience for us. We thought we should repeat it.

As normal, Bierly had the plan. I made only the most minor modifications to it. We knew that everyone would be in front of a television at 7:00 sharp. We surmised that many girls, and maybe their sisters, too, would prepare for bed early that evening so that they could be in their pajamas and hair curlers to watch *The Ed Sullivan Show*. We figured that they would eat early, get naked, take a bath, return naked to their rooms, sit naked while they fiddled with those huge curlers, and finally put on their pajamas and go downstairs to hoot over Elvis. If we were girls, that is what we would have done.

And all of this would happen between 6:00 and 7:00 p.m. on that Sunday evening in January, well after mid-winter darkness. Perfect. We knew where our elusive quarry would be at exactly what time. That is all a Peeping Tom can hope for. This was a plan with real potential. We were all keyed up for it.

So, at 6:00 we hit the alleys. We had already decided on our three most likely candidates. Penns Street was, again, a target-rich environment for this pursuit, just as it was for halloweening. Beautiful girls and a complete and shadowed alley system that would provide both cover and any necessary escape route. We had chosen sites that had some high ground behind the residence; after all, the show would transpire in the second floor bedrooms of those old Victorian homes.

We had made some excuse to our folks to get out of the house on a school night. My parents were a bit surprised. After all, didn't I know that my hero Elvis would be on TV tonight? Assuring them that I would be home in time, I met Bierly, and off we went, two twelve-year-old sexual predators. This was not a job for Queeny; we left her at home this night. We were going to be lurking in the shadows, wearing dark clothing, hiding ourselves from the world. Queeny was too white, too well-known, and, well, she was a girl, so it just didn't seem right.

We roamed the alleys like tomcats. We staked out bedroom windows like FBI agents. We speculated about what we would see, creating wonderful fantasies in our heads. We congratulated ourselves on the quality and insight of our plan. We stood freezing in anxious anticipation of what was about to unfold right before our beady, little, voyeuristic eyes.

And we headed home disappointed. If any girl in Millheim, her sister, or mother decided to eat early, get naked, take a bath, return to her room naked, sit there naked while she curled her hair, and put on her pajamas, she did it somewhere we weren't, probably with the shades down.

We struck out.

Frustrated and foiled we returned to our homes to watch Elvis. That is when we passed through the empty diamond. Everyone was where they should be but Bierly and me.

I enjoyed Elvis more the first two times he was on that show.

***

Obviously, we had entered our high hormone period – the veritable dawning of our human sexuality. It wasn't as if we had just made the connection between girls and sex. We had known about that for some time. But now, we were starting to act on that knowledge.

Of course, this was a major change of direction for us. Before a boy reaches that time in life when sex and girls start to be considered simultaneously, there is a period of girl-loathing that, in its own way, is also a rite of passage. Surely, we can all remember that. For those of us who had sisters, this was natural enough, what with all their primping, dolls, girlie interests, and so on. But even those boys who did not have to endure sisters believed that girls were just not "cool." Girls couldn't throw a baseball, they cried easily, they didn't get in "Dutch" with parents and teachers, and they tended toward drama – secrets and journals and tattle-taling to teachers about our misconduct on the playground. In many cases, their physical and intellectual growth was exceeding our own. Worse, girls inhibited some of our regular routines and boyhood ventures. We couldn't involve them in our newly-concocted schemes because they seemed to have some sort of internal detector that signaled them when the plan spelled trouble. They would offer lame, not so exciting alternatives and, failing that, would simply fade away. No girl I knew in Millheim was ever in trouble with the law, school, or parents. Almost every boy I knew in Millheim was. Until the sex thing reared its head, we treated girls as some sort of aliens. Aliens with "cooties," whatever they were.

We'd stone them if we had to. And that is just what happened one summer morning on the hillside behind Donnie Walker's house. The tale captures one of the stupidest and most dangerous-to-others things in which I was ever engaged. I offer it only as a cautionary tale.

Bierly, Donnie, and I assembled at the big cherry tree half way up the hill behind Walker's house. Donnie had a plan. He wanted to hike up to Cauldwell's pasture field, on up behind the town park, and review the newest Sears Roebuck catalog, what with all its female models in their new, more revealing brassieres. He also had three bottles of Nehi Grape Soda, just to make the expedition more comfortable.

That sounded good to Bierly and me. Except for one, actually two, problems.

Darlene Confer and Suzie Brindel had chosen that day to shadow us, so that they could report us for any heinous act we might commit. Somewhat younger than us, these two girls were small and slight, nothing like the Sears Robuck models. We had no interest in them. In fact, they represented just those icky things we didn't like about girls. When they appeared on the hillside, remaining about twenty yards from us, we simply and kindly told them to leave us alone. In reply, the smarty-pants girls started giving us "lip." "It's a free country. We can be anywhere we want to be. Where are you guys going? We think we will just go along."

"Not with us." We had some women to admire, and no pre-pubescent girls were needed for that. So, we bickered over that for a while. We took a few steps in the direction we were headed; the girls followed. The more we told them to get lost, the more solidified became their refusal. They were just becoming more and more stubborn by the moment.

Inevitably, the moment finally arrived when one of us had had enough. That 'little heathen" bent over, picked up a "goonie," our word for a stone about the size of half-used cake of soap, and hurled it in the general direction of the girls. He meant to hit nobody, and he didn't. That'll end it we thought.

It didn't. The girls persisted in this passive-aggressive response to our growing frustration. They fed on it, actually, and repeated their intent to follow us, wherever we were going.

Bad choice. With the deadly force option already engaged, the inevitable just happened – no one really thought this through, no one verbally called the other two to arms. We witlessly picked up goonies and launched them in the direction of the girls. I do not believe, even to this day, that any of us were really trying to hit them. We just wanted to scare them straight. That strategy must have been apparent to the girls because, undaunted, they insisted that they were going with us. They wouldn't give it up.

So we began a more pointed and fateful attack. Frustrated, all three of us gathered goonies and focused our aim. In firing squad formation, all three of us uncorked targeted shots. Two of us missed. But one flat piece of shale, probably Donnie's, but we never knew for sure, found Suzie Brindel.

It hit her right on the forehead, at the hairline slightly left of center. The damn thing seemed to stick momentarily on her before most of it fell away. For a long second we watched Suzie clutching her head and the instant flow of blood trailing down her face. Suzie screamed, sunk to her knees, pulled her hair back from the cut, and started to cry. We ran over to see how she was faring. Although dazed and in some pain, she hadn't lost an eye, wasn't unconscious, and was able to communicate. As soon as I saw blood on her blouse, however, I knew that parents were going to be involved. I told Donnie that he ought to go home immediately and start working on his story. He left immediately. Meanwhile, Bierly, amazingly, produced a cloth handkerchief from his pocket and used it to stem the bleeding. Where was that stupid first aid kit when we really needed it? Even armed with only a handkerchief, Bierly was the single one of us to come out a hero in the later denouement of the escapade. His ministrations brought thanks from Suzie's parents.

We did not get to Cauldwell's pasture that day. We did not ever ogle the brassiere models while drinking grape pops. Donnie and I did get to visit the Brindel household, however, to offer our deepest sympathy for any inconvenience that we might have caused her. Suzie, luckily, escaped with a wound Doc Henninger could fix with iodine, two stitches, and a bandage. I know that my dad paid Suzie's four dollar office visit fee to Doc Henninger. At fifty cents a week, it took me two months to square my debt with my dad.

I also know that my parents and I had a rather long, heated, and instructive conversation about the incident, rock-throwing in general, and just how closely we all, not just Suzie, had avoided a tragedy that might have scarred participants for a lifetime. Dad did the long and heated part. Mom did the instructive part.

"So, what did you learn from this?"

"I learned not to throw rocks at people."

"What do you think of your behavior in this instance?"

"Stupid."

"Ever again?"

"No. Never again."

"Remember this: The boys throw rocks in jest, but the frogs die in earnest."

"I know, Mom."

I remember thinking about the Rae McNair incident. Here it was again.

***

Bierly already had an extensive collection of girlie magazines stashed in the attic of his home. Most were *Playboy* magazines, but there were several other publications also. He was also in possession of a few nudist club magazines that were really revealing – although the photography was poor and the paper grainy. They had full frontal nudity, banned in regular publications in those days. Everyone was naked. Now that was our new idea of fun, even though we agreed that most of the nudists did not look that great au naturel.

Bierly hid this stash under some loose floorboards in the low-ceilinged attic just off the bedroom he shared with his brother. We'd go in there with a flashlight and review his trove, snickering and delighting in our cache. We would choose our favorite models in each issue and then have an elimination contest until we arrived at our "Naked Girl of the Day" award. She would then be treated to adoring gazes and intensive verbal review, using all those nasty words for female body parts that we had been picking up from the older boys.

We believed Bierly's secret collection was just that – a secret. It turns out, of course, that his mother knew for a long time that those magazines were up there. One day she just casually wove that fact into some non-related conversation. Bierly and I were stunned and momentarily embarrassed. Then we realized that she was not angry or particularly disappointed in us. She seemed to treat it as just about normal. So, we did not even really or directly respond. We just sort of stammered about for a few seconds about how late we were for an appointment down at the old mill and exited with flourish.

I never really determined how Bierly came into possession of this stuff. Actually, he had a bunch of other sexual-oriented novelties. He had a matchbook that, when opened, presented the user with the protruding rubber penis of a miniature cartoon character drawn on the inside cover. He had several little cartoon booklets with Popeye-type characters performing all sorts of depraved acts on each other. He had a deck of playing cards with a beautiful nude on each – fifty-two naked women held in the palm of one's hand.

He'd say only that he had a supplier, someone he had promised not to identify. I always suspected an uncle of his who drove a long distance big rig and lived a long way from Millheim. That guy would stop by sometimes on his way through town, and I thought, perhaps, he was bringing Bierly these trinkets on his visits. Maybe not. Bierly never revealed his source.

My contribution to such naughty contraband was meager in comparison. Mom had given Bari, who was older and a girl and someone who, for both reasons, needed to know more about sex than I did, a medical book that described human anatomy and sexuality. Complete with some centerfold color plates of women's breasts and detailed drawings of the genitalia of both sexes, it was an old brown-covered tome of hundreds of pages. I think Mom obtained it from my Aunt George, one of her younger sisters, who used it when she studied to be a nurse. Bierly and I would pore over those pages when no one else was in our house. We would read about the menstrual cycle women endured every month and congratulate ourselves for having the good fortune not to have to deal with all that. But mostly, we centered our attention on those color plates.

My dad, for a few years, belonged to some book club that would send him a novel every month or so. For some reason, I got to thumbing through the pages of one of them, *The Tumbling of the Sun,* by Whit Cannon. I guess it just looked to me to be the kind of book that was going to contain some sex. I was right. On pages 72-74 there was a titillating passage about the hero, Dick Abbott, and a somebody's sexually-neglected wife, named Essie. In vivid and graphic language, Essie attempted to seduce Abbott, removing her clothing and begging him to service her. I read this passage over and over, wondering whether I might ever meet a lady so interested in what I might provide her. Dick Abbott, however, being our hero and all, overcame this temptation and left Essie standing there unrequited and wondering what the problem was. Fool, fool, fool, I thought.

All this scandalous literature was augmenting our personal experiences. We had started admiring the female body years ago. Bierly and I worshiped those pretty older girls in town, the ones already in high school when we were in third and fourth grades. Girls like Dorothy Thiebolt, one of the very prettiest.

Dorothy simply had striking beauty. Her hair was jet black. Her skin was silky smooth and cream-colored. This doe-eyed beauty had a hearty and easy laugh, and a personality that made her very popular.

And the figure of a movie star. She was well endowed, with large, pert breasts that pushed against any clothing she wore. She was seductive. Dorothy liked me, and tended to treat me like a little pet. I loved her.

If we wanted to see gorgeous girls, we just had to go to Dot and Jake's, the hangout for high school kids right beside the high school. The little soda shop occupied the front, downstairs room of what was really Dot and Jake Albright's green clapboard home. They lived behind and above the shop with their two kids, Kathy and Bobby. The front yard was a crushed stone parking lot capable of accommodating about eight cars.

During the hours right after school and all day Saturday, that lot was filled with the customized hotrods of "cool cats" from the lower part of the valley. Many of them sported v-8 engines, known in the car world as "bent eights." Most cars in the lot could lay a patch of rubber anytime these dudes would peel out of the last place they had been. For some reason, that was important. A few hopeful lotharios were stuck with the family car, perhaps a Studebaker, a Nash, or a rather basic Chevy.

These would-be Casanovas would slide into place outside and then enter the pop joint with great swagger, dressed in style of the day, white, cotton undershirts (they weren't elevated to "Tee shirts" yet) and blue jeans with white socks and black loafers.

Usually they started at the door with a string of teenage slang in utterances such as, "Hey, Daddy-O! What's shakin'? Anybody here crusin' for a brusin'? Hey, Stud, I heard you got shot down last night. Can you dig it? Stud thought he was going to score, but same old, same old."

Some of these guys had credentials all right. At different times, different ones of them owned the timing record for driving up the Centre Hall mountain at full throttle without ever hitting the brakes on that snake-shaped corridor. That was tricky and dangerous. Others held the speed record for the Woodward narrows, the mostly open, but deer-infested, route out of

Penns Valley into Union County. Also dangerous. So, we always considered these heroes and close seconds with admiration of their manliness.

Anyway, they'd enter with great flourish and thump their mirror images on the back, step up to the counter and order root beer floats and greasy cheeseburgers with fries. Then they would slide into a female-rich booth and begin the mating game, flirting with all my older girlfriends.

Bierly and I, and Donnie, for that matter, loved to go there. We could watch all the athletes and cool guys strut their macho acts before the full-bosomed girls. Many of the teenage boys had crew cuts, the fronts of which where pasted straight up in the air with generous dollops of pink Butch Wax. The girls swirled around in their saddle shoes and scooted into one of the half dozen booths that ran along the front and side windows of the shop. They'd order cherry cokes, slip nickels into the juke box, and sing along with Pat Boone as he crooned *Love Letters In The Sand*. The boys would get into friendly scuffles and become more rowdy than Jake Albright would allow. One could almost smell the testosterone. Jake would tone them down and threaten them with expulsion.

We younger guys would perch on the stools at the short counter beside the huge Hires Root Beer barrel, slurping lemon blends and watching all the activity around the booth that had become Dorothy's throne, one she shared with Audrey Rishel. Sometimes Dorothy would invite us over to sit with her. She clearly knew I had a crush on her, and that I loved some up close and personal time. Audrey was not quite as attentive, although she did tease me from time to time about things that were slightly sexual in nature. These two were forbidden fruit to me, just out of my reach. Sometimes Dorothy would chide me about doing something to make her happy. All she would have had to do was ask. She was desire, on a stick.

On these occasions the bigger guys, the ones with the sleek, old, but newly-painted Hudsons and Fords out in the parking lot, always looked at me as an interruption in their attempted conquest of Dorothy and Audrey. Too bad. I, too, swaggered about that place as if I owned it.

Usually though, we maintained our little perches, observing the courting ballet performed in front of us. We would guess who was making an impression, and who might just get lucky. We would root for our favorite heroes, the guys we idolized like Stuart Brungard, Lee Heckman, Bobby Kudrow, and Jack Weiser. We'd talk with Ruby Stover and her steady beau, Donnie Jordan. Ruby's sister and brother, Linda and Ron, were always there too. Both were just plain noisy, wild, and exciting to be around. We'd beg a dime or so off Bob Seeman so we could re-up our lemon blends. We watched, and we learned.

We liked the games we saw the big kids playing. Flirting and holding hands, necking in the balcony of the theatre, getting girls into the back seats of their fathers' Mercurys – man, these were better than the games we were playing. Girls had become our new thing. For a change, I was ready at the same time as Bierly to change interests.

There were lots of pretty but older girls about town. They were fully-developed beauties who rode around in groups in cars, who were the cheerleaders at the basketball games, and who went to our church on Easter, dressed to the nines in pastel, gossamer dresses. There was Brenda Norris, the pretty cheerleader, and Gloria Childs, a gorgeous gal from Aaronsburg. Lucille Foltz lived in Coburn and later married Dick Carrier. They were probably the two best-looking people ever to live in the valley. I now think they were the models for those little plastic bride and groom figures always placed on wedding cakes. Plus, Lucille was one of the nicest older kids ever to lounge at Dot and Jake's.

We were simply taken by pretty faces and big busts – no big surprise there for an average American male, young though we were. No waiting for these beauties; they had breasts. They were comfortable with boys, they liked boys, and they were looking for boys. We knew they weren't looking for us – we were just too young – but we shared vicariously in their romantic pursuits, fueling the passion of our own budding sexuality.

That was becoming more and more the case with girls my sister's age as well. After all, they were three years older than I, and they, too, were starting to develop and to treat boys in different ways. My sister brought several of these girls to our house for visits or sleepovers. That was good.

Bari and her new bike – and then she got older.

Of these Barb Evans was my favorite. Barb was a fun-loving, bawdy beauty who lived on the hill at the edge of town. Another dark-haired, dark-eyed, clear-skinned lovely, Barb just oozed sensuality. Boys her age chased her incessantly. She and my sister — blond, blue-eyed, very attractive — were two of the most popular girls in their age group, from junior high right through high school. Barb was every boy's fantasy – pretty, friendly, well-dressed, intelligent, and big-breasted.

Most days she came to our house after school, directly from the school bus, and hung out until dinnertime. If a huge snowstorm shut down the schools for two or three days, Barb was sure to get trapped at our house for the duration. She'd simply live with us until it was time to return to school.

She and Bari would experiment with new make-up designs, standing in front of the bathroom mirror for hours, giggling and talking girl-talk. She would change into some of Bari's clothes, sometimes being careful with the bedroom door, sometimes not so vigilant. That was a mistake.

She'd flounce about the house with her crinoline hoopskirts flying. She often wore several at a time. She would suddenly be bothered by all this fullness and decide to discard one or more, which she would do right in front of me. That was cool.

Barb and I would flirt, wrestle, and dance. We'd fool around with the wire recorder that Dad brought home from school. We would record a marriage ceremony that Bari would solemnly read from the back of an old hymnal. Afterward, we would fall into each other's arms like passionate lovers. It was grand, squeezing Barb's supple body and brushing up against her. And all the time, I realized that there were boys her age all over town who would have given a right testicle just to be where I, this little boy, was at the moment.

Darla Schade was another girl my sister's age. She was attractive, although more slightly built than what Bierly and I craved. Still, we stayed in her presence when we could. Bari's other friends came from up the valley, girls she met as she moved to the new school. Connie Bressler and Joanie Weaver visited often. Time well spent as far as I was concerned.

These girls treated me like a younger brother. Younger brothers have some advantages over boys who are trying to win a date. Younger brothers get to see sisters and friends in pajamas, in various stages of undress, in non-glamorous positions or situations. A cat can look on a king.

But we were finally getting around to girls our own age too. I had a crush, one of those puppy-love, non-sexual kinds of crushes, on Nancy Fox almost from the time I moved to Millheim. Nancy was petite, pretty, and friendly. She laughed easily, with a dimpled smile that framed two overlapping front teeth. She rose above that small defect with the fine, carved legs of an athlete. She was willowy and graceful, and totally without affectation.

But I was scared to death of Nancy Fox. First of all, she was a girl, and I didn't know how to deal with girls. Second, she was a pretty girl whom everyone knew I liked. So, they teased me about this. That made her all the more distant to me because I did not want to do anything to let the other kids know how right they were. Third, her dad was Ralph Fox, a well-known farmer at the southern edge of town who seemed to be pretty powerful in Millheim.

I was so afraid of Nancy and her dad that I never, ever went to her house. Not when I was in second grade, not when I was a senior in high school. I have no idea what her house looks like to this day, inside or out.

As much of Nancy Fox's house as I ever saw.

I almost went there – a million times. Her farm was at the far end of Penn Street where it turned hard left to cross the creek and headed toward Coburn. Her house sat on top of a steep bluff, reached by a right-curving lane that cut off the road and rose to the crest of the hill. One could stand half-way up that lane and just see the roof of the house. I know because I did that many times. I just never went the entire way up the lane.

Not that she didn't ask. When we were in grade school, she would often invite me down to her house to play, to do homework, or to create a school project. I just could not bring myself to do it. I'd tell her that I would be there, and I would make it halfway up that lane. But I could not finish it. What if her dad saw me there? He was a stern-looking, wiry, tough dirt farmer. What if I displeased him somehow? He'd have my head, whatever that meant.

But mostly I was afraid of Nancy. Girls fascinated me. They also scared the hell out of me. What if I wasn't cool? What if she didn't like me? What if I spilled something in the house? What if she wanted to kiss and I wasn't very good at it?

She'd laugh at me. Worse, she would tell Peggy Moore, her best friend and the girl I loved second most in the entire world.

I just couldn't chance it. I never went up the hill. Nancy would ask me why I didn't show up. I would say something about getting tied up, or injuring myself, or dying in a car crash – anything that masked the real reason I didn't climb that hill. Just plain fear.

We never dated.

Chapter 13

Early Efforts At The Birds And Bees Thing

"Come on, we're going to buy you a pair of pants." When Bierly announced that, I just stared at him. We never shopped for clothes. I had no interest in pants, and I was bewildered that he would be thinking about pants. It turned out that he was really onto something else, something pretty far removed from our personal wardrobes.

We had been shooting starlings with Bierly's pellet gun. Sometime around our twelfth year, Millheim suffered an infestation of starlings, a mid-sized, mostly black bird that had no social significance at all, aviary or human. Thousands of them descended on the burg, squawking and swooping about as if they owned the joint. Mostly though, they pooped, fouling everything. This had to be unhealthy. The town council had made a special deviation from shooting restrictions that allowed anyone, even within town limits, to pick off any of these annoyances with whatever means found useful. That meant guns, of course.

It was commonplace to see folks walking down Main Street toting all forms of handguns, rifles, and shotguns. They had been attacking, or getting ready to attack, the starling population. Any summer day one could hear the report of weaponry aimed skyward or treeward at the noisy, dirty invaders. Kids could do that too, so that is how Bierly and I spent the morning – ridding the town of about ten starlings. We'd shoot one out of the trees that lined the creek, and the rest of the flock would fly off, returning a few minutes later. These birds were numerous, but they were stupid. We repeated this drill, with the help of the stubborn starlings, about a dozen times. Apparently this manly endeavor whetted Bierly's sexual appetite.

As we grew, fascination with sex figured in many of our daily experiences. Bierly and I had begun to infuse sexual overtones or experiences into events or activities that were not primarily sexual in nature. Real sex is hard to come by at ages eleven or twelve. Apparently, that is especially so if one lived in a small town. Women don't take kids seriously, and the girls are as naive, scared, and unreliable as the boys are.

So, one makes sex out of nothing at all. That is where the pants came in.

Totally by accident, Bierly had stumbled upon a just such a titillating situation. His mom had sent him to Nieman's to buy a pair of pants. He so enjoyed the experience that he decided that I was going to enjoy it also.

Mrs. Gates worked in Nieman's. She was the mother of an attractive high school girl who hung out at Dot and Jakes's. The Gates family also attended our church, so we knew them all well.

Martha Gates, someone's mother or not, was a striking and attractive lady. She was always impeccably dressed, wearing the latest fashion. She had taken recently to those black, plastic, cat-eye glasses that were all the rage. She pulled her black-with-a-little-silver hair back into a tight bun, a style that bared and framed her fair skin. She wore really red lipstick. The result was a bit severe, but she had a warm smile and she liked Bierly and me even though she often had to watch us closely when we dallied in the store. (She and her husband really liked me. They asked me to light the candles – because I was a trained acolyte – at their daughter's wedding. Those parents gave me five dollars for that thirty minute event – a virtual windfall for me.) That Bierly and I were pubescently-charged by both daughter and mother was not lost on us. We knew this was slightly weird, even for us. Maybe it was just those tight-fitting sheath dresses that Mrs. Gates wore. But, what the heck, she was someone else's mother, not ours. What did we care? We felt the same way about "Touch" Minnis' wife who worked in the five and ten cent store. She had little kids, but she was beautiful too. Hormones will be hormones, I guess.

While basically kind and thoughtful toward everyone, Mrs. Gates still stepped up to scold us for disrupting the professional, almost library-like, atmosphere of the store or for fiddling with the meticulous displays of clothing. One of our delights was the women's department, what with its astonishing inventory of brassieres. In those days few items were individually packaged or displayed. Brassieres, for instance, were neatly stacked one on another, with their straps and side panels all splayed out to the sides. They formed large twin-peaked mounds of white, coned cotton and polyester, some with serious wire underpinnings. The bigger the bra size, the larger the pile. Bras intrigued Bierly and me. We would admire the circular, concentric stitching around the increasingly smaller circles of the cups. They really made the garment look sturdy and strong. We decided that breasts must be really heavy if all this support was needed. Oh, yes, we loved bras.

They were integral to our fixation on women's breasts. We studied them everywhere we went – school, church, market, or Nieman's. We'd stand near the ladies' underwear section and watch women – big-breasted and small-breasted women – shop for bras. We developed such knowledge about bras and cup sizes that we could have told any particular shopper which section of the bra table she should be perusing.

"Excuse me, Ma'am, but the 32 A cups are on this side of the counter. You are looking at 38 Ds."

Sometimes Mrs. Gates had to shoo us out of there. More than once we poked big dimples in the cups of the bras on the top of each pile. This made them look sort of useless, if not uncomfortable. Mrs. Gates would run us out of the store if she caught us doing that.

(This might be the appropriate, and defensive, time to say that Bierly and I were not alone in this captivation with the female body, especially breasts. While we might have taken this fascination a bit far, most boys our age were undergoing similar awakenings as our testosterone began to exert itself. A friend told me that he used to play with a nearby neighbor girl. When they were both six or seven years old, she had a habit of playing in the sun without wearing a shirt or any other top. He often laughed that he married the first topless girl he ever saw.

Lucky for my friend, he saw her first.

So, while these tales involve Bierly and me, I submit that American culture has made every heterosexual male in it a student of, and a slave to, the female breast. I offer but one example. Why would virtually every other monthly edition of *National Geographic* highlight some primitive tribe of bare-breasted females in a forgotten land? Hey, folks, I've been to the dentist's office.)

But, back to our story. This day Bierly wanted me to be measured for pants by Mrs. Gates. He really liked his own experience. Not the part where she measured his waist, looping her pliable tape measure around his middle and pronouncing him a "28." No, it was when she measured his inseam that Bierly got excited about his new pants.

He wouldn't tell me much about it. He just said that we were going down to Nieman's and that I was going to tell Mrs. Gates that I wanted a pair of pants like Bierly had just bought a day or two ago. The rest, he said, would take care of itself. I told him I didn't need pants – and if I did, my parents would take me to State College to get them because clothing was cheaper there, and the selection was greater in several stores. Not only that, I could go into one of the two shoe stores, Blaney's, and get a free x-ray of my feet. One just stepped onto the base of this fancy machine and looked into the screen forming its top half. Presto! There were all the bones of one's feet displayed on what later was determined a misuse or dangerous exposure, at best, of X-rays. Besides, I only bought pants once a year, in the fall when Mom bought me two pair for the ensuing academic year. Didn't matter, said Bierly, just pretend I was going to buy them, so she has me try them on.

Now I didn't often have pants to fix. Boys only wore two kinds of pants in those days – blue jeans and "dress" pants. We didn't fix jeans (dungarees). We bought them by waist size only. Length of leg did not matter; we simply rolled them up. Kids in jeans in the '50s always had dark blue pants with baby blue cuffs about four inches wide and as thick as necessary to use up the unnecessary length. When I bought "dress pants," the ones we wore to school, my mom fixed the length. I would stand before her, and she would roll them up to a height that didn't drag on the ground yet allowed room for a year's growth of her little boy. She would pin them, and I would be gone.

But if one acquired pants from Mrs. Gates, she measured leg length differently. Bierly had not prepared me for this. I guess he wanted to see the surprise on my face. He got his wish.

With mock, studied care, I selected a pair of brown twill pants that I told Mrs. Gates would address my current need. I changed into them in the dressing room, returning to the two of them with pant legs dragging on the floor. Mrs. Gates got down on her knees just like my mother did. I assumed she was going to roll up the legs just as Mom always did.

Instead, she took her soft tape measure and, stretching it out between her two hands, inserted her left fist up into my crotch so she could pull the other end of the measure to the floor. It was, for a young lad, an exhilarating and up-lifting experience. Bierly was standing directly in front of me, behind the kneeling Mrs. Gates. My face certainly expressed my initial surprise, momentary panic, and then complete delight. Bierly could hardly contain himself.

Neither could I. This was great. I wanted more. When she had finished, I asked Mrs. Gates to check her work. When she had done that, I asked her if I could see just how long she planned on making the legs. When she had repeated the measurement to show me that, I told her that maybe I ought to look at some black pants also.

At some point, Mrs. Gates had to have figured us out. But she was a consummate professional. Her job was to serve the customer, even a kid trying to take advantage of her. Anyhow, I got measured for those pants about four times – four thrilling times. I have no idea how I got out of Nieman's without buying some pants. I probably told her that they were too black or something.

All that sounds silly in retrospect. But a little boy's first sexual experiences often present themselves as accidental, incidental little opportunities. An unintended touch or brush against a woman here or there, a chance and unexpected walk-in when your friend's sister is in the bathtub or getting dressed, or the momentary view provided when a girl across the room sits in a decidedly unladylike manner. Perhaps one gets up close and personal with someone of the opposite sex — dancing, games, riding three across the seat in a school bus, anything that results in close quarters.

Swimming once provided me with such an early memorable experience.

I was twelve years old. I know this because one had to be twelve years old to become a Junior Lifesaver. Bierly and I wanted to become Junior Life Savers in the worst way. Bierly couldn't resist the appeal of winning a badge for some accomplishment.

Jim Tomkins decided to offer life-saving courses to both kids and interested adults. Apparently, Tomkins (we always addressed him as Tomkins at the pool, but always as Mr. Tomkins at school) was a certified aquatics instructor, allowed to train others in the elements of swimming safety, rescue, and resuscitation. Well, he decided that adults around town, folks eighteen years of age or older, should take an advanced swimming course, earning a lifesaving certification along the way. Meanwhile, he would offer basically the same program to us underage kids, allowing us to achieve the revered status of Junior Lifesaver.

The training for young and old occurred at the same time – right after the pool closed for the dinner hour, at five o'clock. Fifteen or so of us stronger swimmers would stay, joined by about ten adults.

Mrs. Minnis was one of those adults. This was Darlene's mother, not "Touch" Minnis' wife who worked in the five and ten. Darlene was the first girl in our class to wear a bra, or to need one. She was maturing at an advanced rate, something we boys watched with great awe. Even the girls in our class snickered about it. I am sure she inherited this gene from her well-endowed mother.

Mrs. Minnis, like Mrs. Gates, was pretty. She was vivacious. Maybe it was just that she was in a swimsuit. Whatever it was, she was sexy. She would spend some time at the pool, perhaps an afternoon two or three times a month, but she often dropped by to pick up or drop off Darlene and her friend, Bea Musser. So I knew her.

I got to know her better while I was becoming a Junior Lifesaver. After Tomkins would demonstrate a procedure, we would jump into the water and practice, with a partner who would feign drowning, fatigue, or sickness – something that required a Junior Lifesaver to spring into action. We would take turns playing each role so that we could all become accustomed to being heroes.

One evening I was paired with Mrs. Minnis. Apparently there were odd numbers of both adults and kids. I was a strong swimmer, and I had already proven that I could drag someone the size of Mike Toomis or Ed Decker out of the water. So Tomkins put me with Mrs. Minnis.

To practice the "tired swimmers carry." Here is how the tired swimmers carry works. If the hero happens upon a drowning person who is utterly calm, one who is not thrashing about in the water in a panic, and who is compliant and willing to follow direction, the saver orders the victim to roll over onto his/her back. Then, the victim is told to spread his/her legs and to allow the hero to swim up between them. Then the tired swimmer extends his/her arms to rest on the shoulders of the oncoming hero. The saver breaststrokes the victim to safety while the salvaged soul looks gratefully into the eyes of the rescuer.

In the world of sex, it is called the "missionary position."

That was what Mrs. Minnis and I, Eddie Frye, Junior Lifesaver, practiced. I was were given free rein to swim up between Mrs. Minnis' legs and float around there for minutes and minutes.

We were the very last to reach the shallow end of the pool. I was in no particular hurry. On the way, I had to keep apologizing for my sloppy breaststroke, which brought back the original meaning of the term. I could have done better; I just wasn't trying.

Mrs. Minnis was great. She seemed to me to be enjoying herself. When it was time to switch roles, she did not ask for a new partner. She simply did the same thing, smiling wanly at me as I lay there on my back. What was she thinking? Maybe adults in situations like that are just like gynecologists or obstetricians. It all is just part of the role.

Bierly told me later that I could have flown a flag from the front of my little maroon bathing suit.

∗∗∗

Be prepared, as the Boy Scouts say. A boy needed to be ready in case a serendipitous sexual opportunity fell his way. Bierly and I decided we better get ourselves some prophylactics. Prophylactics, specifically, not condoms. "Condoms" was not yet the term for prophylactics. On the street we called them "rubbers" or "strippers," but not "condoms." We also referred to them as "Trojans," because around our part of the country

233

there seemed to be only two makers of prophylactics – Trojan and Excello. So "Trojan" was sort of like calling any facial tissue a Kleenex.

But the proper and commercial name for the item was "prophylactic." I wished it had been "condom," because I could have pronounced "condom." We were stuck with "prophylactic" and sick about it. In some remote possibility that cheap, raw sex presented itself to us, we wanted to be supplied. In truth, we fully expected to carry our prophylactics around in our wallets until the outside packaging wore off.

But Bierly and I could hardly pronounce the word. It wouldn't be bad enough that we had to ask for the damn things, we had to use about the largest word we knew in the English language to do so. It wasn't easy preparing oneself for sex. Anyway, we had to go into a store and ask someone to sell us some prophylactics.

Actually, we had to go to a particular store to get them. They were certainly available in Doc Forsythe's Drug Store, right there on the diamond, but there was no way Bierly and I could go in there and ask Miriam Forsythe to sell us a package of prophylactics. She would laugh at us and tell our parents. No, we had to ride our bikes almost to Coburn to a little store in Frogtown that purveyed our treasure.

We knew the store of course. We had been in it before. It was a tiny little soda pop, convenience joint. One could get bread and milk, aspirin or cough syrup, but mostly, it featured racks of potato chips and candy bars, even an ice cream chest. It was operated by a little old woman with stringy black hair and no front teeth. The first time I ever encountered her – there in her lair – I thought she was the witch from *The Wizard of Oz.* I actually expected her to refer to me as "My Pretty." But she was not as nice as that witch, and I decided she was not as good looking either. We didn't know her name, and, more importantly, we didn't think that she knew ours. Paul Lingle and Mike Toomis agreed that that was the place to go for prophylactics.

We asked them to make the purchase for us, but they said no, it was our job. After all, we were the ones who wanted them.

Couldn't we just ask for "strippers" we wanted to know. No, that would be crude. The lady sells "prophylactics." Well, could we ask for "Trojans?" No, because she might just have Excellos. If that were the case, we would unwittingly necessitate the same conversation one has with waitresses when ordering Coke and they ask if Pepsi is okay. Did we want to prolong the transaction? No. Then ask for "prophylactics." It was important to sound like we knew what we were doing.

So, we mounted our bikes for the short trip to Frogtown to purchase some rubbers. Two kids less than thirteen years old in dire need of instruments of sex that we could not pronounce, did not have a clue how to use, nor had a reasonable opportunity to do so.

For some reason, I had to make the purchase. I suppose we had a contest that I lost, but I don't remember. All I recall is stepping through the screen door of that dimly-lit old shack and circling the candy counter for about two minutes, screwing up enough courage to tell the old lady what I wanted. While I fretted, I practiced how to say "prophylactics" a dozen times. Meanwhile, the old crone stood there behind the counter, studying my obvious discomfort at selecting a candy bar.

Finally, Bierly nudged me forward, and I stepped up to the plate. I placed our order, one package of prophylactics for him and one for me. I did it poorly.

First, I didn't say "prophylactic" correctly. It came out something like "prosifactic."

And, worse, I used the wrong unit of measurement for the deal. That confused the issue. Prophylactics came three to a package – twenty-five cents. In my mind I was thinking about six of the little guys. I meant two packages, of course, one for each of us. But I wasn't thinking about clarifying how many I really expected to get. As if she dealt in split packages of the hermetically-sealed product. I should have known that this was like cigarettes. One didn't order twenty cigarettes; the request was, "one pack."

So, inadvertently, I caused the whole Coke/Pepsi discussion – worse, a great expansion of it — during the occasion when I least wanted to call any attention to myself or the item.

"I'd like six prosifactics, please."

"Six what?"

"Six prosifac . . . , I mean six prophysacties . . . I mean six prophylactics."

"You want six packages of prophylactics?" the old woman snorted. "You must be a busy little boy!"

So, here was this clarifying conversation that just seemed to go on and on. And I had already been deemed a little boy. Oh, man.

"No, I just want two packages. There are three in each one." I assumed she didn't know.

"I know that. Trojans or Excello?" And Mike said she only might handle one brand!

"Uhmm . . . Trojans."

"Excellos are on sale, five packages for a dollar. That ought to give you enough," she cackled.

"No, I think two packages will do it." Do it? Our six Trojans would probably last a lifetime.

So, she began digging below the counter for the Trojans. There was an awkward silence while she sorted out two little boxes from the specially-grouped on-sale Excellos that she clearly thought was the better buy. The silence and pregnancy of the moment created a void that Bierly just couldn't tolerate.

"We use them for the 'prevention of disease only'," he offered, reciting the little message that appeared on all packages of prophylactics. As if she cared.

The old woman swung her head up and around to look at him and snarled, "The only disease you will ever get will come from your own hands."

The urge to flee rose in me, and I almost bolted, letting her stand there with my almost-secured Trojans still in her hands. But we had come this far; no use quitting now.

We finished the purchase and exited sheepishly, out into the bright sunlight beyond the screen door. Outside, we carefully inserted the little boxes into the new wallets we had recently begun to carry. Now I was carrying a spiffy black wallet with an identification card, a crisp dollar bill, my school picture, and a package of Trojans. I was satisfied that before long the box was going to make a raised impression in the outside leather covering. Wait until the girls saw that! Now all I had to do was keep my mom from seeing it. Bierly and I were now prepared for sex.

***

My first date was with Connie Probst. We define date here as meeting a girl at the Millheim theatre, watching a movie together while holding hands, or, better, with my arm around her, and then buying her a coke at the restaurant. The optional part – her option – was walking over to the park, sitting in the bingo stand, and making out.

Well, my first one of those, to include the optional part, was with Connie Probst. The whole thing was really set up by Mike Toomis with whom we were really on a double date. Mike was taking Gloria Rendell, a pretty, sometime resident of Millheim. She and Connie were close friends. Mike understood that the only way he could take Gloria to the movies was to take her joined-at-the-hip friend along also. That meant Mike needed another guy, and I was that guy.

Connie and I were already friends. She and her slightly older brother, Jack, lived on Penn Street and were at the pool everyday. Connie was one year older than I. She was a tomboy — a sinewy, low body fat gal who could play baseball, ride horses, swim, and swear as well as any boy and better than most. For all of that, she was attractive. Because girls tend to develop more rapidly than boys at this age, and given that she already had a year's start on me, she was a pretty imposing date. As friends we were fine; she did not intimidate me at the pool. In fact, we teamed often in games and tag matches. But I went into that Saturday night filled with the inner conflict of the timid and unsure.

Mike had coached me that afternoon. Being two years older than I, he knew all about this dating stuff – what to do, when to do it, how to do it well. He told me to compliment Connie's appearance as soon as we met up with the two girls. He reminded me that I would have to pay for her ticket (That was about the only thing I already knew for sure.) He showed me how to move my hand surreptitiously over hers after the movie started. I asked him how I would know when to do that. He said that she would put her hand on the armrest between us as sort of a "girl message" that I could hold it. When I saw her do that, I should move in for the kill. As for getting my arm around her, the theory was about the same. She would shift her shoulders slightly toward me and turn her head just slightly away. That would be the signal.

What if I missed the signal? What if she didn't signal? Was I supposed to do nothing just because she didn't signal? What if I ticked her off and she slapped me, right there in the theatre where I knew just about everyone. It was already bad enough that they all would be seeing me there with a girl, on a date. I was filled with questions and doubts.

Mike gave me some pabulum about how all girls wanted to do such things. She wouldn't slap me, he promised. He also told me that if I got into a jam or didn't know what to do, I was just supposed to look over at him. I should just do whatever he was doing to Gloria. That crutch would have provided more solace if I didn't know that his date was much more feminine and ladylike than Connie. We had two different cats in this bag – Gloria, the finely combed Angora, and Connie, the tiger cat.

As they always do, this Saturday night finally arrived. I had bathed and combed with great care. I was wearing my baby blue twill pants – the ones with the little metal buckle on the back, right below the belt loops – and my favorite multi-colored striped shirt. I slid into my black leather loafers with the steel cleats on the heel. Elmer Etters tacked those onto the shoes of every boy in town. When we walked down the street, we sounded like Albert Stover's Tennessee Walker. None of this preening and costuming helped. I was still nervous as hell.

Mike and I met our quarry in front of the theatre. Boys our age did not yet make house calls. Besides, both of the girls knew their way to the theatre, and both of them lived closer than we did. I remembered to compliment Connie on her appearance. I think I told her that her teeth looked especially white or something.

The movie theatre part of the evening went well enough. We were watching some western. During the cartoon and the newsreel that always preceded the feature in those days, I kept peaking down at the armrest, looking for and hoping not to miss or misconstrue, Connie's signal.

Sure enough, by the time the first Indian was shot, Connie had placed her forearm on the armrest with her hand hanging loosely over the front. It looked to me as if that hand was just crying out for someone to save it from dropping on down to the floor. It wanted company; it wanted the care and attention of a man.

This must be the moment, I thought. Surely this is the moment. God, I hope this is the moment. Slowly, I raised my arm from the crevice between the seats where it had been lurking, just waiting to be called into the game. With more resolve and force than I intended, I plunked my hand down on hers and felt around with my fingers until I found hers. Then I laced my fingers through hers and squeezed her entire hand pretty tightly. I guess I wanted her to know that she had been snared. As if she could have missed that ham-handed effort.

She jolted a little, almost imperceptibly, but there was a start there. She recovered quickly though, and looked over at me with just the thinnest of smiles. My heart raced. I was filled with the satisfaction of my success. Maybe this dating thing wasn't so hard after all.

More Indians died. So did a few cavalry and one or two horses. Clearly, the white man was going to win this saga. I looked over at Mike and Gloria. He was moving a little faster than I was. He already had his arm around her, and either he had just whispered something to her, or he had actually kissed her neck, cheek, or ear. Too dark for me to tell.

I needed to make my next move. Buoyed by my earlier success with the hand thing, I did not sit in long contemplation. I pulled the "Stretch Move" that Mike had taught me earlier in the day. The "Stretch Move" is as old as dating itself. Some caveman probably invented it after bonking a woman on the head and dragging her to a cave went out of fashion. Every boy, and I imagine every girl in the world, gets some experience with the "Stretch Move."

Still, on the off chance that someone out there has yet to encounter it, I will take a minute here to describe the version Mike taught me.

The boy, basically the assaulter, shifts his body weight so that he is leaning slightly to the side opposite of the unsuspecting assaultee. The boy sighs audibly, mustering a yawn if possible, and stretches both arms as far up and away from his body as possible. This should be done with such extension and flair that the people in the seats behind are actually watching the movie for a second or two through outstretched arms, hands, and fully extended fingers.

This full extension is really the critical part of the maneuver. Mike had stressed that over and over in the training session. If the arms are not fully extended, the elbow can become a weapon in the next phase of the move. The trick, of course, is to get that arm ready to pass behind the victim. If it is not out there, far and straight, there is the danger of inadvertently elbowing the prey when attempting to get the arm past and behind her. That would be sloppy.

The move is finished effortlessly. The hormone-enraged boy brings his arms down, slowly, and turns just slightly toward her. This is easy because of that previous body lean. Done by experts it is now an almost imperceptible move. The snare is finished by dropping the arm behind her shoulders and resting it casually on the back of the seat. One does not go directly to the shoulders. That would look planned and purposeful, and the "Stretch Move" has as its charm casualness and nonchalance. It is like saying, "Oh, I often rest my arm in an outstretched manner just to keep from getting stiff. Think nothing of it."

Executed well, the girl is not even to notice what has happened to her. Soon, the boy can slowly drop the arm down from the backrest and feel the inviting warm flesh of her nape, shoulders, and arms.

Of course that isn't the case. The girl certainly knows when that arm is around her. She knows it is not incidental or accidental. Heck, she knows when the weight shifts, certainly by the time the arms are sticking out in the air like the twig arms of a snowman.

But most girls pretend not to notice. It is part of the ritual.

Connie, outspoken, bawdy tom girl that she was, did not even pretend not to notice. As soon as I had completed my well-rehearsed maneuver, pretty well I must add – probably an 8.9 on the judges' scorecards – she looked at me, grinned broadly and said something like, "Are you comfortable now?" Well, yes I was. This was going great.

The white men won – they always did in the westerns of the '50s. Afterwards, the four of us went to the restaurant and had Pepsi Colas and potato chips from a family-sized bag, the cost of which Mike and I later split. That may have been the best part of the whole night. It was a social situation most like the pool or school. We were all comfortable with each other's company, and conversation came easily. There was not nearly so much of that sexual tension, that boy-girl stuff that gets in the way of enjoyable chat.

But that tension was still to be part of the evening. After all, this was a date, right? That boy-girl stuff was the whole object of this drill. The theatre activity was just prologue. It was now time for the pubescent version of going back to her place.

We left the restaurant, cut through the alley across the street, walked right across the ball field from first base through centerfield, crossed the wooden bridge, and entered the park. Somewhere along the way I had taken Connie's hand in mine. We were a couple, no doubt about that.

As prearranged, Mike and I led the girls to the long wooden tables and benches of the bingo pavilion. Mike and Gloria slid off to the far left corner. Connie and I chose an area closer the front. We sat down on the tabletop, our feet resting on the bench below.

We sat there almost mute. Neither of us knew quite what to say. The easy conversation at the restaurant was now a real chore for both of us. We knew what we were supposed to do next. It was time to make out – to kiss, to kiss again, and then to — who knew what.

Mike had also coached me on the art of kissing. Here again, the trick was to make the act simple and natural. Actually, it seemed to me that there were a lot of mechanics involved. Both parties had to cant their heads just so. Someone had to make a decision about the noses. They couldn't just go straight at one another. Someone had to take the right lane and someone the left. Was there a rule for that? Then the lips. Open? Closed? How open? And oh, by the way, there was the breath thing. What sixth grader ever worried about that before? Was a mixture of Pepsi and potato chips an accepted odor? And Mike said some people actually used their tongues. What? Sounds gross. And don't forget that kissing was done with closed eyes. I remember thinking that I was not yet good enough at this to do it with my eyes closed. I could throw a ball back to the pitcher with my eyes closed. I could get dressed with my eyes closed. I could walk through my house with my eyes closed. But this . . .

Well, after lots of talk about kissing, and with a planned preset for my head, nose and lips, I made my move. I turned to Connie, pulled her to me by the shoulders, and planted a kiss on her.

One that almost broke her front teeth. Too late I remembered that Mike had also said, "Gently, gently, gently." I was so focused on all those other details that I failed to attend to the large movement involved in bringing our heads together. We had started pretty far apart, with Connie looking away from me. When I turned her, I bore in on her face with my own like a bulldog would grab a steak. My mouth was partially open, lips pulled back some, my head turned hard left so that she'd know which lane I had selected. I had moved too fast; I had misjudged the distance to her mouth. I hit her head-on at about fifty miles per hour. It wasn't a kiss so much as a train wreck. There was the loud click of teeth on teeth – she must have had her mouth open too. I didn't know because I had my eyes closed as Mike had instructed.

The kiss rattled her teeth. I know it rattled mine. It was a poor effort, even for a first one.

Connie was not overly sympathetic. She said something like, "Are you trying to kiss me or knock me out?" But she had to take some of the responsibility too. Kissing is not a one-sided deal.

We tried it again, and then again. We were getting better, but I had the feeling that we were practicing instead of really kissing. Somehow the thrill was gone. We didn't try any of that "second base" stuff that Mike said might just happen. We sat there quietly and waited for Mike and Gloria to finish. It seemed to be going better over in that corner. They soon did all they were going to do, and we all walked back downtown. We pretty much left the two girls where we found them, on the street near the theatre.

That was my first date. I had to overcome all of that to try it again.

***

"All you have to do is get them 'hot'."

Mike Toomis was trying to convince me that girls liked sex too. That was news to me. They always seemed to be rebuffing the efforts of all my cowboy heroes on the big screen and those of the big boys up at Dot and Jake's.

But Mike said that wasn't so. He told Bierly and me that not only do girls like sex; they can actually go out of control over it. Mike said the trick was to get a girl "hot." If a girl got "hot," she was absolutely powerless over her sexual urges. The problem for the boy, however, was how to get a girl into that zone.

The easiest way to accomplish that, of course, was through chemistry. If one had some "Spanish Fly," he could simply slip the drug into a girl's Pepsi and the rest of the evening would resemble a mauling. Mike told us that a girl could actually become disoriented and oblivious to her own senses and welfare. She would simply be overcome by sexual desire, unable to stop, no matter whether the boy wanted to or not. He shared some particularly ornery stories about girls who got "hot" and the vile deeds they performed while under the influence of "Spanish Fly."

The trouble was that no one we knew in Millheim had any "Spanish Fly." So, we were going to have to induce this state of "hotness" the old fashioned way. How did we do that?

Mike said that was the whole trick to romance. The role of the boy was to get a girl all worked up with some Casanovian tricks he was going to impart to us. He then described to us the traditional progression of kissing and heavy petting that offered the best possibility of success. He described foreplay and fondling, stroking and cooing, love bites, and lovemaking techniques. He described the positions that girls seemed to like best, body orientations and juxtapositions that had never even occurred to me. It was heady stuff. I wished I had taken notes. I couldn't wait to try some of this, even if I was feeling a bit inadequate to the task. Never fear, Mike said, the girl probably hasn't been there before either. Just get her "hot," and the rest would take care of itself.

Sometimes getting her "hot" was more than just a matter of proper technique. I was fresh off that previous experience with the "Stretch Move" and, while successful, it did not exactly cast Connie Probst into the ecstasy that he was describing. Well, Mike said, the place and time had to be conducive also.

And that led to The Great Graveyard Endeavor.

Mike and I decided to try another double date. Mike had an interesting theory – a scenario really – that he wanted to test. The rationale was built on the everlasting notion that fear is a great aphrodisiac. That is, if a girl gets scared and a boy rescues her from a perilous situation, she is both grateful and enthusiastic in her repayment for the gallantry. We saw it in the movies all the time.

Mike's idea was to place the girls in a terrifying situation and then to save them. In their efforts to show their gratitude, they would be susceptible to our considerable charms. We would have them in a position in which we stood the best chance of getting them "hot." They would allow us to do all those things involved in foreplay – "foreplaying" is what Mike called it. Then, because we would be so effective at "foreplaying," the girls would submit to our wishes. They couldn't really help themselves. After all, they would be "hot." What a finish to the evening that would ignite.

Mike's plan was to take two girls up to the Union Cemetery at the western edge of town. The graveyard was home to a great and scary mystery that we would explore with the girls. It would be so scary that, given our lovemaking skills and the time and place, we would literally scare them out of their pants.

Union Cemetery and Mr. Long, R.I.P.

A great old tale in Penns Valley lore involved one Daniel A. Long who was buried in Union Cemetery. There were several versions of the Long legend, all of which ended pretty much the same way. It seems that Mr. Long was a prominent and successful businessman, around the late 1800s. In fact, at the time of his death in 1888, he owned two of the town's grist mills and several parcels of land scattered about the area. His problem was that he was accused of murder.

Some of the versions had him butchering his lovely young bride with a knife. Others reported that he killed someone in a bar fight in the Millheim Hotel; still others describe a young maiden, pregnant without the luxury of marriage. Whichever it was, Daniel Long proclaimed his innocence at the time and vowed proof of that fact upon his death. Whether or not he was ever convicted, hanged, or punished in any way is not a matter of public record. No old newspaper articles ever confirmed any parts of any version.

What is known is that he was buried near the front entrance of the cemetery, his grave marked by a huge, ornate, and impressive obelisk that towered above all other tombstones in the graveyard. Supposedly in his dying words Daniel A. Long warned that he would send a sign from "the other side" that would prove he had been falsely accused. The quote attributed to him at the time was, "If I'm innocent, you shall know, a knife from my gravestone shall grow."

According to legend, not long after his execution that seems to be just what happened. Inexplicably, a dagger-shaped image appeared in the stone, well up the towering monument. Several residents of the time reported actually seeing blood drip from this formation, leaving a residual trail streaming down the face of the obelisk. Naturally, this phenomenon caused great consternation in town then and for years to come. Townsfolk argued about whether or not the presence on the stone was proof of innocence or guilt. Fact and fancy over the matter accumulated such that the truth of the crime itself and the resulting symbol on the tombstone got all mixed together.

Over the years Mr. Long's family took steps to put the matter to rest. First, they tried to prove his innocence. Then they tried to remedy the situation on the gravestone. They cleaned it with acid, they etched out the knife-shaped specter, and they turned the stone around. No matter, the knife kept reappearing. Nothing seemed to help. Later generations finally fitted heavy metal plates over the offending area, front and back. Their purpose, they said, was just to hold the stone together, which they insisted was cracking.

But the knife, visible or not in that granite monument, was forever lodged in the folklore of the community. Naturally, seceding generations of young people were raised with that story. It fascinated us; it scared us. We quickly accepted the notion that the graveyard was haunted by the spirit of Daniel A. Long. It was not a place that kids went to play. Going there at night would obviously be the height of sheer folly, a death wish none of us had any desire to fulfill.

All of that made the Union Cemetery the perfect venue for Mike's plan. He and I would get ourselves a couple of girls and make a nocturnal foray into the bone yard. The girls would be terrified. We would scare them even more if the place was lacking in that regard.

We practiced the version of the story we would tell them. We added horrific details of the terrible bloodletting that Daniel A. Long perpetrated. We would find new signs of the knife on the tombstone and try to get the girls to go near it, perhaps even touch it. They would be scared witless.

Then we would save them. We would boldly encircle them in our arms and protect them from the spirit of Mr. Long. We would assure their safety; we would give them succor.

And they would be ours.

We would march them out of harm's way to the rear of Union Cemetery. We would select separate soft patches of grass underneath less intimidating tombstones, and we would beguile them. They, in turn, would get "hot", and life would take on an entirely new meaning.

That was the plan.

247

I admit to having the same qualms about the graveyard and the sinister Mr. Long as all the other kids in town. I did not make it a habit to go there. Bierly and I had visited the grave marker once before, but it was daytime, and there was lots of traffic on the nearby road. This time it would be dark. It made sense that if Mr. Long were going to pull any shenanigans, he would do it when nobody could see him. The situation gave me pause.

However, my judgment was overcome by my raging hormones. I judged that there would be four of us after all, and the prospect of "foreplaying" outweighed any temporary inconvenience I had to endure to get to it. Sometimes, valor is the better part of valor.

I do not know if Mike harbored any anxieties or not. I chose not to ask. He chose not to tell. So, we proceeded with The Great Graveyard Endeavor.

Getting two girls was not too difficult. It helped that we did not tell them where we were going. We simply told Darlene Minnis and Bea Musser that we had something we wanted them to see the next night, sort of implying that they could consider it a date if they wished. We made it clear that Darlene would be paired with Mike, because she already liked boys, especially the slightly older ones in town. Bea drew me. That was fine with her. A year younger than I, she was not yet particular about the company she kept. Bea was a petite blond with sharp features, a budding body, and blue eyes that seemed fixed always in a far-away stare. Perfect for what we had in mind.

The next night we somehow maneuvered the two of them to the upper end of town. They were good sports and asked few pointed questions about our destination until we left the light cast by the homes along the street. By some dumb luck, the night was moonless, dark enough for the debauchery Mike and I had in mind. This was going to be great. I was so excited by the prospects that awaited us that my earlier fears of the site couldn't shake me off the mission. I was a bulldog who had caught a meat truck. When the line of homes and the sidewalk petered out, there were a few anxious moments when the girls seemed to be catching on to our goal, but Mike sloughed them off, and we got to the cemetery before either girl really identified our destination.

At first, both girls demurred about entering the cemetery, but not adamantly. After a few taunts about "sissies," we won their reluctant agreement, and in we went. Mike and I thought we had them right where we wanted them.

We did not. Instead, our plan began to deteriorate.

Neither of them had ever been in the cemetery before. But now, dark or not, both were emboldened by the safety of numbers. Darlene pointed out that there was no record of Mr. Long ever attacking anyone, especially four people at a time. This fact had never occurred to Mike and me. Darlene simply grabbed the flashlight that Mike had secreted away for just this moment and dashed right on over to the Long monument. She screeched out the information on the stone — the name, the dates, and so on. She directed the light onto the metal plates that presumably covered the dripping knife and retold the version of the tale she had heard.

Bea was only a bit more bashful. She stayed beside Mike and me, but she slowly followed us up to the stone and touched its base. Darlene was already trying to climb up onto the small ledge where the lower square narrowed to form the pillar that rose from it.

Both girls were almost excited to be there. Neither of them appeared to me anywhere near being scared or "hot."

"Hey, Mike, just when should we proceed in saving these two from Daniel A. Long?"

Mike gave it his best shot. He tried to scare them. He told them some cockamamie story about it being bad luck to touch the haunted stone. He told them to be quiet for a moment because he thought he heard some moaning from behind the marker. He felt the bottom stone and pretended to wipe some liquid off his fingers, speculating that it was probably blood. All this to no avail.

The girls simply were not frightened. Neither was I. I was just utterly deflated. The Endeavor was already dead. There would be no saving it – obvious enough. I could feel my hormones receding deep in my body. The anticipation I had been harboring all day long was shrinking into disbelief and disappointment. I vowed to acquire some "Spanish fly" just as soon as I could learn how that was accomplished.

Mike did not give up as readily. He kept trying. He was wedded to that theory of his, and his pride would not let him quit. By now the girls had finished with Mr. Long's place in history and had moved to other graves, again reading the engravings and making morbid jokes that rhymed with the name of the deceased.

Five minutes later I officially declared the time of death of The Great Graveyard Endeavor and proceeded to Plan B. Plan B was my own, on-the-spot invention. I now refer to it as "The Direct Approach." I walked back into the graveyard where the two girls frolicked and got directly in front of that far-away stare of Bea's and asked her something akin to, "Hey, Bea, want to make out?" To my profound amazement, she shrugged her shoulders, quietly said something that I took as an affirmative. We headed for a small tree growing in the middle of the graveyard. We sat down and repeated my experience with Connie Probst. I was better this time. I remember that and two other things. One, there were mosquitoes. Two, their annoyance and bites were worth it.

Mike and Darlene had disappeared also; we rejoined them some time later and headed back downtown. It was done before 9:30 p.m.

May Mr. Daniel A. Long rest in peace.

Chapter 14

Nothing Gold Can Stay

Matt Dillon shot Millheim in the stomach. The righteous lawman coolly and casually pulled the trigger on her at point blank range.

The bullet hit her with a whoosh and knocked her to the ground, stunned and bewildered. Gut shot, she lay in the dust of a hundred horses, wounded, bleeding, and inglorious.

She would survive the attack, but her recovery would be slow — years in rehabilitation. She would never be the same vibrant and comely lady. The shot ended an era. The Millheim diamond would never again be the focal point of valley social and commercial life.

The shooting occurred somewhere around 1958. Its multiple effects lingered into the next two decades. It would be well into the 1970s before the town could sit up straight again, grow something new and useful, and regain some of the dignity and vitality of her illustrious youth.

Television had left its infancy and had entered that awkward adolescent period of rapid growth and development. *Gunsmoke* was helping to change television, and television was already changing how America lived. The pre-television lifestyle of Millheim was already doomed. Matt Dillon sealed the deal.

Gunsmoke, with James Arness playing Dodge City's infamous marshal, began its first season in 1955. It was to run for twenty years, six hundred thirty-three episodes of which the first half were in black and white. And those episodes affected the lifestyle, the commerce, and the viability of small towns across the land.

It didn't start out this way. In fact, for the first years of its incredible run, the program was actually a boon to the lifeblood and economy of towns such as ours. In the earliest days of the medium, of course, most homes were without a television set. If people wanted to see *I Remember Mama, The Sid Caesar Show,* or *I Love Lucy,* they had to find a friend or relative who had a TV set. Or they had to go to town where many of the businesses – and all the bars – had a set.

That fact helped keep Millheim a vibrant town through the mid 1950s. Of course the bars were open every night. But on Wednesday, Friday, and Saturday, so were the stores. Commerce on these evenings was brisk.

And if shoppers wanted to watch that popular new show, *Gunsmoke,* all they had to do was drop into any of the four bars and buy a beer. There they could watch Matt, Miss Kitty, Chester, and Doc Adams clean up the West. Lots of people in town, lots of money, plenty of business for the theatre, Nieman's, Cooner's, and the hardware store.

Life was grand. But then more and more people purchased television sets for their homes. The appetite for the new medium was insatiable. The price was coming down, and reception was improving. For whatever reason, T.K. Arbor's FM radio no longer was an issue. (I often wondered if Bierly and I had really solved a townwide problem with that assault on the old man's house.)

Curiously, television affected the lifestyles of our parents and older people more than those of the youngest in the family. We liked television, of course, and we watched plenty of it. But we were no more attracted to it than our parents. Our parents were intensely intrigued by both the wizardry and the shows. My father quit going to the Elks Club in State College because he didn't want to miss Saturday night television, especially *Gunsmoke.* Folks around town would plan entire family visits around favorite television programs, especially *Gunsmoke.* Folks loved *The Lawman,* Jackie Gleason, *Four Star Playhouse,* and *Your Show of Shows.*

Meanwhile, Betty Furness knew how to sell a refrigerator, and Loretta Young knew how to swish a dress as she passed through that rear stage door. Americans were discovering their favorite shows, but allegiance to *Gunsmoke* was singularly universal.

And folks stayed home to watch it. They quit coming to town on Wednesdays, Fridays, and Saturdays. The entertainment on the small screen was just too fetching. The tube was a seductive mistress. Mothers were getting hooked on the soap operas, and so they ventured downtown during the day less often.

Four years after its start, the CBS Television Network lengthened *Gunsmoke* to an hour and moved it to Monday nights. But the damage had been done. Lifestyles had changed, and Millheim was a victim.

In tandem with the effect of *Gunsmoke* on the town other changes started to weigh in. Supermarkets came next, pretty much killing the small independent grocery stores like the MRM Market, and Boob's IGA. They both closed as the Weis Store and the A&P in State College drew shoppers from across the county. Plans were made to build a mall between State College and Bellefonte, just twenty minutes from town by car, and everyone had a car, even the kids. The small businesses in town were mortally wounded when that opened. Even the Millheim restaurant closed.

And Dot and Jake's closed. When the four small high schools in the valley merged to form the Penns Valley Area High School, East Penn School became an elementary school. Elementary kids don't drive to school. They don't hang out in soda shops after school. They get on buses and go home to play. The commerce generated by being located beside a high school was lost to the Albrights, and there went that haven.

The theatre hung on until sometime in 1958. Then it closed, to reopen briefly under new management until 1961, but ultimately to close again. Nieman's lasted until 1968 but only because the Mamolens stayed on just long enough to retire from it. No one took over the store, and that was that for one corner of the diamond. Across the street, John Cooner quit the business, the 5 & 10 closed, as did two of the grocery stores. The diamond lost its glitter. Even the green, cast iron water fountain in front of Nieman's quit working, and nobody bothered to fix it. The diamond was now the deserted center of a burg that cast bluish-gray light from the parlor windows of the homes up and down both streets.

Naturally, the bars survived. But *The Millheim Journal* didn't. Nor Ulrich's barber shop, nor Elmer's shoe repair shop. Lost they were, all of them, to progress and to television – especially that western of westerns.

The Millheim Pool had closed, or better said, had been closed around this time also. The governmental agency that took all those water samples had simply run out of patience with local efforts to keep enough chlorine in the large asphalt hole. In doing so, they eradicated swimmer's ear in our lifetime.

We had to find other places to swim. We first tried a spot in the creek just below the entrance to the park. Ivan Rendell built a stone dam across the stream where it passed between high embankments on both sides. The beauty of this location was that there was a huge tree overhanging the creek, with half of its root system exposed from the erosion of the spring run-offs. We tied a rope to a branch of that tree and swung out over the five-foot pool of water we had dammed, dropping into the water from a height of about six feet.

We also begin to swim – well, not really swim as much as dip – in the creek right at the bridge.

But neither of these was much of a substitute for the pool. Swimming any length was impossible, games of tag impracticable, no concession stand, no nice place to sunbathe, not nearly all the kids there everyday.

To top it off, Queeny died. On day I was crossing Sheep Hill in search of Bierly. I saw him coming toward me, carrying Queeny. "She gets tired and stiff," he said, "and then I have to carry her home. She's just getting old, I guess."

She was dead within two weeks. Bierly and I never discussed it. Never. Bierly never got another dog.

***

After forty-five years of marriage, I offer this advice: Marry a farm girl. Ed and Doris, a.k.a. The Duck.

There wasn't much left for a kid to do in Millheim. No swimming pool, no theatre, no storekeepers to terrorize. About all that was left to us was grand theft – auto. Paul Lingle and I began to steal cars and go for "joy rides."

We ran the slickest joy ride system in the history of the town. Even if it weren't the first.

Lots of kids have commandeered vehicles before they were old enough to drive them. Ben Hollock and Fred Walker, Donnie's older brother, had set the standard in Millheim years ago when they climbed into Mr. Walker's car, so old that it had a running board. Townsfolk who were out shoveling tons of "mostly cloudy with a possibility of flurries" remember fifteen-year-old Ben driving the car through a foot of snow one Saturday night with Fred hanging outside on the running board. It seems that the wipers could not handle the snow, so Fred hunched on the step below the driver's door to tell Ben where to steer. So, right through the diamond they went, in the middle of the season's biggest snow, trying to get that car home before Fred's dad realized that it was gone. They made it across the bridge and up the hill, even into the garage behind the Walker home.

But the day of reckoning still faced them because of the snow they brought with them. When Fred's dad saw the car the next day, snow still covered the roof and trunk. Puddles of water surrounded the tires. Clearly, it had been in the snowstorm, and Mr. Walker had not. Little as he was, Donnie still remembers the verbal beating his older brother took that day.

Johnny Maher once tried, unsuccessfully, to take his dad's huge, chrome-finned Plymouth station wagon out on the town. Bierly and I had a ringside seat for this folly because we were playing "HORSE" at the Maher's outdoor, professional-grade basketball hoop.

Johnny was about twelve years old at the time and was a short kid even for his age. He could barely see over the wheel of the behemoth; he certainly couldn't see out over the two back seats which was required to exit the garage. Of course, Johnny would have had trouble going forward, but steering backward is seldom the acquired skill of a twelve-year-old. He somehow got the monster clear of the garage, but he could not negotiate the curving driveway to it. Instead, he backed into the front lawn, soft from the spring rains, leaving a tire-tracked trail everywhere he went. Which was across most of the big lawn. He kept backing up and going forward in an effort to return to the driveway. The more he did this, the worse his position became. In frustration, he would gun the engine, spin the wheels on the wet grass, and spew large clods of sod into the air. Finally, he came to rest, stuck in a small depression of spongy yard, sitting crosswise to the driveway. He got out and stomped into the house to plan his defense.

That defense turned out to be blaming Bierly and me. First, he tried to tell his dad that we were driving the car – Bierly, no, Frye, no, Bierly, well, both actually. But his dad, that great district attorney, lawyer, and baseball umpire, saw through that immediately. Bierly and I never had to file a counterclaim. Mr. Maher looked at us, and we simply shook our heads. We were off the hook.

Anyway, Paul Lingle and I got into the joy riding business. Unlike Ben Hollock and Fred Walker, we knew better than to return a car with incriminating evidence melting off it. Unlike Johnny Maher, we brought more driving skills to our new endeavor. We could both drive a car pretty darn well. We were trained professionals.

And we had an entire car lot from which to choose our ride.

Paul's family lived right next door to Donnie Walker. Two years older than I, Paul was a stocky lad, compactly built. He was large for his age, and when he played second base for our little league team, opposing coaches used to question his age. Boyd Blazer had to carry around an official-looking paper certifying Paul's birthday.

"Paulie", as his mother used to call him to his great chagrin, was muscular, with broad shoulders, each of which had a chip on it. He took offense easily. He had a temper, a foul tongue, and a reputation around town as a tough kid. He smoked at an early age. He wore his hair in the popular ducktail style and kept a pack of Lucky Strikes rolled up in the sleeve of his tee-shirt. He always reminded me of the bad guy in an Elvis Presley movie. With an impish smile that included a little dimple on one cheek, he and his reputation made him a hit with the opposite sex. Just as the song says, "Ladies love outlaws, like little boys like stray dogs."

Paul was a fount of knowledge of all those arcane topics that come up in a boy's life. Like Mike Toomis, he taught me about sex, the plumbing, the roles, the rules, the tricks, the taboos – the whole shooting match. It was Paul who assured me that Bierly did not come from that tube of K-Y Jelly.

Paul knew about machines and fixing things. He knew about alcoholic beverages and cigarettes and chewing tobacco. He helped me coordinate the James Dean look I was perfecting, with the jeans, white tee-shirt and a wisp of hair on the forehead. Paul Lingle mentored me on those topics my parents just weren't going to broach.

Paul was fascinated by cars. Like all of us boys in town, he knew about cars. Actually, we all did. In those days most car manufacturers made only two or three models. There were only a few manufacturers – all American. Several of these were slowly leaving the business. Studebaker was still hanging on with its new Starliner edition, but it wouldn't last much longer.

Hudsons were gone, Willys and Kaisers were gone. The Nash was gone. So, if one knew about Chryslers, Chevys, and Fords, one was pretty much on top of the car scene in Millheim.

We kids knew all those models. We knew the small design changes made from year to year so well that we could identify any car on the road at a distance of one hundred yards, no matter which direction it was moving. We could tell the difference from a DeSoto and a Dodge, a Ford Custom and the higher priced Fairlane 500. We could identify the year a car was manufactured by the paint color. We could hear a car start outside and tell if it was a Ford, Chevy, or Plymouth.

There were probably not more than five "foreign" cars in Millheim the entire time I was growing up. Dick Peterson drove the first Volkswagen in town. Eugene Porter's dad gave him a Renault that he was too embarrassed to drive. Tom Gillette came home from college with a white Volvo that looked like an old up-side down bath tub.

In fact, I was in that car one night a few years later when Wayne Wagner almost shot a whole carload of us to death right up at The Right Deal Garage.

Wayne was enraged because Tom had driven us drunken revelers through Wayne's cornfield with its six-foot stalks flying up over our hood and roof. For some reason, this young farmer was still awake at midnight or later, heard the defoliation outside, and gave chase. We didn't know he was coming, so Tom nonchalantly drove his agile little import up onto the sidewalks of the diamond, just to show us how nimble it was. When Wayne came up Penn Street and saw us on the sidewalk instead of the roadway, he knew he had found the culprits. He gave chase. We stopped at the garage just above my house to reason with this known hothead.

Mistake. Wayne was waving a rifle around, promising to shoot whomever couldn't get hidden behind that Volvo. I thought I was a goner – in the prime of my youth and only a few hundred yards from the safety of my home. The several minute stand-off was finally ended when Sheldon Bressler bravely walked out from behind that trunk and talked the gun out of Wayne's hand. It was an act of either incredible bravery or stupidity.

Well, Paul's dad had a used car business on up the road, in the field that adjoined Vic Stoler's garage. That location was too close for two kids itching to drive motorized vehicles.

It was a small business. At any one time Paul Lingle, Sr. might have a dozen old cars lined up in a single row. He installed a line of blue and white plastic pendants over them on a wire that also ran electricity to three or four naked light bulbs, bathing the used vehicles in a not so complimentary light. An eight by eight foot, homemade shack served as an office, complete with two folding chairs, a wall-fastened key rack, and a wooden desk.

Behind the string of cars was a large, unfarmed field. Paul Lingle Jr. and I had turned that into a sort of racetrack, complete with a figure eight in the middle and two outer loops near the edges of the premises. His dad often allowed us to take one of his older models onto that field.

That is where I learned to drive. I was about twelve at the time; Paul would have been thirteen or fourteen. We would tear around that field in some old clunker, pretending to be in a big race or just trying to shave one second off our previous best time in the figure eight. Few cars in those days had automatic transmissions, certainly not the old beaters we were allowed to use. We drove old Plymouths, Fords, and Studebakers from the late '40s. So, we learned to change gears, turn on a dime, back up, spin the wheels, slide into a turn – all that stuff required of a racecar driver. We were good. Too good to be confined to that field.

Paul asked me one day if I was ready to go out on the road. He had an idea about how we might get the keys to one of those cars. We would wait for nightfall, and then, under the cover of darkness, we would "borrow" a car from the lot, and off we would go.

This sounded like a good idea.

Paul would simply lift a key off the board in his dad's office around closing time – dusk – apparently after his dad was not going into the office again. Maybe it would be for an old GMC truck, maybe for a '49 Buick. Once he pilfered the key to the only convertible I ever saw on his dad's lot, a late model red Chevy that had no business on that line of losers. He would hide one of several dealer plates under the back corner of the shack for later retrieval.

After dark, we would head out. Usually, we headed toward Aaronsburg. That was a left off the lot and away from both our homes and the downtown. We didn't want to cruise down Main Street and have to stop at the light and let everyone see us. So, we would head east, out over the hill and onto the back roads that branched into the countryside. This route also served to get us off the highway, out of sight of police who may be on routine patrol.

The "outback" as we called it was laced with intertwining roads and lanes that provided all sorts of driving challenges to novice drivers. There were sharp turns at the tops or bottoms of long, steep hills. There were narrow places in the roadway that had to be shared with oncoming traffic. There were dirt or crushed stone lanes in which we could turn around and spin the tires and make stones fly as we popped the clutch and hit the gas. There were little parking spots tucked along the road that the high school kids used for spooning and love trysts. We were always on the lookout for cars that were backed into these little love nooks. More than once we found one, always someone we knew. We would drive up to them with the lights on high beam and beep the horn. Elbows and kneecaps would appear first, followed by peaking heads with shaded eyes. Then we would peel out. We knew who they were, but they didn't have a clue about us. We were in a rented – okay, borrowed – okay, stolen — car.

We'd do this for about an hour at a time. Paul always drove first. I usually got a fifteen-minute stint in the middle of the drive. Paul acted like a mother, lecturing me about steering, braking, accelerating, and all those sorts of things that the bigger boy always has to tell the smaller boy. I didn't mind though. I was driving a car.

Once, we found ourselves beyond Coburn, on the creek road toward Centre Hall. We had requisitioned a '52 Oldsmobile, light and dark green, with an automatic transmission. After going by Rote's Mill, we passed a sign warning us of a narrow, low-sided bridge that lay ahead. "One Truck At A Time" read the sign. Apparently, there was a weight consideration for this little twenty-foot bridge. So, when Paul saw that sign, thought about that weight problem, and saw an approaching set of headlights, he took measures to ensure that we didn't arrive on the bridge at the same time the other guy.

Normally, such consideration would represent good, defensive driving skills. Working against all this, however, were two negatives. First, the road was wet, the night misty. Second, we were traveling at Paul's normal rate of speed, about sixty miles per hour on this narrow little band that sliced through lower George's Valley. When Paul hit the brakes, too hard, the car did exactly what one might guess: it fishtailed, spun fully sideways, perpendicular to the road, and teetered toward its right side – my side — ready to roll. The wet road probably prevented that. It allowed the car to slide because the tires couldn't gain a bite on the pavement to finish the flip.

So, we slid broadside across that bridge. I twisted sideways in my seat, facing Paul, so that I could crawl over his soon-to-be-mangled body and out his window if we went shiny side down. When we could feel that we were not going over, I switched my concern to the bridge abutments. Where were they? Were we going to slide by these three-foot high concrete walls or take one at midships? It turned out that we went between them, still sideways, just like a perfectly executed field goal.

That was good, but now where was the on-coming car? Its lights shone into that green Oldsmobile enough that I could have read a map. Were we going to hit it? I braced, wondering how many people were in that car.

All of this happened fast, of course, but it unfolded as if in slow motion. It seemed as if it were a dream – not in Technicolor, but in black and white, with the glaring headlights creating bright, sharp, almost eerie light.

Sitting sideways, I was actually looking out Paul's portion of the windshield and part of his side window. After what seemed a long time, I saw the top half of the other vehicle slide across my view. Somehow, the other driver had pulled his dark sedan to a stop just off the roadway. This ruddy-faced, middle-aged farmer (I could see the tops of the blue straps of his bib coveralls stretched over a checked flannel shirt) sat braced for impact, with his mouth agape as he watched us slide by him and his flivver. I could see both his huge hands encircling the steering wheel in a death grip. His wife (I assume it was his wife) was leaning toward him, and us, with her mouth forming a perfect circle. She had both hands clapped against the sides of her head as if she was going to attempt to hold her head onto her body if we hit her. She was not attractive. She was scared.

So were we. We never really did come to a stop. In fact, I believe we still might have rolled over if we had done nothing except ride it out. But Paul had all those hours on that figure eight back in the field. As we slowed, we started to rocker again. Paul whipped the steering wheel toward me and stepped on the gas pedal, but evenly rather than simply flooring it. The car fishtailed again, slightly, and then regained an attitude more in line with the roadway.

We did not stop. We did not go back to tell that couple we were okay nor to ask if they were. We were kids, and no good could come out of that. We thought it best to just move on. Paul tramped on the pedal, and off we escaped into the rainy night.

But more slowly this time.

Of course our joy-riding careers ended badly. We were finally caught. Actually, Paul was caught. He was the bigger fish his dad wanted to land; I was just small fry – no pun intended.

What happened was a combination of little things, details that, when Paul Sr. added them up, pointed rather clearly to his son. First, we got an old black Dodge into some mud one night. Paul Sr. did not remember that much mud around the fenders. Dusty sure, but where did the mud come from? He also distinctly remembered putting a dollar's worth of gas in that car just the other day. That was almost four gallons. How could the gas gauge be reading almost empty again? And look at the inspection sticker and bill that he had just obtained from The Right Deal Garage next door. How did more than forty miles get on that car in the course of a week or ten days? No one had even test-driven it.

Something was wrong here, Paul Sr. decided, and the evidence pointed to an inside job. No thief would steal and then return the car. No one except the Lingles had access to the keys which were still hanging in the shack. None of the businessmen down at the restaurant in the morning coffee klatch were reporting strange disappearances of vehicles or equipment.

Could it be Paulie? He chose to find out one afternoon when Paul and I walked into the house. He told his son to have a seat at the kitchen table. I was ignored. I leaned against the basement door and waited for what I already knew was coming.

First, though, Paul Sr. tried something that would have been laughable if we hadn't been as guilty as Adam and Eve. He launched into his theory that some of his cars had been taken off the lot during the nighttime hours. Instead of using all the information he already had garnered – the mud, the mileage, the gas gauge – he pulled a handkerchief from his pocket and said he had found it in that old Dodge. He recognized it as one of his old handkerchiefs, now belonging to Paulie. His wife, who was standing not far from me in the kitchen, reminded her son that he now used that white handkerchief with the brown and blue border. Paul Sr. waved that old snot rag about for minutes, slowly coming to a boil. He was getting angrier and angrier about the situation, and he expected Paulie to confess immediately when confronted with this damning evidence.

Well, that wasn't going to do it. Paulie wasn't going to cop a plea over that handkerchief. He knew he hadn't used that rag recently, or maybe ever. He knew it was never in that car, and he knew his dad was bluffing. He shot me a gangster look that indicated his official stance: "We are going to stonewall on this. The feds don't have enough to put us away."

But of course they did. When the handkerchief gambit failed, Paul Sr. reverted to the real evidence. For some reason he must have felt that these coincidences did not link Paulie directly enough with the crime. So, he finally gave up on the manufactured scenario and got to the real stuff.

The jig was up. We knew that evidence would do us in. And we probably telegraphed this realization to his parents by our body language. Without actually confessing to the crimes, Paul confirmed their worst suspicions.

His dad snorted in anger and looked skyward for strength. His mother, a small, fine-featured and fragile woman named Grace, leaned against the wall and covered her eyes with her hands.

I thought this would be a good time to leave. No one had actually said one word to me throughout this several minute inquisition, and it suddenly occurred to me that no one had yet suggested that I was even or ever with Paulie during these raids on the car lot. I smelled freedom on the other side of that kitchen door, and I made for it.

I stammered something about needing to get home and said good-bye to everyone. None of them even looked at me. I realized then that no one cared if I was along or not. Paulie was in no more or less trouble with or without me. His parents would never even think that I influenced Paulie into doing the wrong thing. He was the older kid; everyone knew the hierarchy here. I was simply cut loose, like a four-inch trout. I crossed the street to my house thinking that I would never see Paulie alive again.

Of course I did. His parents did not kill him, nor did they disfigure him in any way. As I recall, they did empty their arsenal. They threw the book at him. No allowance for months, no television, in by dark, no gift this Christmas, and, of course, no more driving cars up on the figure eight. No more friends in the house, no new clothes for school – whatever they had, they used.

It all lasted about two weeks. Slowly, "Paulie" whittled away each new sanction as the heat of the moment died. His parents just were not fully committed to persevere in the adherence to these impositions to his lifestyle.

In the end, life went on.

***

And that is the way it was for all of us in Millheim. Life went on, ever changing, ever more modern, and ever more complex.

Bierly's and my journey featured elements probably lost to next generations. We ran freely, we made our own mistakes, and learned from some of them. Our experiences and the people with whom we shared a small town reflected both our youth and our futures. We became what we became. We are products of the last time in America where a child could, and was expected, to forge his or her own way. That is how the adults around us did it. We knew that we were headed for adulthood. We just had to be kids first.

Our parents understood this. Their responsibilities manifested themselves more in temperance than control. In fact, today's necessity for close oversight would have unnerved our parents. That freed us. I haven't known that freedom since.

Millheim in the 1950s was an extraordinary time and place probably lost to us now. Things, simply, have changed. The lifestyle of the times represents a high water point in adolescent self-manufactured fun, impossible now. There is a loss here, make no mistake about that. As Larry Gatlin once sang, "Somebody loses every time freedom changes hands."

Bierly and I made it past age thirteen, and several thereafter.

Bierly and I made it to our thirteenth birthdays – actually, both of us have done considerably better than that. Some sort of intervention, divine or sublime, helped us achieve that lofty goal. Mom was probably right about fools and children. Whenever the two of us look back on our early years, it is with less nostalgia than awareness. We were smart enough then to realize the grand life we got to live. We are both smart enough now to value those days as a time that only our contemporaries will ever enjoy. We know that we are lucky to be alive. As any era, the 1950s provided us with milieu that will not be seen again. We were given the opportunity to make the most of it. And, we did. We Spock children are who we are because of who we were.

Meanwhile, the glorious adolescent years of our youth and our town passed to the next phase, changing as the seasons. And with them, longed for now, went naiveté, some youthful freedom, and yes, the recklessness, all the crisp new leaves of the Spring of our lives. Ah, Robert Frost captured the thought very well:

> Nature's first green is gold,
> Her hardest hue to hold.
> Her early leaf's a flower;
> But only so an hour.
> Then leaf subsides to leaf.
> So Eden sank to grief,
> So dawn goes down to day.
> Nothing gold can stay.

We lived out our schooling years. We grew up. Many of us left town, some to return, some not. Some of us left for years, coming back only occasionally to see our aging folks.

We look at the town and sigh. We remember.

And then we visit a store, stop in at the hotel, or attempt to pick up our mother's mail. And we are remembered.

Millheim.

266

About The Author

Edward T. Frye, Ph.D. served in several teaching and administrative roles in Pennsylvania schools for thirty-two years. During that time he also provided speaking, writing, and consulting activities to educators across America. Since 1999 he has operated his own consulting firm while he continues to teach in the graduate school of Penn State-Harrisburg. Married with two grown daughters and three grandchildren, he lives and works in Mechanicsburg, PA.